D0044626

README.txt

Manning, Chelsea, 1987-
Readme.txt : a memoir /
2022.
33305254292877
ca   11/21/22

README.txt

A MEMOIR

CHELSEA MANNING

FARRAR, STRAUS AND GIROUX

NEW YORK

Farrar, Straus and Giroux
120 Broadway, New York 10271

Copyright © 2022 by Chelsea Manning
All rights reserved
Printed in the United States of America
First edition, 2022

Library of Congress Control Number: 2022942651
ISBN: 978-0-374-27927-1

Designed by Gretchen Achilles

Our books may be purchased in bulk for promotional, educational,
or business use. Please contact your local bookseller or the Macmillan Corporate
and Premium Sales Department at 1-800-221-7945, extension 5442, or by email at
MacmillanSpecialMarkets@macmillan.com.

www.fsgbooks.com
www.twitter.com/fsgbooks • www.facebook.com/fsgbooks

1   3   5   7   9   10   8   6   4   2

The views expressed in this publication are those of the author and do not necessarily reflect the official policy or position of the Department of Defense or the U.S. government. The public release clearance of this publication by the Department of Defense does not imply Department of Defense endorsement or factual accuracy of the material.

This book is dedicated to the brave trans kids who struggle to live as themselves in a hostile world. You make me proud.

AUTHOR'S NOTE

I must confess: I grew up extremely online. In the U.S. Army, I was trained to be an all-source analyst. I'm used to collecting the full context and getting—and sharing—as much detail as possible. I am also an advocate for transparency and open government. This memoir, by contrast, is only a single source and perspective, and there are points at which I am deliberately vague about specific events or groups. Some names in this book have been changed (I will note when this is the case). There are things the media has made public about this story that I can't comment on, confirm, or deny. Certain details remain classified. I am limited to some degree in what I can put on the record.

I know this can be annoying. However, I have already faced serious consequences for sharing information that I believe to be in the public interest. This book is an honest accounting of what I witnessed, what I experienced, and what I felt.

README.txt

1.

The free internet at Barnes & Noble is . . . not fast. Especially if you're on an encrypted network, pinging nodes all over the world to mask your real location and ensure anonymity. But it was what I had to work with. I needed to upload almost half a million incident reports and significant activity logs (SIGACTs) I'd brought with me on a memory card from Baghdad. This was every single incident report the United States Army ever filed about Iraq or Afghanistan, every instance where a soldier thought there was something important enough to log and report. These were descriptions of enemy engagements with hostile forces or explosives that detonated. They contained body counts, and coordinates, and businesslike summaries of confusing, violent encounters. They were a pointillist picture of wars that wouldn't end.

The upload meter bar slowly filled up. With a blizzard hitting the mid-Atlantic states, power outages, and the ticket I had for a flight scheduled to take off in twelve hours, this was my only option.

I had brought the documents back to America in my camera, as files on an SD memory card. Navy customs personnel didn't blink an eye. To get the data out, I'd first burned the files onto DVD-RWs, labeled with titles like *Taylor Swift, Katy Perry, Lady Gaga, Manning's Mix.* No one cared enough to notice. I later transferred the files to the memory card, then shattered the discs with my boots on the gravel outside the trailers and tossed the shards in our burn barrel, along with the rest of the trash.

Sitting at a chair in the bookstore café, I drank a triple grande mocha and zoned out, listening to electronic music—Massive Attack, Prodigy—to wait out the uploads. There were seven chunks of data I needed to get out, and each one took between thirty minutes and an hour. The internet connection timed out so often that I had to restart several times. I began to worry that I wouldn't be able to get the whole thing out before the Barnes & Noble closed at 10:00 p.m. If that happens, I thought, I'm done. This is over. It just isn't meant to be. I was going to throw the memory card in a trash can and never try again.

But the Wi-Fi finally did its job. At nine thirty, the final file was uploaded. It wasn't a moment of celebration, though; I was dead tired and needed to leave for the airport at four thirty in the morning to start the several-days-long journey back to Iraq. I left the Barnes & Noble. My bags were in my rental car, so I just slept in the back seat, in the freezing cold, in the parking lot, then dropped off the car and took the Metro out to Reagan National in the strange, empty predawn hours.

I wasn't thinking about what might happen to me. I was just trying to survive every day. Compartmentalizing is something I was good at. I was grappling with my gender identity and working inside an army that didn't officially allow people like me to serve openly.

When I landed in northern Virginia at the end of January 2010, I was both physically and psychologically exhausted. I was excited for this short leave, for a break from Iraq and from work—and to see Dylan (not his real name), my boyfriend at the time, who was a college student in Boston. When I went to see him, I'd been overseas for less than four months. But he was caught up in the social life of college, and was emotionally distant from me during the few days I spent there. He didn't want to talk about anything that involved the two of us in the future. I worried our relationship was ending. I went back to my aunt's house in Maryland.

I took the D.C. Metro out to Virginia, to Tysons Corner Center. I'd been there plenty of times before—that's what you do in the suburbs, go to the mall. This time, though, I snapped a photograph of myself in the car on the way, wearing a blond wig. It was the photo that would later, to my chagrin, be broadcast all over the world. I wandered around the mall, shopping: I went to Burlington Coat Factory for a purple coat. At Sephora, I bought makeup. I wanted to buy a business casual outfit, so I tried on clothes at Nordstrom and Bloomingdale's, telling the salesperson that I was shopping for my girlfriend, who was about my size. I ate fast food for lunch, and then I went home and put on my new clothes and the long blond wig. I spent the rest of the day wandering around to coffee shops and bookstores, dressed as a woman. I took pleasure in the freedom, the escape, the ability to wear the clothes I wanted, to present myself in the manner I wanted.

For me, at least, being trans is less about being a woman trapped in a man's body than about the innate incoherence between the person I felt myself to be and the one the world wanted me to be. In the weeks before my leave, I had imagined what it would be like to walk around with long hair instead of my buzz cut, wearing something femme instead of my standard-issue uniform. I'd watch YouTube videos of trans women documenting their transition alongside my usual web-browsing circuit: video games, alternate histories, and science videos.

But I didn't just want to unburden myself of the restrictions of a judgmental world. There was something else even more urgent on my mind, and it's why I sat down with my computer at the Barnes & No-

5

ble. There were critical revelations about the government, and the complex nature of war, in those files.

Uploading those files wasn't my first choice. I first tried to reach more traditional publications. It had been a frustrating ordeal. I didn't trust the telephone, nor did I want to email anything; I could be surveilled. Even pay phones weren't really safe. I went into chain stores— Starbucks, mostly—and asked to borrow their landline because supposedly my cell was lost or my car had broken down. I called switchboards at *The Washington Post* and *The New York Times*, trying to get transferred to a reporter who would understand what I was offering them. I reached one at the *Post*, and we talked briefly. I left a message with my Skype number at the *Times*, but I never heard back. I said only that I worked in Defense. I tried to get them to understand. *What I have is everything about two wars*, I said over the phone. *This is what asymmetric warfare looks like, uncut; this is the whole thing.* I wanted this information published in a widely read outlet that could defend itself.

But I wasn't getting anywhere. The reporter I reached didn't understand the sensitivity of what I wanted to expose, that I could only give them the information digitally, and that I didn't have enough time to establish a meaningful line of secure communications. They also didn't understand end-to-end encryption—this was before Signal, an easily accessible, fully encrypted text messaging app, was commonly used by the news media—and more than that, they didn't seem to understand the magnitude of what I was offering them. (It probably didn't help that I was being so vague and nonspecific.)

After striking out with the *Times* and the *Post*, I returned to my aunt's house. It started to seem possible that after all that risk, I wouldn't be able to connect with a reporter before I had to go back to Iraq. But there was one last publication I wanted to try, *Politico*. I planned to drive to its headquarters in northern Virginia and try to just walk in, get a meeting, and hand over the data in person.

Then the blizzard started: Snowmageddon, as Twitter and the local news called it. Washington—not a town that was prepared for winter weather—was quickly covered in two feet of snow, and my aunt's house lost power. It was as if I'd lost two more days of my leave. I was completely snowed in. The internet went out. I couldn't wait for service to be restored. I was about to go back to Iraq. And if I didn't do what I wanted to do before I left, I'd never be able to do it.

On the last morning of my leave, I woke up and dug myself out of the house using only my gloved hands because I couldn't find a shovel in the house. I walked two hours into Rockville, where I rented a car with a ride-sharing service, Zipcar—but that car was stuck in a giant mound of snow. I spent two more hours digging it out, again using only my hands. I finally got the car loose enough to drive it out of the snowdrift and began searching for a business that was open despite the storm—a place with internet access. Driving all the way to *Politico*'s offices in northern Virginia would be virtually impossible. Even driving nearby was hard with the road conditions. But there was one last option.

In 2008, during intelligence training, our instructor—a Marine Corps veteran turned contractor—had told us about WikiLeaks, a website devoted to radical transparency, and then instructed us *not* to visit it. (The instructor later denied doing this.)

While I shared WikiLeaks' claims of a commitment to transparency, I thought that for the purposes of what I wanted to do, it was too limited a platform. Most people back then had never heard of it. I worried that information from such a site wouldn't be taken seriously. But I hadn't gotten anywhere with journalists in traditional media and I felt it was the only option I had—the whole point of exposing this information was to get Americans to actually pay attention to what we were doing in Iraq and Afghanistan. I posted to one of the chat rooms I was in. I told them that I had information that needed to be shared with the world, about the true costs of the wars in Iraq and Afghanistan. In reply, someone in the chat posted a link to WikiLeaks' online submission form.

This website was the publication of last resort. But with half a day left on my leave, it was now or never. I felt totally alone, but I was optimistic that society would benefit—if only the information could get the attention it deserved.

I tried a couple of Starbucks stores in the area, but had no luck. Finally—at around 2:00 p.m.—I drove by a Barnes & Noble that I knew offered free Wi-Fi. I sat down, pulled out my laptop, and opened an anonymizing browser.

Everyone now knows—because of what happened to me—that the government will attempt to destroy you fully, charge you with everything under the sun, for bringing to light the truth about its own actions. ("Nuts and sluts" is the term for how the government often tries to portray leakers—as being crazy, drunk, or sexually off in some way.)

But what I was trying to do had never been done before, and therefore the consequences were unknown. Daniel Ellsberg, who had disclosed the Pentagon Papers during the Vietnam War, avoided prison because of illegal evidence-gathering by the Nixon White House (which had ordered a break-in of his psychiatrist's office, in search of information that might discredit Ellsberg). Nobody had gone to prison for this sort of thing; I hadn't heard of Ellsberg at the time but I was very aware of Thomas Drake, an NSA whistleblower who had been prosecuted under the Espionage Act. He'd faced charges that carried a thirty-five-year jail sentence, but shortly before trial he'd cut a plea that left him with only probation and community service.

I certainly weighed the potential consequences. If I was caught, I would be detained, but I figured at most I was going to be discharged or lose my security clearance. I cared about my work, and it was frightening to imagine losing my job—I had been homeless before enlisting—but I figured if I were court-martialed, it would only damage the government's own credibility. I never really reckoned with the notion of a life spent in prison, or worse.

The four months I had spent in Iraq had changed the way I understood the world and these wars. Every night, I woke up in the desert at 10:00 p.m. I walked from my tiny trailer to the office, a Saddam Hussein–era basketball court the military had converted into an intelligence operations center. I used three different computers, two of which contained classified information, reading email updates and watching video feeds of what was happening in east Baghdad.

Monitoring reporting was like drinking from a fire hose: the military used at least a dozen different intelligence, surveillance, and reconnaissance assets, each giving the analysts a different view of the city, of the people and places we were watching. My job was to analyze, with emotional detachment, what impact military decisions and personnel movements were having on this giant, bloody "war on terror." But the daily reality of my job was more like life in a trauma ward.

I'd spent hours learning every aspect of the lives of the Iraqis who were dying all around us: what time they got up in the morning, their relationship status, their appetites for food and alcohol and sex, whether they were engaged in political activities, every single person they interacted with electronically. I watched each bit of their lives. Sometimes, I knew more about them than they probably knew about themselves. And I'd realized that we—the occupying military force—didn't actually give a fuck about them. I couldn't talk about my work with anyone outside my unit. Nor about this conflict that looked nothing like the one I'd read about back home or watched on the TV broadcast news before I enlisted.

The idea that the information I had access to held real power began to flash into my brain more often. I'd try to ignore it, and it would come back. People had begun to pretend that the seven years of conflict had been worth it, all the lost American lives and the still-uncounted lost lives of Iraqis and Afghanis. The establishment had moved on. There was the recession to deal with. People at home were losing everything. The health care debate was on the news every night.

And yet we were still fucking there. Still dying. In every scenario I gamed out, we'd be there for many more years. Even if we tried to draw down troops, every flare-up—and there would be flare-ups—would require a return to a large troop presence, and more death. The whole system was set up so the general public would never really understand that.

I was constantly confronted with two different realities—the one I was looking at, and the one Americans at home believed. So much of the information they received was distorted or incomplete. The irreconcilable differences became an all-consuming frustration for me.

It is not possible to work in intelligence and not to imagine disclosing the many secrets you bear. I can't pinpoint exactly the first time the idea crossed my mind. Maybe it was when I was exposed to actual classified information, right after basic training in 2008, when I was first learning to be an intel analyst. It's as if there's a line you've crossed, a partition you've opened, this knowledge that you can't un-know, and it gives you power over the government—but it also gives the government power over you. You're trained and tested and vigorously inculcated with the notion that you can't tell anyone anything about what you do, ever. This begins to control how you think about everything, how you act in the world. But the power of prohibition is fragile, especially once the lines seem arbitrary.

Or maybe the first germ of the idea was planted when I was stationed at Fort Drum, in upstate New York, before I'd ever set foot in Iraq. I was transporting a cache of classified hard drives in a large box in the summer heat, and I began to worry about what would happen if I screwed up and left the box unattended. If someone picked up a stray classified hard drive and accessed it, what would happen? For me personally, of course, I knew there would be consequences. A serious investigation, negligence charges, maybe a demotion. Perhaps even discharge.

But what would be the ripple effects if the actual information got out? Would anything really happen if these obscure memoranda and rambling reports were made public? I knew the official version of why they had to be kept secret—we were trained to see classification as life-and-death—but I struggled to think of the real-world consequences, whether anything actually harmful would happen. More and more, I began to question the rationale for keeping so much information classified. Why were we keeping so many secrets? There seemed to be no consistent internal logic to classification decisions.

But just how arbitrary the lines were didn't become fully clear to me until six weeks after I'd arrived in Iraq. Our press office had asked me to create a historical report, a huge assessment: an analysis, complete with detailed examples, of all the significant actions that had occurred in Iraq during the previous two months.

Seven hours later, I gave it to a major and a lieutenant colonel, in a classified courier box. The public affairs officers went through it fast and liked what they saw. In a single swoop, they removed the classified stamps. I asked them what they were doing.

They were sending it to the Iraqi press. I was shocked. The intelligence report that I had produced for internal purposes only was now a public affairs assessment. Casualty numbers, incidents, details, all of it.

We'd had a successful couple of months, compared with the status quo, and the public affairs office wanted that known. The report would make the military look good. There was no sensitive information, they'd decided, nothing that would cause global consequences—but then why was it labeled as classified in the first place?

I asked a press affairs officer why he took off the classification markings and how he could do it so quickly. His reply—an honest, succinct one—has lingered in my mind: the classification system exists wholly in the interest of the U.S. government, so if it's in the interest of public affairs to declassify something, we will. In other words, he seemed to say, the classification system doesn't exist to keep secrets safe, it exists to control the media. I realized that not only did *I* not think this stuff needed to be secret, neither did the higher-ups, at least not when it suited them. In that instant, I began to consider whether the public deserved to have the same information that I did. If we were briefing journalists on the full picture when it suited us, why not all of the time? This was, after all, historical information.

That month, I began the process of downloading reports of all the significant activities (SIGACTs) from Iraq and Afghanistan—an expanded version of what our public affairs office had been willing to release. They contained, in their aggregate force, something closer to the truth of what those two wars really looked like.

2.

Images of central Oklahoma sit in my memory like beautiful, dusty snapshots. There is an endless golden glow reflecting from the landscape, over the sunburned-brown grass and rusty-red clay soil and even on the modest house I grew up in, with its black-and-white exterior and its little hobby farm out back: hogs, horses, a cow, chickens, staple crops.

We lived on five acres in a small gully just off Oklahoma State Highway 74. The area was mostly scrub and mud, but we had a little pond and trees on the outskirts of a shrinking former boomtown called Crescent. My father drove his red-brown Nissan pickup truck the forty-five minutes to Oklahoma City and back every day so he could live in the country while making a city salary. Crescent had been settled in the first Oklahoma land rush, stolen from the Indigenous people who lived along the Cimarron River. Decades before I was born, the railroad company built a long berm near our house to lay tracks on. It was the only thing that broke up the plain, and when you stood on top of it, you could see corn and wheat fields, scattered oil derricks, and the tidy railroad tracks headed straight into town. There were about a thousand people in Crescent, and everyone knew everything about everyone—a blessing or a curse, depending on who you were.

My family had no real roots in the plains. They'd come there for my father's job—electronic data processing for the Hertz Corporation—in the eighties, a few years before I was born. Brian Edward Manning, my father, grew up in a working-class Irish American family in the western suburbs of Chicago, and bounced around in his late adolescence. He left home at seventeen and tried college in the Florida Panhandle for a short time before dropping out. School wasn't for him, but partying was. Back in Chicago, instead of waiting to be drafted into the army toward the end of the Vietnam War, he and my uncle Michael both decided to enlist in the navy—after a particularly boozy weekend, as he tells it. He always credited the navy with giving him structure, a path in life.

My father made the military sound glamorous. The U.S. Navy stationed him in the United Kingdom as an analyst at a Royal Air Force base a few minutes' drive east of St. Davids, in Pembrokeshire, Wales. He rose to petty officer third class and worked with classified intercepts, monitoring a network of undersea microphones between Iceland and the UK, on the lookout for Soviet (and sometimes NATO) nuclear submarines. He told me that he'd worked with classified documents and worn a Royal Navy uniform to blend in and confuse spies— it sounded like a spy movie or Tom Clancy novel to me, growing up in the quiet, empty plains of Oklahoma.

Wales is where he met my mother, Susan Mary Fox. She was from a working-class family from Haverfordwest. It was a town built around a Norman castle, in a region where the hills were as sharp and green as the Midwestern American plains are flat and beige. She was one of nine children, eight of whom were girls. They lived in a tiny three-bedroom council flat, each room barely big enough for a single bed, and so when she met my father, the American, drinking at the tiny pub on Castle Square, it must have seemed like a fairy-tale way out. They married the day after his twenty-first birthday. Later that year, my sister, Casey, was born, and I followed eleven years later, to the exact day, on December 17, 1987. I was given the name Bradley—my dead-name, now.

My parents didn't live happily ever after. They acquired the trappings of a comfortable middle-class life—my father got a community college degree in computer science, which eventually led to the Hertz job—but their marriage was unstable. As a child, I didn't notice my parents' struggles. To me, the family just made sense—it was just the way of the world, like the sun rising in the east and setting in the west. But both of my parents were hard drinkers, the kind who drink to escape their daily life.

Dad drank cheap beer. He left stacks of aluminum cans in the trash. Within moments of arriving home, after setting his things down, he'd slide an ice-cold can into an insulated foam holder and crack it open. On weekends or holidays, he'd drink so much he could barely stand by early afternoon. Mom drank vodka and rum, with shots of Absolut or Bacardi in every drink. She started every morning with liquor poured into a mug of hot English tea. She drank even during her pregnancy with me. She told me she had two miscarriages in the years between Casey's birth and mine. I now wonder how that sadness weighed on her.

During my childhood, my mother was disarmingly gentle, and had a simple, warm smile. She always took people at their word. But she was also cloistered, and sometimes incapable of behaving like an adult. She never learned to drive or to balance a checkbook, and her alcoholism eventually made it even more difficult for her to function in the world. My face takes after hers, but she was frail, with the rosy cheeks of a heavy drinker. She chain-smoked menthol Salem 100s, and it left her teeth—dentures, actually, after a bar fight in her youth—deeply yellowed.

My parents could both be charming, but my father had a selfish streak. At five foot two—a little shorter than my mother—he was funny and smart, and probably came across as mild-mannered to most people. But at home he'd lash out, suddenly blow up, take out his frustrations on my sister and me. He cared a lot about fitness, about looking good, and so he'd run and do sit-ups, push-ups, and pull-ups every day, religiously. He was also a master of the art of saying utter bullshit totally convincingly.

Casey had to grow up fast. My parents' drinking was the backdrop to her adolescence; she became my caretaker and babysitter, and also took care of my parents when they drank too much. One quiet gray autumn day, my mother sat down on our porch, chain-smoking her menthols, watching a squirrel nibbling in a pecan tree above us. Some pecan shards fell down, and one hit my mother on the head. Casey walked inside the house, then came out brandishing Dad's pellet gun. Standing below the brown and orange leaves, with sharp posture and both arms extended, she aimed the pistol at the squirrel. The echo from the shot bounced off the hills in the distance. She missed, corrected her breathing, and tried again. Pop—crack! The squirrel fell out of the tree. Casey just took care of business.

Casey—blond and blue-eyed, like me—was already a teenager, driving a sky-blue Ford Tempo, by the time I was in kindergarten. She means the world to me now, and I idolized her then. She had her own telephone line, nineties polka-dot and zigzag sheets, and walls that were plastered with posters, magazine clippings, and collages. She spent days at a time solving thousand-piece puzzles, and pasted them on poster board to hang on the wall. Her room doubled as a zoo, filled with dozens of animals—birds in cages, tanks full of lizards, frogs, toads. She loved reptiles more than anything.

I didn't just want her room; I wanted to *be like* my sister: when I was five or six, I'd sneak in and try on her things. She played around with a cowgirl look in her early teens, and I still remember the boots and the belt buckles and the T-shirts with the horses and the frilly fringes that I'd try on. I loved her makeup station, with a mirror and light bulbs that changed color. I'd stare at myself for long stretches, seeing if I looked different with this lipstick, that foundation, this lighting. After I'd left a mess enough times, Casey installed a lock on her bedroom door. I still tried to pick the lock so I could play with her things.

My childhood now feels like it was all lived under rigidly cisgender sensibilities. Even my explorations followed a binary path. When I was four, I asked my father if I'd get to live like my sister, with her makeup and her clothes, when I grew up. He told me that I needed to go outside and do "boy stuff." He banned me from watching my favorite movie, *The Little Mermaid*, and filled my room with military toys: model fighter jets, G.I. Joes with plastic tanks and rifles. Even my coverlet was military themed, decorated with drawings of F-14s and F-16s. I put Casey's hand-me-down Barbie in G.I. Joe's uniform and sent her on missions. Eventually, my father explained the biological difference between boys and girls to me, after I pressed him, over and over, about why I had to be a boy. His pained description boiled down to the awkward phrase *the plumbing is different*.

Gender roles in Oklahoma were as hard and fixed as the land, and I didn't fit in. "Girly boy! You're such a girl—why?" kids would say. "Are you bent or crooked?" (In other words: Are you gay, or *are you gay*?) My father wanted me to fight back—he'd been short, and he'd been bullied, and he wanted me to react as he had, with fists and taunts in reply. I was fast and smart, and he thought I should use that.

When I was six, my father gave me a better form of escape: a big beige IBM desktop computer. The games I played on it felt immersive and high-tech at the time, more creative than anything else available in the middle of nowhere. I played SimCity, an early simulator of urban development—building towns and cities by zoning residential, commercial, and industrial districts, and connecting them with roads and power lines. In games with characters, I'd always make mine a girl: Jessica, Alice, Chelsea. My father got me into military flight simulation games. I piloted the American F-15 Eagle and F-16 Falcon, and the Soviet Su-25 and Su-27. I learned about aerial combat maneuvers— bombing, strafing, flying in corkscrews, deploying chaff and flares. It was thrilling, and it was a way to be closer to my father.

So was programming. My father showed me how to code not long after I'd learned to read. At first I didn't really understand it—I'd simply type in exactly what the instruction book told me to do—but by the time I was ten I was imagining and creating my own simple games, like a ski jumper zigzagging down a mountain. I built my first website when I was ten, too—a simple fan site for a popular Nintendo 64 game.

That was also the year I first kissed a boy. I'll call him Sid. Sid, a bicycle ride away, white-blond and tanned and pencil thin and obsessed with the spectacular pageantry of the World Wrestling Federation. We used to wrestle on a big foam mat at his house, with bungee cables he'd set up as the ring's ropes, pretending that we were pros. One day, while we were play-fighting, I gently moved in and kissed him—it wasn't premeditated, just a yearning impulse. He kissed me back. And then some other kid saw us. Once Sid realized we were being watched, he pushed me off. *Get off me, you faggot.* I couldn't stop weeping.

"Homosexual sex" was a criminal offense in Oklahoma until 2003. And so, when word got around about what I'd done, the bus driver reported what he heard from other children, and the school intervened. The next day, the principal pulled me from class. Dad, the bus driver, Sid, and Sid's father sat in his office. The school weighed suspension as a possibility. I'm not sure whether my father even paid enough attention to me to think about the question of whether this was a real sign that I was gay. The fact that he was called out of work, and had to drive an hour to my school, was all he cared about. He seemed embarrassed.

I told my parents and the school officials that I wouldn't do it again, and they decided not to enforce the suspension, but I wished I had been sent home. Then I wouldn't have had to face the teasing and the rumors. I didn't even know what *gay* meant at that point, and I bet the kids calling me that didn't really, either. It was just a *bad thing*, we all thought, the worst insult you could use. I just wanted the whole thing to go away.

My mother told me years later that she'd always thought I was gay. She was kind about it. She didn't understand my gender identity, though, and I think she wanted to believe it was a phase, something I'd grow out of. She lacked the language to talk about it. But unlike many of our neighbors, though she did go to Mass on Sundays and probably would have voted Republican if she'd ever become a naturalized U.S. citizen, she wasn't a conservative Christian in her bones.

My father, while also outwardly conservative—you couldn't *not* be, in central Oklahoma—had something of a libertarian streak. He'd talk about how terrible Bill Clinton was, and how you couldn't trust "the Dems," parroting points he'd hear on the talk-radio shows that were just starting to become popular. What really bothered him, and a lot of people like him—libertarian conservatives, I guess you'd say— was that the federal government had killed people, including women and children, in Waco, Texas, during their botched intervention there in 1993, when I was six. The words *Waco, David Koresh, Janet Reno,* and *ATF* left most of us with a bitter taste. Our community shared a pervasive fear of the feds coming in again and interfering in our lives, taking away our firearms, going from house to house and forcing a new way of life on conservative, working-class people. I don't think people who are not from that part of the world understand just what a formative event the standoff at Waco was, or that it still feels like recent, urgent history to many.

My father did own firearms—like almost everyone in rural Oklahoma, where it was common to hear gunfire from hunting or recreational shooting—and that was important to him, but he rarely weighed in on other social issues. The few times he ever talked about Christian or family values—and only ever in front of company—it felt contrived. It was theater, satisfying his need to fit in. Dad's strong anti-authoritarian stance drove his preoccupation with a vast and dangerous government invading our homes and interfering with our lives. Government was far off and alien, anyway; we were out in the wilderness. I hardly ever even saw police cars or ambulances. The closest things to the government were my school bus and a local-government-operated leveler that would grade the dirt road we lived on once a month or so.

And yet the larger concerns, and dangers, of the outside world came alarmingly close to Crescent. One hot spring day when I was seven, a clear day without a cloud in the sky, I heard a huge boom outside. It wasn't a freak storm, it turned out, but a Ryder rental truck loaded with ammonium nitrate exploding in Oklahoma City, thirty miles away. Our teachers were bone-scared, panicked: they gathered us all in one room for a head count, and I remember watching the TV news coverage explaining what had happened, but all I really understood or heard was that somebody had killed a lot of people—168 of them, including small children at a day care center in the federal building that Timothy McVeigh targeted. He did it on April 19, two years exactly after the deadly end to the Waco standoff.

Terrorism, thanks to the close-to-home tragedy of the bombing, loomed large over my childhood. I saw from an early age that loss of life could be senseless, and that Americans could damage our own country as much as or even more than an outside threat could. After all, my first taste of terrorism was the work of not foreign radicals but a common American white guy, a right-wing extremist in the middle of nowhere.

Violence, by then, was the undercurrent to my life. My father beat the crap out of me; he abused everyone close to him. He used a belt or a flyswatter on me, and sometimes the beatings felt random, confusing, unrelated to anything that I'd done. He was mad at the world, and taking it out on me. What had I done wrong? Why didn't he love me? I never got answers. When I'd cry from the pain, he would tell me he wouldn't stop beating me until I stopped screaming, stopped showing weakness. I would force myself to shut down, my skin bruised blue all over.

The worst night was when I was eleven—a year after I'd gotten in that big trouble at school. I was working on homework at the shared family computer in the dining room, a full-page essay for my fifth-grade social studies class. As the sun fell under the horizon, my father arrived home and started drinking extra hard for some reason. Within an hour, his eyes were bloodshot and he could barely stand. He tried to kick me out of the dining room. "Get out of my way!" he yelled. I told him I was doing homework. "This is my house, pay rent or get the hell out," he said. I was confused. I was *eleven*. And I needed to finish my homework.

He stomped off to my parents' bedroom and came back with his belt, threatening me again. But the belt no longer fazed me. He shoved me down, pulled my pants down to my knees, and started to hit my buttocks. While he was striking me, I grabbed the belt from him. Then he grabbed me by the shirt collar, lifting me off my feet.

Years of being fast and smart against bigger kids in wrestling matches paid off. I noticed Dad's mistake: his arms were straight. I reversed his arms, pinning him back. "Get the hell off of me!" he screamed. He slammed my body against the wall, and I could feel the blood vessels breaking under my skin. I twisted his arm, and as he screamed in agony, I let go and walked away, then sat back down at the computer as if nothing had happened.

When I looked up, my father was standing over me, drunkenly waving his twelve-gauge shotgun. I tried to run out the front door, but my father, in his paranoia about the government coming to get us, had installed a dead bolt. My mother, who was also drunk, tried to intervene, to tell him to stop. He turned to her and started to yell, and I was able to finally get the door open. Outside, the sky was pink and green—a storm was on its way. I picked a random direction and just ran, trying to get away from his anger, trying to get mine out. When the storm got closer, I walked home and went back inside. My mother was sitting on the floor near the abandoned shotgun, staring blankly. My father was drooped over, mumbling to himself.

It wasn't the end of that incident. I didn't get my homework done, and I was bruised—both of which my social studies teacher noticed. She pulled me aside and I told her what had happened. The teacher got the state involved: a social worker came to the school to investigate, but that wasn't what I wanted. As difficult as things could be with my parents, I loved them, and I couldn't imagine living anywhere else—especially not at a foster home. I lied about the assault to the social worker, clearing my father's name. Still, our relationship remained distant. He never showed affection, never gave me the validation I so desperately sought from him.

With puberty came a new set of complications in my life: I fell in love with my best friends and felt overwhelmed, especially around one boy. I thought maybe I felt something back from him, and besides, it was too painful to hold it all inside. I told him, finally, what I felt. He was kind but firm in telling me he just didn't share those feelings—and he kept my secret. But I also told another friend about my crush, and he spread the news all over school. I denied everything, and threw myself back into repression.

In private, I harbored an even bigger secret. My experimentation with gender presentation had expanded beyond sneaking into my sister's room. I'd go to little stores in town—the mall was too far away, and I didn't want to ask one of my parents to take me there—and steal things to try on in front of my mirror at home: makeup, bras. I'd stuff socks into the bras to see how I looked. But when I was done, I'd throw it all away and promise myself I would never do it again.

The internet was the only place I could explore my identity without worrying about the consequences. My family got AOL dial-up service early—1993 or so—and the chat rooms I navigated through our 14.4k modem started to fill up with people who felt like *my* people. I understood this world, felt free in it. There were no consequences here. The rooms were full of tinkering hackers, and we'd talk about games or movies in between questions about troubleshooting and coding tips and hardware setup suggestions. Often the conversation would turn to regular life, ideas—it was intelligent conversation of the kind that I craved.

I was an adult on the internet, or at least that's what I pretended. When I was twelve or thirteen, I started going into queer chat rooms, talking to people there about hookups or "cybering." They'd ask for ASL—"age, sex, location"—and metrics about your body shape and size. We asked one another for photos, but I always managed to avoid sending any. I never met up with anyone from the forums, either; I was far too scared. The internet was more useful to me as a source of information. I can't count the number of times I typed the word *gay* into search engines. (It was mostly porn that you got back then.) I searched *transgender* a couple of times, too, although I didn't really know what the word meant. Those results were even less useful. *Transsexual* was the word I'd heard, but it didn't have good connotations: they were always the prostitute characters on *Law & Order*, or a bearded man in a wig trotted out as a source of amusement on *Jerry Springer*. I didn't identify with those people, and so, in the absence of role models, I didn't identify as trans.

Besides searching for information on gender, the thing that really excited me about the internet was file-sharing, especially for music. I was into Eminem, and other rap that I thought was edgy, different. I liked the way it upset the TV newscasters and drew controversy. Like the electronic music I was also starting to explore, it was attractively far outside the norm in Oklahoma City, where the radio stations played mostly classic rock and country. The CDs at Walmart were way too expensive, and usually the censored versions anyway. So when I did get my hands on something good from friends, I'd burn it onto CDs. When Napster came out in 1999, it felt like both a natural progression of that sharing and a revelation, a promise of access to music I'd never have come across otherwise. And I didn't just download music; I mixed it, using early DJ software and audio-editing tools to cut up, loop, remix, and totally re-create music of my own.

And then one day I went to check the status of my downloads, only to see that Napster had been shut down. The promise of free music had attracted too much attention, had threatened powerful corporations. And so my most important creative outlet was gone, just like that. The reason for it, copyright law, sounded as ancient and strange as a horse-drawn carriage, or churning your own butter. And I *really* couldn't believe that people—my friends—could go to jail just for downloading music.

The idea was absurd. Copying data seemed like the most natural, normal thing in the world. The notion that downloading music or sharing information was the same thing as stealing felt intellectually dishonest to me; it just intuitively didn't make sense. Information isn't a tangible thing that can be packaged and sold at a Walmart.

I began to read about the ideas of Richard Stallman, who famously said that information should be free like free speech, not like free beer. For the first time, I began to think in earnest about the way government could affect my daily life, and to consider how my reaction to that could be political. I stopped using Microsoft products, with their expensive licensing fees, and switched to Linux, the idealistic experiment in open-source software. The user interface wasn't as good, but it was free—a concept I believed in. You could make modifications, and the more people who were involved in improving the code, the better it got. That was revolutionary then. The open-source community felt like a movement. They were people who affiliated with one another without regard to geographic location. The internet expanded.

I was a pain in the ass as a kid. I was smart, and I was arrogant. Standing out academically—especially in geography, science, math—became something I depended on to make my different-ness a good thing. I won the science fair, held down the academic-bowl squad, and became the first person from my school to ever win that competition at the state level. I thought I could learn anything, and if I didn't know something, it was just a matter of time until I would. I read the encyclopedia for fun, to teach myself facts. When I was a little older, I began methodically working my way through the Western canon of philosophy, starting with the Greeks.

Outside my closed bedroom door, it was harder to make sense of the world. My parents weren't getting along, and it had become clear to me that neither of them was able to take care of themselves. Sometimes they could barely get dressed or feed themselves without huge difficulty. They'd get blind drunk and fight, sometimes becoming physical. I would sit alone in my room, crying, as I listened to my father yelling, threatening my mother—threatening to hit her, to leave her. I could hear him grabbing her sometimes; the sound of his feet stomping around her echoed through the paper-thin walls of my bedroom. I could hear my mother's footsteps, too. It was an awkward, creaky dance. She'd stumble as she poured more drinks.

Drinking had taken my mother hostage. Vodka destabilized everything. She slid into a deep depression, which only made her drink more. She saw psychiatrists who prescribed her Paxil, which didn't mix well with alcohol. She'd stopped doing much of anything—a little bit of cleaning around the house was all she could manage, some microwave dinners. When I was twelve, my parents starting talking about divorce. They were secretive at first, whispering. When they finally told me, my whole world shattered. My mother's did, too. In the middle of the night, she went into the bathroom and swallowed an entire bottle of muscle relaxants my father had been prescribed, washing them down with a vodka screwdriver.

I heard something from my bedroom. My mom was passed out, half naked, on the green rug in the hallway. She was still breathing, sprawled, her dentures slipped loose. "Dad!" I yelled. He didn't answer. My sister took charge of the situation. Casey called 911, but we lived too far from the hospital to wait for an ambulance. My sister woke up my father, who was passed out drunk. Casey piled us all into her car and drove as fast as possible to the emergency room. My dad sat in the passenger seat while I held my mother in my arms in the back, still unconscious, her gut full of pills. I couldn't process what was happening to her, so I concentrated on Casey: she had never seemed stronger, more in control.

My mother stayed in the hospital for ten days, and after she came home, still wearing her white plastic hospital bracelet, we never spoke about the incident again. But for me, the fear that my mother was going to die colored everything. I now knew how difficult it was for her to take care of just herself, let alone me. By the time she died, in January 2020, I had been reckoning with what that would feel like for decades.

After my mother's suicide attempt, my parents' marriage fell apart even more profoundly. My mother wanted my father to know how much he'd hurt her, how much he was to blame for their—and her—troubles. One night, she theatrically packed up her bags and left. She didn't go far, just to a neighbor's house, but it frightened me, and I wondered what might happen if she never came back. It was a dark line of thought I'd been entertaining since her hospital stay, an earth-shattering shift, one that would change my whole reality. Before this time, I couldn't imagine my parents splitting up, not having both of them with me. I thought that my family was always going to be the exception in central Oklahoma, where so many kids I knew had one parent, or a new stepparent every few years. We were special, I had believed, despite our obvious problems. Our family unit was a force of nature. My parents' marriage was special, I'd thought. But not anymore.

3.

One warm, sunny September day in eighth grade, I lay down on the couch after breakfast. My parents had separated the year before, and my mother had temporary custody. She and I had moved together to a new house in town, a short walk from school, which gave my teenage body more time to sleep. I half dozed while she watched TV news, the sunlight streaming in the windows. And then the panicked, confused voice of the announcer woke me up. Something frightening was happening. The planes had hit the towers.

My town's rural libertarians thought that Bad Things were coming, and would arrive in Oklahoma directly by way of the Middle East. I remember passing a gas station on my way home and seeing a line of cars fifty deep, people filling up not just their cars but plastic canisters, in case the supply ran out. My father was among the people who worried that the collapse of society, even a supposedly stable one like ours, could happen in the blink of an eye.

I put a flag up on my locker after 9/11, one I'd printed out from the internet—and I certainly wasn't the only student who did that. It felt like the appropriate thing to do—but I did worry, even at that age, about the consequences of our new heightened fear of Islamic terror-ism. I got into an argument with a history teacher—who doubled as my basketball and track team coach—about whether this militant jin-goism would end up leading to martial law or restrictions on freedom of speech. He didn't think it would, but I had seen the movie *The Siege*, starring Denzel Washington and cowritten by Lawrence Wright, a few years before that: it imagines a series of terror attacks in New York City, in which the official response is to round up Muslims and detain them in stadiums. The intense xenophobia, justified by calls for secu-rity, felt familiar. I had the movie's central question circulating in my head: Do we become monsters in response to monstrosity? My teacher said that we would someday go back to normal—but I worried nothing would, or could, ever be normal again.

It was a difficult autumn, a full and final rupture with my child-hood. Two months after 9/11, my parents officially divorced. Within a few weeks, my father remarried. The wedding was a quick civil cere-mony at a courthouse. I wasn't invited, but they told me about it after-ward. It was unclear how long my father had known the other woman before my parents split, or if their relationship might have been a fac-tor in the divorce. Neither one of my parents ever seemed honest about what had occurred, and they each wanted me to believe their own, different version of what had happened between them.

After the divorce went through, my mother had to support herself for the first time in years, or maybe ever. I saw clearly how little idea she had of how to take care of herself. She began to drink even more, and her health deteriorated. She took on odd jobs: janitor, house cleaner, babysitter. She even worked in my school cafeteria for a while. My mother couldn't handle life on her own. At age fourteen, I started to handle her bank account, her tax forms, the monthly checks for our bills. She was on the other side of the world from where she'd grown up, scrubbing toilets and failing to make ends meet, and the man who'd been her whole reason for leaving home had left her for another woman. But even as I knew this, I felt left out of the picture. My sense of security, of knowing where I fit in the world, had evaporated. Ten months after their divorce, just as I was set to start high school, my mother bought airplane tickets we could barely afford: we were moving to Wales, back to the scene of her childhood, to a place where there would be people to take care of her. I didn't want to leave.

My mother's family had little to give: we stayed with her sisters, in their small, cramped houses, and it quickly became clear that we were an additional strain on households that were already close to the edge. The novelty of her return wore off fast, and all the ancient grudges and feuds came back. I couldn't follow all the arguments—and my mother struggled to catch up with the decades of complicated intrigue she'd missed—but it was obvious within a few weeks that we'd overstayed our welcome. She found a tiny apartment in town, but we couldn't afford to furnish it beyond a couple of beds and a couple of chairs. It was a quiet existence: just the two of us in a bleak, empty square. My mother was not yet fifty, but the drinking and smoking had taken a toll on her body. She had a series of strokes not long after we'd moved into the new apartment. Rather than frightening her into taking care of herself, the strokes led to a fear of medicine; after one mild stroke, she refused to go to the hospital. It was as if she were embracing slow decay, and forcing me to watch it happen. I started to tune my home life out, to try to think as little as possible about the mess of it. I spent time alone, filled the hours with video games, music, and skateboarding.

I wasn't totally provincial. My family had traveled a lot when I was young, and we even lived for the summer of 1995 in France, when my father was helping the Hertz Corporation set up for the Eurozone switch-over. But in Wales, as the new American, it took me a long time to adapt to high school. I'd been teased for being girlish my whole life, but in Oklahoma I'd had lifelong friends who would defend me, a spot on the middle school basketball team, and a pretty good jump shot. They didn't even play basketball in Wales. The school, a vast 1950s labyrinth of glass and brick, was ten times larger than the high school in Crescent. We wore uniforms with green, white, and red ties to class—the colors of the Welsh flag. A boy at school had to show me how to tie a simple half-Windsor knot. On the first day of class, I met a girl named Emily, a pretty brunette with brown eyes who became my first fast friend. She had a boyfriend, and I was attracted to him—and to her. But I couldn't quite figure out whether I had a crush on both of them, or whether I wanted to be her and date him. I became obsessed with the strange complication of those feelings, and drew away from both of them—if I could stop thinking about them, maybe I could stop the feelings themselves. Open sexual experimentation was much more normal in the UK than in Oklahoma, at least if you were straight. But even with the general air of permissiveness, I struggled with how different my own experimentation would be. I had crushes on boys; the longing I felt when I looked at girls was not rooted in a desire *for* them.

One girl in my physics class giggled at all of my jokes. Once, as I did a bit—impressions of famous actors—she laughed so hard she fell out of her chair. She liked me, everyone said. It became a source of gossip, and a friend gave her my number. Several weeks later, she texted to ask me to a party. It was in a backyard, with no parents, just a dozen of us holding red plastic cups with alcohol, listening to Blink-182 buzzing through distorted speakers. We jumped on a trampoline, higher and higher as we got tipsier and tipsier. We pretended to fight, pawing at each other, and then she grabbed my hand, for real this time, and led me behind a shed. She kissed me, and I froze: Where do my hands go? What should my tongue do? Why doesn't this feel good? I tensed my whole body, and she stopped. "I'm gay," I said. Where did that come from? I hadn't been ready to say it. She kept holding me, and I waited for her to mock, or to recoil. But instead, she asked me which boys I fancied. I laughed, and she offered me another drink, but I went home instead. What I wanted more than anything was a relationship, stability, someone to connect with, confide in, depend on, and trust.

And yet I lacked even the most basic opportunities to experiment. The nearest queer bar was forty miles away in Swansea, and mostly had an older clientele, and I was still underage, anyway. And so I turned again to the internet. There seemed to be a new chat room for every new aspect of my life. I tried porn, but it was too extreme and not for me. I'd sometimes help friends find what they wanted from triple-X sites in such a way that their parents couldn't find out, and what I saw was always pretty creepy, a bunch of topless girls with cartoonishly large breasts.

Sometimes the churn of world events broke through the cloud of my self-loathing. I was in Wales in 2003 when the invasion of Iraq began; I watched the post-9/11 world unfold from outside America, which gave me a different perspective. My classmates put the weight of American foreign policy on me; I got blamed for anything the George W. Bush administration did. *All you Americans are the same.* The complexities of our domestic politics were lost on everyone. And so I was put in the position of defending something I saw as complicated, not clean. I wrote about the invasion in a paper for school. My arguments weren't moral; they were financial. I did not argue about whether or not there had been justification for the war, but focused, in a detached way, on the expense; I argued that the cost wasn't worth it. I wasn't deeply antiwar by any means, but I was struck by how many people I knew who were. My classmates gave the paper a small standing ovation.

During the summer of 2005, I needed to go to London to get my American passport reissued: I felt vulnerable, trapped, and I wanted to make sure I had a way out if I needed it. It was early July, and I was staying in a tiny, closet-sized room at a cheap hostel in Bloomsbury. I walked down the spiral staircase, with my backpack on my shoulder, and headed out. I was on my way into the King's Cross Underground station, just under the grand façade and through the turnstiles, when all hell broke loose. I didn't see any fire or explosions, but I knew something was horribly wrong. I followed everyone else running away, back out to the street. The sky buzzed with helicopters. I'll never forget the police and fire sirens; the tone and pitch of the city changed in an instant. I didn't have anywhere to go or anyone to talk to. I was just a dumb kid with a backpack. Public transit was shut down, so I walked toward Grosvenor Square. I paused at a hole-in-the-wall bar, and perched at a stand outside, where I could see the news through the window—every TV was tuned not to sports but to the blanket BBC coverage that blared TERRORISM, alongside images of a destroyed bus. That was how I found out what had actually happened: a four-pronged bombing of three subway trains and one bus throughout the city—and one of the trains had departed from King's Cross. If I had gotten to the train station a few minutes earlier, what might have happened? I couldn't stop thinking about it, replaying the worst-case scenario in my head.

I decided to keep going to my appointment—I'd come all that way from Wales, and I didn't know what else to do—but the entire American embassy (and the city) was on lockdown. I was one of the few civilians on the streets. It felt like the prelude to a battle. There was security everywhere. I stayed near the Paddington station overnight, slept on a bench, and took an early bus in the morning back to Wales. My mother was freaked out. She was worried that I might have been killed, and I hadn't called her. With typical teenage logic, I figured that she knew I'd call if something had gone wrong. I tried not to let my anxiety over something that hadn't happened overwhelm me.

I had begun to think about my future. My only goal was to be rich, secure. It wasn't any more specific than that. Tech work seemed like the best way of getting there; I had come a long way since my father and I had programmed little downhill ski games. By now, I was a good programmer, and I'd done things like set up my own secure server, at a time when that was unusual. I knew about the intricacies of database management, the importance of user experience and good design. I also understood the security of online infrastructure. Knowing how to defend servers meant knowing how to exploit them, in an era when weaknesses were everywhere.

Mostly I learned about computers by fucking around, hacking. There were a lot of vulnerabilities then, and I just viewed them as problems to be solved. In other words, get complete control of the system, acquire the ability to be an administrator, edit any file, and view anything I wanted. Any random server in California or Italy could become my personal Rubik's Cube.

The chat rooms where I was spending more of my time had gotten sharper, more technical—and also more political, in a sense, as the government crackdown on the sharing of music and proprietary software got even more harsh. My hacking started to overlap with my ideological commitment to freedom of information: I'd go after targets that I thought *deserved* it. I'd take down the websites or sabotage the web servers of organizations in the recording industry that had acted to limit the ability of people to download files or share information. I didn't do it alone. Groups of mostly bored, vaguely nihilistic teenagers and young adults had begun to form, out of the murk of the chat room, into semi-autonomous cells of like-minded people. We'd use an app called Internet Relay Chat (IRC), which let us talk privately. We'd deface the public-facing sites of targets: I'd add a banner that said something like "this system is owned" or set up a spoof of an organization's site full of things that would be a PR disaster for that organization. We left in-jokes, game and movie references, or just plain nonsense on the sites. All for "the lulz," as we put it.

There was one person in my real life who understood computers like I did. Wallace, the name I'll use for a boy in my grade, had become both my best friend and my deepest rival: we competed academically, always trying to outdo each other. We both also bluffed our way through stuff, pretending to know things we didn't, and each of us could catch the other in his bullshit. Over time, we realized that there was something else to our strange affinity, our competitive sniffing out of each other: we were both being only partially honest with the people around us. Wallace was gay and closeted; I was trans and self-repressed. As a result, we had more to prove to the world and to ourselves. We had big ideas: once, we tried to start a social network together—this was before Facebook, in the Myspace era. We declared that I'd be the chief technology officer, while he'd be the public-facing chief operations officer, and tried to sell advertising to local businesses. But we fought over everything—how to do it, who would get credit. Before we'd really gotten anything off the ground, we ended the venture, and, for a few months, our friendship.

We explored what else we could do with our skills. Once, Wallace dared me to see if I could break into the digital files of a local public figure he didn't like. I wanted to prove to him that I had a level of skill he lacked. So, one night, under the cover of darkness, I went to that person's office. I picked the lock, then copied the hard drive from his desktop to a portable disk drive. A quick search of the disk image revealed very little: a computer used mostly for internet surfing and memo writings. We went through the emails together. Meetings, policy, and absolutely nothing scandalous. I ditched the copied drive. Still, it was a triumph for me. I'd shown Wallace I could do something he couldn't.

My sister was married on New Year's Day, 2005, to a law student, in an elaborate ceremony at the Tropicana casino in Las Vegas. My father and aunt had offered to pay for the plane ticket back: it had been two and a half years since I'd been home. I took my father's money, but instead of visiting him in Oklahoma City before the wedding, I stayed with my aunt and three cousins near Washington, D.C. Back in America, everything came flooding back. This was home. The way people said hello on the street, the accents—all of it brought up a homesickness I'd been ignoring. The Maryland suburbs of Washington felt warmer, friendlier, and more familiar than Wales, and even than my hometown of Crescent: there were tall green trees, colonial houses, quaint suburban parks, and quiet schools. It felt like the sun shone brighter, the clouds were somehow fluffier. Among the dignified cul-de-sacs, opportunity and financial security seemed possible.

Once I was in Wales, my mother had another stroke. She still wasn't taking care of herself. I figured something worse was bound to happen soon. The last straw for me was when I came home one day and found her passed out, dripping wet and naked from the bathtub, at the bottom of the stairs. I thought she was dead. It is a terrifying, indelible image—I can still close my eyes and see myself, this tiny blond teenager, checking my mother's pulse and breathing, wrapping her in towels and blankets, trying to figure out who I could call. There was no one. I picked her up over my shoulder and walked her to the bed, where I propped her up in the recovery position. She vomited onto the towel I'd laid beside her. This was the moment when I finally knew for certain that I would—that I could—never be taken care of by my mother ever again. And I knew I didn't want to be the one to have to take care of my mother. I wasn't ready for that. I was seventeen.

Later that year, I finished school, with AS-level certificates in physics, economics, history, and mathematics. The first thing I did was come out as gay on Myspace. My attraction to other guys was no longer something I had to hide for social reasons, and finally just telling everyone felt like releasing the longest-held breath of my life.

But I missed America. And so, when I got my diploma, I decided to move back to Oklahoma City. I wanted to go to college in the States, and since I was only seventeen, I had time to apply. Instead of a warm welcome home, I got an icy reception. My father's new wife had no use for me. It became clear I wasn't wanted in their home. My father seemed to view me mostly as a financial burden, telling me that he wouldn't support me through college. Meanwhile, his new wife rarely acknowledged my existence unless I was breaking an arbitrary rule. I was an interloper in the life that they'd built together, a reminder of the marriage he'd had before theirs. Her son from her previous marriage also lived with us. Caring for him was her main purpose in life; she saw me as a bad influence, and believed I was exposing him to the wrong things when I played video games with him or just answered the questions he'd ask. The way I saw it, I was the only person who talked to him like he was a human being. Everyone else treated him as if he were stupid or six years old, rather than a teenager with social limitations. My father's wife and I would get endlessly angry at each other, my depression and surliness butting up against her need for total control and her complete lack of empathy for my situation.

My father got me an interview with one of the few tech companies in Oklahoma City, a photo-hosting service. I'm pretty sure he just wanted me to get a job as quickly as possible so I could afford rent and move out of his house. I got the job on the spot, as a paid intern. I liked the work well enough, but the real excitement was finally having an actual dating life. I started going to the gay clubs down in the Thirty-Ninth Street district. Two out of the three spots were twenty-one and over, but at the third, there was an eighteen-and-up nonalcoholic lounge, connected to the actual bar by a breezeway. Thursdays—the college party night—were the best nights to go. People would drive sixty or seventy miles just to come to this dank little club in Oklahoma City. By this time, I was more androgynous than I'd ever been. Now that I didn't have to wear a school uniform, I was experimenting with how I presented myself to the world, pushing boundaries. I favored a full-on emo-Goth look. Eyeliner with black hoodies and dyed black hair, Chucks or Doc Martens.

I came out to my father several months after I moved back. For weeks, I worked myself up to it, imagining the best way to phrase it, the precise moment to unburden myself. I was afraid of his reaction, but still ached for his approval—would this mean giving it up forever? When I finally told him, struggling to get the words out, turning red, stopping and starting, he just said, "Okay?" and threw up his hands. It was meant not in a reassuring way, but in the most neutral way imaginable: he wasn't surprised, he wasn't even upset, he just didn't care. It hurt how matter-of-fact he was. Even a negative reaction, yelling insults or worse, would have meant that he cared enough about his child to be angry.

It wasn't an easy place and time to be queer. Just two years before, in 2003, the Supreme Court's ruling in *Lawrence v. Texas* had finally overturned all of the anti-gay-sodomy laws. So the gay-bar raids by the vice squad had officially stopped, but the Oklahoma City police still had a huge presence in those Thirty-Ninth Street clubs. Even if they weren't arresting people, they'd routinely kick us out, test for underage drinking, and hassle us for noise complaints with every bullshit excuse under the sun. My earliest memories of trying to flirt, of holding hands, and of kissing are tied up with knowing that the cops were watching the whole thing happen, surveilling our exploration. Still, the sense of shame I'd felt when I was younger about being gay had begun to melt away.

The first person I ever really dated was a guy I'd met online. He lived around ninety miles away. He was a year younger than me, still a senior in high school, and had been born in South America. His family ran a restaurant, but we went to the Olive Garden for our first proper date together. It felt pretty high-end for where we lived, and I felt like a big-deal big spender with the money from my internship. His car had a panoramic moon roof, and I remember, on an early date, going through a McDonald's drive-through in it together holding hands. We even kissed a little bit while waiting in line, under the orange street-lights. That was a risky, even scary move in Oklahoma in 2005.

Despite the thrill of a new social life, I got depressed. I turned up the volume on my tiny iPod Nano as high as it would go, listening to electronic music, trying to drown out the rest of the world. Even in my fashion experiments I was trying out Goth clothing: I went to Hot Topic and bought a corset that I told the clerk was for my girlfriend. I wasn't angry, I was just full of darkness, and I was trying to make my outside match my inside. It was nihilism mixed with loneliness—I felt like I'd never find anyone to build a secure life with, never have a job that got me away from central Oklahoma, with its judgment and bore-dom. I felt barely human. Most of the free time I had I spent alone on my computer, with multiple screens for gaming. My mother had an-other stroke, and this one was bad. Casey and I flew to London because the doctors said it was likely she would die. We thought we were buy-ing tickets to attend her funeral; our aunt picked us up from the air-port and drove as fast as she could to the hospital. I looked at my mother in the gown, disoriented and pale, and I thought about all the times I'd seen her passed-out drunk on the floor. It was horrific and frightening to see her that way. She didn't die, but I had started to think of her as gone, and to think of myself as someone without a mother. I felt hurt and alone.

Back in Oklahoma, I lost my job. The CEO was targeting his photo-sharing service to stay-at-home moms, which I thought was all wrong, considering that the user data showed our market was mostly teenage girls trying out their new camera phones. I yelled, and it escalated. I was eighteen years old and trying to tell the CEO of a company how to run his business. I deserved to be fired. There weren't many other options for tech positions in Oklahoma City, though. I got a job in the electronics section of Walmart, where I lasted for six days. In every way, it was the shittiest employer in the world. I quit, which left me jobless, home all day, and depressed. My father's wife hated having me around. She felt entitled to boss others around. Our fights snowballed. My father tried to pretend they weren't happening. He didn't react to things with visible emotion at the best of times—the only feeling I really ever saw him exhibit was anger—and he was especially vacant during that time period. He had been trying to quit drinking, which took up a lot of energy. He'd also had prostate cancer that had required surgery, which meant he was bedridden and majorly medicated on painkillers.

It was just a week after that surgery that my father's wife and I got in our last, worst fight. I'd gone into the kitchen to make myself a sandwich, sometime around sunset, and she decided to impose a new arbitrary rule: you can't be in *my* kitchen after eight. Fuck off, I thought. I sliced my sandwich and yelled at her for her stupid manipulation, waving the knife as I talked. I put it down as soon as I realized, but she dialed 911 and told them that I was threatening her. My father tried to get up to intervene, but he was so drugged out from the pain medication that he fell from his chair instead. I tried to pick him up, and this only made her angrier. My father was mumbling about his surgery, about his pain, and she ran into her bedroom.

I walked back to my room with the sandwich. Five minutes later, the doorbell rang. I opened the door and stepped outside, closing the screen door behind me. "What's up, officers?" I said calmly. "Call about a domestic dispute," one of them said. "She's back there," I said, pointing to the bedroom. My stepmother had weaponized the police against me.

The police told me I couldn't stay in the house: Oklahoma state law required them to remove the accused person from the premises in domestic disputes. The police, in effect, have to arrest someone in these calls, although they don't necessarily have to press charges. They put me in the back of the squad car and told me they weren't booking me. *That fills me with so much joy* was my sarcastic reply. It was my first time in handcuffs, and as I watched the familiar streets and buildings fly past the window from the back of the patrol car, I felt unwelcome everywhere.

The police took me to a domestic dispute center. By the time I arrived, Casey was already there. She was beyond pissed at my father's wife and at my father. This was the last thing she wanted to do that night.

I stayed with her for a couple of days in her tiny one-bedroom house, where she was living with her husband. My father dropped off all my worldly belongings, which he and his wife had packed up into plastic boxes.

I was officially kicked out, homeless. Casey said I could stay with her, but her house was small and I felt like a burden. I had no job, no home, no parental affection to speak of. But I had the keys to my father's truck, an old beater that he didn't really care about. I took the truck, a red 1992 Nissan Hardbody, and headed out to Tulsa for a couple of weeks, ninety miles from Crescent. It was the only place I could think of; Jordan, my best friend from elementary school, let me crash with him. He helped me get a job at Incredible Pizza, where he worked. It was a brand-new place, so they were hiring in bulk. Pretty soon, I got the vibe that this was a "family-oriented" company—a Christian company. In a million little ways, I began to feel uncomfortable. People spotted me at gay clubs, or with men; there was a rumor mill and I had no sense that the company's management would be at all supportive of my "alternative lifestyle." I needed to leave Oklahoma, where this was the undercurrent everywhere. Besides, Jordan was living with his parents, and they wanted me out.

I didn't have other options, but I still had that truck. So I just got in and drove north and east, away from Oklahoma, overnight without stopping. My plan was to stay in the first big city I hit, St. Louis, about seven hours away. I had no agenda, no local knowledge, so I went to the Gateway Arch, the one thing I knew about the city. I wandered around for a day, then spent the night sleeping in a parking lot out by the airport. I didn't want to stay. Fuck it, I'd made it this far away from home, from everything and everyone I knew. I might as well keep going.

4.

The Illinois countryside, with its corn and wheat fields, looked golden in the summer morning light. I drove past the grain silos and power lines into the outskirts of Chicago, where the scenery turned dingy, the low buildings blocky and brown. Somehow, I felt safer already.

Finally, the city skyline came into view. Slowly and carefully, over-whelmed by the number of pedestrians and the downtown traffic, I drove to the Sears Tower. It was the tallest building in the country at that time, and I figured it was the best place to get my bearings—it was also one of the only things I recognized about Chicago. Inside the tower's gift shop, I bought a guide to the city that offered a general lay of the land and a detailed rundown of where I could find just about everything I might need: maps, food, libraries, laundry. It was a dream for a recently displaced young person.

I thumbed through it until I found a section marked "gay and les-bian." I headed straight to Boystown, the "gayborhood" near Wrigley Field. It was a different world. Men held hands and kissed on the street, and a whole economy had sprung up to serve them. From my point of view, it was as close to liberation as I could imagine. I spent days there in coffee shops and on park benches, watching openly gay people go about their lives, trying to imagine such a life of my own. But I didn't have anywhere to sleep other than my car. Finding a place to live seemed impossible. The price of rent in Chicago was outrageous compared to Oklahoma City, and I didn't have any money regardless. And there was a part of me that liked and desired the autonomy and anonymity of living on the streets, alone in a city where I knew no one.

Most of my admittedly fuzzy memories of Chicago are of the Boystown clubs, chaotic and warm in the summer heat, filled with rainbow flags and Mardi Gras beads. My spot was Crobar, which held a weekly event called G.L.E.E. Club. (*G.L.E.E.* stood for "gay, lesbian, everyone's equal.") I would sneak in, with a fake ID I'd bought from a graphic designer in Cicero, and let guys buy me drinks. The clubs were fancier than any bar I'd been to before, hot and dark and full of men, packed together on a huge dance floor in front of a smoke machine and a real sound system. Steve Angello's remix of Eurythmics' "Sweet Dreams" played constantly that summer. Rihanna had just blown up the pop charts. "S.O.S., please someone help me / It's not healthy for me to feel this," she sang as I danced all night. The lyrics from that summer are seared into my brain; I lost myself in the music, in the scene, and the freedom was everything I'd ever dreamed of.

I'd spent my childhood and most of my teens swinging between hopeless desire to be myself and seeing myself through the eyes of people who, at best, did not understand me. In Chicago, I was able to see myself as desirable, and to be comfortable in who I was. The freedom and the music enhanced each other, and the whole experience was further enhanced by the unrestrained attention of men, and the drugs that were sometimes on offer at the clubs. I tried cocaine, but the thing that defined my experience of those clubs that summer was ecstasy. The comedown was soul-crushing, but in the moments of that high, I felt what it was to have real desire. Even more than that, I felt like my life had purpose and meaning.

The Boystown clubs allowed me to survive that summer. They gave me an anchor and a community, but they also enabled me to meet my basic needs. I could go home with someone at the end of the night and have a roof over my head, a place to shower in the morning. Sometimes they would give me a little gas money. I always told them I was "between places," but they probably knew how desperately I was struggling. Even then, I was looking for true love. I believed every person might be the one, and was inevitably and repeatedly disappointed. I did end up spending a lot of time with a young professional in the suburbs, as well as another guy who was a bassist in a truly terrible Fall Out Boy–wannabe band, but most of my visions of romance ended after a single night. Naïve as I was, I did know that not everyone I went home with was a keeper. After some uncomfortable situations I learned how to say no, and somewhat to my surprise, it usually worked. But I always had a Smith & Wesson knife on me, too, just in case.

The club was filled with kids like me, white Goth twinks, on the edge and on the prowl. People who had already carved out their territory for their hustle felt disrespected by my presence and signaled their displeasure. But still, they looked out for me. And we all looked out for cops. Just about everyone was a potential undercover trying to entrap unwary club kids for anything resembling sex work. Club lore was that cops couldn't actually expose themselves, and that the only way to figure it out for sure was to ask a potential client to flash you. Of course, the idea that cops were constrained in this way was nonsense, and I think at some level we all knew it.

But the danger wasn't limited to the club. Avoiding cops colored my whole life. I found a free parking lot near a Guitar Center on North Halsted, so the cops couldn't hassle me. For a while, that was where I slept. I hung out at the store during the day, talking about amps with the staff. I even worked there, briefly, but I couldn't stay hygienic enough to fly under the radar. I tried my best, grabbing showers when I could get one at a guy's apartment, and I'd do my laundry at a place on Addison where you could get a whole load done for a dollar. But my coworkers at the Guitar Center kept indicating that my smell was a problem. No one there knew my situation, and I didn't want to explain. I stopped working there, and I stopped sleeping in their parking lot.

I'd eat one meal a day, most days. When I wasn't getting dinner or a midnight snack from someone I met at the club, I lived off the McDonald's Dollar Menu, which was actually a dollar back then. The McDouble—one of the most calorie-packed meals on the planet— was my superfood. It's not the greatest nutrition in the world, but it'll keep you alive for a while. I still shrank from 120 pounds to 95, with deep circles under my eyes that made me barely recognizable to myself in the mirror. My fair skin was fried: it was summer, and I couldn't afford sunscreen.

If I didn't find someone to crash with for the night, I shanked out forty bucks for a cheap hotel out in Schaumburg, a suburb by the airport. On the nights when I didn't have the money for that, I'd drive all the way out there anyway. It was isolated and I was less likely to be hassled by cops while I slept in the parking lots of giant shopping complexes. The harassment was constant—every week or two I'd be awakened by a cop shining his light into my truck and telling me I couldn't sleep where I was. They'd ask about drugs, or weapons, or clients. If I got lucky and slept through the night, I'd wake up the next morning sweaty and baking in the hotbox of my truck. The fun and the feeling of freedom were beginning to wear off.

I started to dumpster dive, not just for food but for objects that I thought might be useful. I'd drive to big apartment complexes on the northern edge of the city, the kind of places with big dumpsters and lots of people moving in and out, trashing their stuff. I'd pile it up in the back of my truck and give it to people I encountered—to friendly people as gifts, to hostile people as peace offerings. The video game Fallout imagines a postapocalyptic universe in which you collect trinkets that serve no obvious purpose, but that might help you scrounge for survival. In my own personal apocalypse, that logic made a lot of sense, and worked out pretty well.

I needed money. I started making cash by trading on my tech skills, selling bullshit to people who didn't know enough to realize I was full of it. I'd meet someone, chat them up, and promise websites and databases I had no intention of delivering. HOMELESS HACKER, I wrote on poster board attached to the tailgate of Dad's pickup truck. I'd explain that I didn't have my bank account set up, so I'd just ask for a small down payment, say a hundred dollars or so, for the work I swore I would do fast and cheap. And then I'd disappear. Once, I found some old software cases trashed in a dumpster, so I bought shrink wrap at a hardware store and used a lighter to seal it around the cases; I'd bootleg the key code using a generator I found online. I set up next to a guy on a street corner selling watches of questionable provenance and authenticity in Greektown, and I sold the discs to passersby, who thought they were getting an unbelievable deal.

I wasn't just living on the margins, I was falling off the edge. I figured that I was going to end up in jail sooner or later, and that it wouldn't be that bad. I didn't care about having a record. Three hots and a cot sounded about as stable as sleeping around for food and shelter. I didn't regret coming to Chicago, but I needed this particular adventure to end.

I hadn't been in touch with anyone from Oklahoma while I was in Chicago. But I had the possession most important for survival: my laptop. I used the free internet at the Chicago Public Library (I couldn't check out any books; because I was homeless, I couldn't get a card), or unprotected wireless networks. My parents weren't looking for me, as far as I knew. I told just one friend that I had moved there, and gave him my new cell phone number, though we didn't stay in touch. Having the phone was complicated—the bills had to go to an address, so I rented a PO box for a couple of bucks a month.

One day, toward the end of the summer, I got a call from a Maryland number I didn't recognize. I answered out of curiosity. "Oh my god, I've been trying to reach you!" said a woman on the other end. It was my aunt Debbie, my father's sister. She'd tracked me down because my mother had asked her to. She was furious with my father for kicking me out. This was relief I hadn't realized I wanted. I cried. She cried. She said she had just wanted to make sure I had a place to stay, and when I told her that I was on the street, living in my father's truck, she suggested I come stay with her in Potomac. She wired me money at a Western Union, enough for gas and food, and I drove east, with no plan beyond showing up on the doorstep of a woman I hadn't seen in years. It was raining, and I was followed by a thunderstorm. It was chasing me down I-80, pouring dense, windy sheets of rain at my back. I'd drive for a while, outpacing it, then I'd see the storm again in my rearview mirror, and I'd have to stop for a while. The radio was broken, and so I just let my mind wander. Near Pittsburgh, I stopped for gas. I sat in my truck by the pump and cried for twenty minutes. My truck was good to go, but I was only starting to understand how long I had been running on fumes.

Potomac, Maryland, is an upper-middle-class neighborhood full of big houses owned by doctors and lawyers. I was self-conscious, arriving in my beat-up truck, smelling like I had spent the summer living in it. I couldn't find my aunt's house at first, and I drove around feeling more and more nervous, worried someone might call the cops on me. Finally, I pulled up to my aunt's, a big brick house on a street with tall, leafy trees. I knocked on the door and my aunt helped me inside. The first thing I told her, before anything else, was that I needed a shower.

And sleep. My cousin was away at Penn State, and my aunt told me I could sleep in her room as long as I wanted.

I tried to build a new life, slowly. One that would give me a future. With a new Maryland driver's license in hand, I enrolled at Montgomery College, a community college. The plan was to study there until I could transfer into the University of Maryland and get a degree in physics, a field that I have always loved. I needed money, so I looked for a job that would use my tech skills, but just about everything in the D.C. area required a security clearance. I assumed my period of homelessness would pop up in a background check, and besides, most companies don't want to invest in getting a person a new security clearance when it's not a sure thing. I got a job at Starbucks to pay tuition. The benefits were good—health care!—but the work was exhausting. As a barista, you're expected to be chipper and outgoing all the time. People want you to recognize them, to know their drinks and their names. The emotional work is taxing, and the schedule is grueling: "flexible," in a way that accommodates the ever-changing needs of the company. Between the unstable hours and the enforced cheerfulness, I spent as much time grinding my teeth as grinding coffee.

The Dupont Circle club scene quickly became a release for me. Once again, I found temporary euphoria in sex and ecstasy. I bought my ecstasy from a chemistry graduate student who was going *Breaking Bad*, and I chose boyfriends more carefully, now that I wasn't desperate for a place to sleep. The quality of both was vastly better than in Chicago, but they still left me feeling strung out afterward. This time, though, I started to think that my social skills and hookups could be my way into a better job. All I had to do was sleep with one person who could hook me up with a connection that would deliver me to the next big thing, anything that would get me money or stability. I was sure that a better job was going to appear if I leveraged my sexuality just right. I would suddenly be able to jump through a certain kind of door and breathe more easily, get away from the exhaustion of shift work. On the club scene, everyone but me seemed to have a great job—the State Department, the diplomatic corps, careers I saw as a path to a bigger life, one of stability and significance. I tried for a year, and it just never happened. I'd go as people's date to fancy parties filled with politicians and diplomats, but it never led to what I wanted.

Through it all, my already debilitating gender dysphoria was getting more acute. The best explanation I've ever heard is that it's like a toothache that never goes away. You're not always consciously thinking about it, but it's this persistent thing you can't totally shake, that keeps holding you back. I started to buy women's stuff. I was making more money than I ever had before, and I had free rent, so I could afford better makeup, better clothing. I'd take the makeup that I'd bought and try it on with the clothes that my cousin had left in her closet when she went to college. I'd stare at myself in her full-length mirror from every angle. I felt better, but the prospect of being discovered was terrifying. It felt a little like the first time I smoked a cigarette: there was peer pressure to smoke and also to hide it. Only this time, all the pressure was coming from me. And it was immense.

I had more security and freedom than I'd had before, and I didn't want to ruin that. I could go out and party all I wanted, but in my aunt, I now had someone who loved me like a parent. Through everything, my aunt Debbie has had my back, but at the time I was afraid that if she found out about my gender, she'd kick me out. I didn't know whether my aunt was entirely comfortable with my sexuality, because while I certainly didn't hide it, I never officially came out to her. But I had no read on how she would react to the revelation that I was trans. She was politically liberal, but sometimes people like that, especially then, were simply more secretive about their prejudices. I'd just found a safe harbor, so I saw thin ice everywhere I stepped.

The feelings outweighed the fear. I began, for the first time, to research hormone therapy, which I'd first learned about from a flyer I'd seen at a club in Dupont Circle, alongside all the condoms and dental dams. I wanted so badly to see if it was feasible, but the cost seemed prohibitive, and I was working a low-wage job and going to school. I tried to forget about it.

There weren't a ton of openly trans people in the queer scene then, but there were some. Once, I met a trans woman at an after-party. She sat alone, smoking a cigarette on the balcony of someone's high-rise apartment. I was fascinated by her, and she, in turn, clocked me immediately as an "egg"—a trans baby who hasn't "hatched" yet. She called me out; I pretended not to know what she was talking about. She winked at me, and hugged me. "When you're ready," she said. I turned the moment over in my mind obsessively; it was one of the things that finally led me to seek out therapy. I found my therapist by searching online for therapists in the D.C. area who specialized in LGBT issues. She was dark-haired, young, and thoughtful, and I thought she could help me work through whether I wanted to transition. I knew from my research that I would need a letter from a psychiatrist in order to get the hormones and surgery covered. But, in the five or six sessions we had, I talked to her about everything *but* gender: my difficulty feeling safe after having been kicked out and sleeping in my car, my job, my general insecurity, my family. I avoided the subject of gender, and there was plenty of other stuff to keep us busy. Panic attacks plagued me. They had started when I was a teenager, and had accelerated while I was homeless. We ended up talking about all of my problems as simply anxiety and depression, going into the symptoms and ignoring the root issue. I was afraid of being judged, even by my therapist, and of what acknowledging my feelings could set in motion. I worried that if I said it out loud, if I acted on it, I would set off a chain of events that would end with me getting kicked out of my aunt's house, unable to finish college, and back on the streets of yet another city.

I wished desperately that my therapist could look at my face and just understand what I needed to say. I'd stare at the art on her walls, avoiding eye contact. Once, I sat there, completely silent, as she waited for me to say something. I was speechless, for minutes, endless minutes, unable to unburden myself.

I revisit that moment often. What if I had come out as trans then? What if I had lived my life in a more ordinary way in suburban Maryland? Maybe a few more sessions and I would have broken my silence.

But I didn't, in part because I was thrown into despair over something much more ordinary, a series of professional disappointments. I was passed over, twice, for an assistant manager position I'd been promised at Starbucks. The second time it happened it felt like I'd be stuck with that apron forever, a wage worker with unpredictable hours in a scummy corporate horror show. I felt trapped by the impossibility of improving my position, of getting to the salaried job with the regular hours.

Even with in-state tuition, I was struggling for cash. I'd even gotten a second job, at Abercrombie & Fitch, during the summer of 2007 to try to supplement my income. I liked the décor—black-and-white photos of cute, shirtless guys—and I was good at the job. On my first day there, they handed me a scan gun and asked if I knew how to use a database. I did a store inventory in two days, and the store manager offered me a higher-paying job as a stock manager—but the hours conflicted with school.

That was my breaking point. I was spending one hundred hours a week either at school or working these two jobs. By the time I had a moment to study, I was falling asleep. College stopped seeming worth it. I didn't sign up for the next semester and started reconsidering my options. I didn't know what I wanted to do, I just knew I couldn't sustain that life anymore. I met a corporate headhunter on the club scene who got me an interview with a tech company that was building a password manager. I went out to a big anonymous office building in Virginia, where the CEO, an older white man, hired me on the spot—but it quickly became clear to me he had no idea how to actually build what he wanted to build. He was just a venture capitalist who thought starting a company sounded cool, and had ended up with a Defense Department contract he was trying to fulfill in a hurry. The amount of information they planned to give the government about their users seemed sketchy as fuck. When he told me that I'd be the one writing the feasibility plan—that is, they didn't even have proof of concept yet, despite the big contract—I turned it down. I didn't want to be part of that kind of con.

I got on the Orange Line back to the city, thinking the whole way about how stuck I felt, how hopeless it all was. I knew I had the ability to do something real, but I just couldn't get a solid foundation. At Metro Center, I waited on the platform to switch to the Red Line back to Maryland, and fixed my gaze on a woman in a makeup ad. She was obviously photoshopped, and I knew it, but I stared at her image and saw only perfection—total, unattainable perfection. A train was coming in, and I thought, Should I just jump in front of it right now? I don't want to do this anymore. I can't live in this netherworld. Everything I do ends up not going far enough, not being enough. "Doors opening," the familiar voice recording played. "Step back to allow customers to exit. When boarding, please move to the center of the car."

"Are you going to go in or what?" an older woman scolded me from behind. I stepped in. The doors closed.

5.

I had begun talking to my father on the phone, trying to repair the damage, to have a relationship with him again. Things started smoothly. He liked small talk. Then he offered advice—how could I build a life, grow up into something steadier? Join the navy, he kept saying, join the navy. Hell, join the air force. He saw the military as the fix-it-all solution to my problems: the military offered stability, tuition money down the line, a career. And it would man me up, he kept repeating. It had done that for him.

The Iraq war was on TV in the background constantly. Every night, my aunt came home from her job as a lawyer for Fannie Mae, the government-sponsored mortgage company, and watched the news in horror. Her defense contractor husband was opposed to the war, too, and they'd talk for hours about what President George W. Bush and Vice President Dick Cheney had done wrong. But my own views on Iraq and Afghanistan were less formed. I took the mission at face value. I didn't dig too deeply into the reasons our country was in Iraq. I believed the narrative that the media was pushing: we needed to boost our troop numbers in order to tamp down the violence.

My aunt's bookshelves were filled with histories of World War II and the Civil War—as my father's had been—and so I read about troop movements, battalions, tactics, strategy. And I spent a lot of time playing combat video games, like Call of Duty. The technical aspects of fighting interested me; insurgency and counterinsurgency were intriguing theoretical, tactical problems.

Enlisting, I began to think, might solve a few problems. For one thing, it would get my dad to stop needling me. And I wanted his respect. For another, I thought it would be a good way to externally enforce my own masculinity. I figured I wouldn't have the desire to wear women's clothing in such a regimented environment—if there was a uniform, I wouldn't have to think about gender presentation at all. Then, as my father had pointed out, there was the job security it offered, along with the GI Bill. I was killing myself to make in-state tuition at a community college; when I got out of the service, I could go to college for free. And because of the surge, the military was offering extra inducements on top of all that.

Maybe most important, enlisting would allow me to feel once more that my life had meaning. I *wanted* to go to Iraq. I wanted to experience the fight firsthand. Be there. Smell it. Even risk my life. If I died in Iraq, I wouldn't die in a way that would embarrass my dad. I also wouldn't die of the targeted violence so many queer people like me fear and experience. Instead, I'd die for equally pointless reasons overseas. I could live with that.

In late September 2007, I drove out to the joint recruiting center near downtown Rockville. There were two competing cardboard cutouts—one in a Marine Corps uniform, one in an army uniform—and a rack full of brochures. As a naval officer, my father looked down on the Marine Corps, and in one last little rebellion, I'd decided it was my first choice. I knocked on the Marine Corps door, but the office was closed for the day. I grabbed a brochure, and noticed that the army recruiting center was open across the hall. I stuck my head in the door and asked if they had any pamphlets. Every head in the office turned at once. The room smelled like Windex and new construction. Three soldiers in green, tan, and gray digital camo stood up quickly to greet me, as if I'd made their day by showing up.

I'd been worried military recruiters would laugh at me. Not because I was queer—I had a sense from the men I'd met in the Dupont club scene that Don't Ask, Don't Tell wouldn't actually be much of a practical issue—but because I was scrawny. I was just five foot two at the time, still a couple of inches short of my final height. Instead of ridiculing me, they gave me the gold-star treatment. I think they were thrilled to get an actual walk-in recruit. "We've got way more than a brochure," they told me. "Sit down, have some coffee." I'd never really spent much time around enlisted soldiers before that afternoon. These guys were friendly—they offered institutional support, even empathy. They specialized in offering a way out for people who were way down on their luck—people like me. And they'd once stood where I stood. My recruiter was a staff sergeant and veteran of two tours in Iraq, who had a dark sense of humor and easy friendliness that appealed to me. We sat together and created my career, my life plan, on the spot. They asked me what I wanted to do, what I was good at, where I saw myself living in ten years. I had rarely had people ask me those questions in my life, had rarely had someone sit and listen and think through the answers with me.

They drove me to Fort Meade right away to take a forty-five-minute battery of aptitude and academic tests. I excelled. An official sat at a desk with a generic form on his computer, interrogating me about what I wanted to do in the army. "You have no limitations on what you can choose as your job, since your scores are almost perfect," he said.

What *did* I want to do? I had computer expertise, but didn't want to get sucked into IT, just sitting behind a screen and fixing people's software problems. And I knew I didn't want to get placed in signals intelligence at Fort Meade, where I thought I'd be doing math problems in an office. I wanted to see the world, to be in the fight itself. So instead of saying that I liked computers, I said I liked to work with databases, and that military intelligence sounded good to me. I signed up as a 96 Bravo: all-source intelligence analyst. That sounded good to the officer, too. In the last two minutes, he introduced me to the concept of green-to-gold: you go in as an enlisted person and come out as an officer, and from there, a whole world of career options is open to you.

Everything happened quickly. Instant test results, instant everything. The recruiters seemed to be in a hurry, like they didn't want me to walk out the door and think it over. They promised a twenty-thousand-dollar bonus if I signed up on the spot, which waived the forty-day waiting period—the surge needed soldiers, after all. All I had to do was get a physical. They picked me up from my aunt's house the next morning—the burden of getting there yourself might make you have second thoughts. I spent the rest of the day filling out the background check form called SF-86, and tracking down dozens of people and addresses. As it turned out, after all my worrying about what might pop up on a background check, they assured me the army's security check would be no problem whatsoever, and thanks to their instruction, they were right. I was blunt with them about having been homeless; instead of shaming me and telling me I could never get a security clearance, they were supportive and sympathetic. I asked them what to do about my drug experimentation. Write nothing, the recruiter told me. "Everyone's done something," he said. The forms also asked whether I'd seen a psychologist, and I explained that I'd seen someone to deal with panic attacks. He assured me that wasn't what they were worried about—as long as I hadn't been in inpatient psychiatric care, it shouldn't be an issue. "When in doubt, don't write it down," he joked. It was technically against the rules, but this, after all, is how the army officially dealt with other uncomfortable issues: at several points, the paperwork reminded me that the military was not going to ask me about my sexuality, and that I could not disclose my sexuality, engage in any "homosexual acts," or get married in a same-sex relationship. This uncomfortable balance seemed like no big deal then. I would do my best to hide my sexuality while still working and getting paid, no questions asked.

My physical approval, however, was delayed because I had a mole on my back that they wanted to have biopsied. The recruiters were pissed about that; they thought the medical officer, who they referred to as "Dr. No," was a pain who just liked slowing down the process. But a few days later, after a trip to the dermatologist, the medical officer gave me a yes. I would be shipped out to basic training at Fort Leonard Wood, Missouri, as an E-1, with a monthly salary of $1,204 for six months, and three automatic rank upgrades within two years. I was given one day for goodbyes.

I didn't tell my family until after I'd signed the papers. My aunt was blindsided. She wanted to know why I hadn't come to her first, why we couldn't have talked it through together and figured out another plan. My father, though, was proud of me. He still wished I'd gone for the navy, but mostly he thought I was doing something smart for once. I didn't call my mother—talking to her, just then, would have opened too many wounds. My sister seemed genuinely concerned, and loving: she told me I was a dumb-ass, making a stupid, impulsive move, and that no matter how talented I was there was no way I'd fit into the culture of the army, given my history of clashing with authority figures. Her care was reassuring, but irrelevant in the face of what I had already set in motion.

Fort Leonard Wood is a two-and-a-half-hour drive from the St.

Louis airport, down gently rolling Route 44, in the Missouri Ozarks. Gone was the friendly, supportive atmosphere of the recruitment office. From now on the drill sergeant, a guy with prominent eyebrows and a fierce, authoritative bark, told us what to do, with a yell that instilled both fear and motivation. The bus from the airport filled up with other recruits—tall people, short people, guys and girls, with short hair and long hair, mostly young but at least one as old as thirty-eight. Most of us had just finished high school, in the Midwest or the Deep South. Hardly anyone spoke. I just leaned my head on the glass of the window, with my backpack in hand, watching the trees roll by. It reminded me of riding the school bus.

Our first stop on base was the Reception Battalion in Grant Hall, a long building with rows of benches, where the sergeants gave us ten minutes to say our goodbyes over our phones, before they ordered us to dump out our bags and empty our pockets of all electronics and civilian items. They carted out a large bin labeled AMNESTY, giving us one last consequence-free chance to turn in any contraband—drugs, cigarettes, alcohol, or knives. To fill out the essential paperwork, we were allowed only black-ink pens. "There are no blue pens in the army," the drill sergeants repeated, as if it were a metaphor for the control and rigor we'd learn to adjust to. "No talking," they'd add, although the room was silent. Anyone who didn't follow directions was taken aside for push-ups. Over the next few hours, the drill sergeants issued our essential army gear: utility uniforms, bags and packs, boots, physical training outfits, and gloves. We wrote our last names and the last four digits of our Social Security number on everything. The drill sergeants marched us to our barracks bunks for the night, but we didn't get to sleep for long. At 0500, long before dawn, we were called for breakfast formation, with the drill sergeant barking orders. But no one knew the ranks or the files; we were just a confused gaggle of scared people in the dark. There was another long day of in-processing: Most of us, including me, had to shave our heads. For vaccinations, the nurses took large groups of us into a medical room. They directed us to face the wall, lean forward, and pull down our uniform bottoms and underwear, with our buttocks exposed in a long line. Nurses walked around with giant needles.

On ship-out day, I was assigned to a training company in the Third Chemical Brigade. (The *Chemical* part was a historical name, not an indication that it was a specialized unit.) The drill sergeants split us up and marched us to our respective buses, with our new military-issue gear in a heavy duffel bag. The newly designed gray-green digital camouflage uniforms looked ridiculous, even for the military. We joked that standing against the rough stucco walls outside a barracks, or lying down in the rocky side roads and parking lots, were the only situations in which the pattern could perform well. From the second you put on fatigues, everything around you works to instill a mindset, program you to be what is needed, rebuild you from the ground up to perform as part of a team. *Basic soldiering* is the term: the goal is to prepare you to be taught. The hard drive is wiped. We'd all learn different skills eventually—a lot of the other recruits were going to be truck drivers, since there was a huge need for them in 2007 in Afghanistan, and a big bonus for signing on to do it—but first we had to learn what it was to be a military person.

Technically, in 2006 the army had banned the use of derogatory language during basic training, following a decade of hazing scandals. But the culture lagged behind official policy, and I quickly got used to humiliation, insults, misogyny, the casual use of words like *retard* and *faggot*—all coming from the people in charge. "Stand at attention, you ain't in the fucking hood," I heard one sergeant say to a person of color. We sang cadences, including the infamous Jody calls, named for a fictional character who pops up in some of them as the man a soldier's wife is cheating on him with back home. They sound like disgusting cheerleading chants, meant to make you laugh like a frat boy and pump you up for war. "We went to the market / Where all the ladies shop / I pulled out my Ka-Bar / and I began to chop," we'd sing. Or "I don't want no teenage queen / I just want my M16 / This is my rifle, this is my gun / This is for fighting and this is for fun," then we'd point at our junk. *Left, right, left, right.*

There's a basic-training technique called a shark attack, meant to establish psychological dominance: a drill sergeant starts yelling insults, telling you what to do, daring you to talk back, prodding you into a formation you don't know how to make. "Move, cocksucker! Pick up that bag, you maggot!" Every mistake, and even sometimes a thing done correctly, leads to an intense verbal attack from a drill sergeant, who isolates every slightly unusual characteristic of your appearance, your personhood, and picks it apart, in front of the whole crowd. One of our drill sergeants had a thick Korean accent, which seemed at first to take a little of the bite out of the attack—until two idiots in my group decided to start mocking her under their breath, giggling. They were instantly destroyed. "You think my voice is funny? Off the bus, motherfucker." They had to do push-ups, crunches, and the dreaded mountain climbers until they couldn't anymore, and then *she* mocked *them* for being weak. It was our first lesson in control. Power in the army is all about authority, and if the staff sergeant whose accent you think is so funny has all the authority here, she will make your life miserable. The rest of us suffered, too, which was the second lesson—you're a team. If one person fucks up, everyone is punished.

The drill sergeants targeted me from the beginning for my slight, childish appearance. I heard one of them say loudly to another, "That one takes it up the ass, I bet." Or more directly, to me, they'd say slightly more coded things like "All right, mama's boy, you're in the army now. It's not your bedroom."

The main way the army breaks down recruits is through nonstop, punishing exercise all day long. Picking up a duffel bag and running around in circles. Constant running. Drill sergeants sounding off: "Front leaning rest position. Move!" Tens of thousands of push-ups. Pull-ups. The side straddle hop. Every exercise approved under the old field manual, and even some made-up "home brew" exercises.

The hardest part was the lack of sleep. We'd spend all day doing intense physical training in an environment that was meant to deliberately strip you of your ability to think for yourself, and our bodies got just five hours to recover from that. You end up in survival mode, too exhausted to think or question anything. Soon, the orders start to feel like a relief. They teach you how to strip down an M16, force you to memorize the contents of a five-hundred-page book, grill you on rank structure and hierarchy. And being yelled at helps instill it into your bones. "Stay awake, stay awake, stay awake! I don't want to see your eyes closed!"

I am now convinced that what the army is actually trying to do in basic training is mimic the effects of low-level PTSD. They need to ingrain you with the deep-grooved reflexes to behave in certain ways under pressure, and the easiest way to do that is to burden you with an enormous amount of stress; then, once you're already weak and tired and afraid, they give you things to do. And even though all you want to do is go home, you know you have to keep going. Something about the trauma makes you retain the instruction more, teaches you how to react on autopilot in a high-stress environment.

I survived chow to chow. I craved food like never before in my life. We had to eat whatever we got in under ten minutes. Spoons, we learned, were the fastest option for shoveling in as many calories as we could as quickly as possible. Eating wasn't a bonding experience; nothing was. There's no such thing as a social or sex life during basic training. Libido evaporated completely, and the drill sergeants shut down any flirtations they saw developing.

For me, it wasn't just my sex drive that shut down during that intense period. My gender stopped mattering to me; all the feelings about identity and existence that had so preoccupied me were gone. Maybe joining the army *had* done what I'd wanted it to on that front, I thought. I knew what tomorrow was going to bring, and that gave me some sense of security—although not enough to sustain me in the long term.

Basic training broke my body. Ten days in, I was struggling through the morning's physical training when I realized that something was off. I wasn't just tired. My right arm and left foot were completely numb. All feeling was gone, and it was terrifying. The drill sergeants began to scream at me: I was lazy, I was faking it. Malingering, they called it.

They eventually let me go to the sick hall, where they, too, operated under the assumption that I was making up an injury—a common enough tactic for soldiers who couldn't take the stress of boot camp. The sick hall is set up to be unpleasant, and to weed out the fakers. Sick call started at 0450, earlier than the normal wake-up and breakfast call, and we had to stand in a line hundreds of recruits long. The standard prescription was eight hundred milligrams of ibuprofen and a "back to duty" slip. When it was my turn, in the early afternoon, the nurse gave me an ibuprofen and sent me back out to train, as if I'd pulled a muscle. The next day, I signed back up for sick call, in spite of the drill sergeant's sarcastic comments. "You're broken? You must not be very good. You must be a shit-bag soldier." This time, a physician's assistant sent me to a specialist, who referred me to a hospital for a neurology appointment. It confirmed that there was something real going on, but offered no explanation for why; it seemed that my nervous system might have just collapsed from shock and stress. I was terrified. What if my sensation never came back? What if I was paralyzed for life?

Most people in the rehabilitation company were waiting for discharge papers. A smaller group was going to head back for training after their injuries had healed. The training brigade began to process me as if I had sustained an injury before joining, and thus should be discharged. It just wasn't true: training had caused the injury, and I didn't want to be sent out into the world with no insurance, no job, and nonfunctioning limbs. Besides, I didn't *want* to quit. I asked for a lawyer when administrators gave me a piece of paper to sign that would out-process me. They weren't used to someone fighting discharge. Instead of giving me an attorney, they withdrew the paperwork.

I had never felt so bored and trapped. We just sat there—no TV, terrible pulpy books, no cell phone or internet, nothing to do but clean the barracks. The other soldiers started calling me Thumper, because of my numb foot just dragging along behind me. I lived in limbo, and fought for weeks to stay in the army. At last, my first appointment with the neurologist arrived. At the hospital, the neurologist administered an electromyogram (EMG) test—poking needles and shocking me at different points across my arm and leg. He confirmed I had suffered nerve damage of some kind. I needed to heal for a few more weeks and come back for another exam. Luckily, as fall turned into winter, I started to heal. Sensation returned to my arm. Soon, I could write again. Two months after I went in, they sent me back to restart basic training. The second time around, it was less overwhelming, and I was more levelheaded. I knew what to expect, and I was even in better physical condition—as I'd recovered from my injury, I'd begun to exercise and build up my strength. It was still difficult, and isolating—but I was too exhausted to feel lonely. We alternated between field training and classroom instruction. We practiced rifle marksmanship at the ranges, learned how to use radios, worked through obstacle courses designed specifically for teamwork and cooperation, and drilled with a simplistic form of mixed martial arts. We did live-action role play using our rifles with attached infrared lasers on the barrel and sensors that would detect any blanks that hit us. I was good at small-unit combat maneuvers. Most people hesitate, or freak out, even during train-ing. It's a lot of long walks under cover, and my size, the thing I was most derided for both in and out of the military, suddenly became an advantage. I could duck, crawl, run, and avoid getting hit. I could shoot accurately under pressure. I could think clearly, and tactically—even with others yelling and screaming in panic. At the end of an exercise, I was often the last one standing.

My father drove up from Oklahoma City for graduation. He had never been that visibly proud of me in my life, seeing me in my green dress uniform, with my new military bearing. For me, seeing his pride felt like a hole inside of me had been filled, if only temporarily. My aunt came, too. She was there to be supportive, and to make sure that my father and I didn't fight—but I could tell she hated the whole thing, especially all the talk of Iraq and Afghanistan. I knew she thought something bad was going to happen to me now that I was a soldier, and she blamed my father for steering me this way.

A guy I'd had an intense two-week relationship with in D.C. also flew in to see me. He was plugged in to the D.C. political scene, work-ing for the Human Rights Campaign. Now he was on the Hillary Clin-ton 2008 presidential primary campaign. We had been casual, but I'd started to write to him every few days during boot camp, to slake my loneliness, and the correspondence had deepened things between us emotionally, at least for me. He had kept me updated on current events, the election—getting cut off from the news was one of the more jarring things about going into training. I felt disconnected from the world without a computer, and he was my lifeline. And then, he'd dropped into a letter that he was getting engaged. I had been letting my roman-tic imagination run away with me; meanwhile, I'd been just a fling for him. I was devastated. He felt terrible. Coming all the way out to see me was a way of showing me that I mattered to him—even if he loved someone else. And it worked, sort of. His big grin soothed my heart, and even seemed to charm my dad somewhat. We all got a day pass to be with our families and celebrate, so the four of us went to lunch at the same diner where every single other basic training graduate had gone with their family.

Packout started the next morning at 0400; the drill sergeants oversaw an out-processing inventory of every item—each boot string, sock, and undergarment. Some recruits tried saying goodbye to the drill sergeants, only to be met with stern warnings about getting close to anyone in this world. And then I flew off, with just two other trainees, to Fort Huachuca, in Arizona, almost at the Mexican border. This was our first time out in public in a really long time without drill sergeants watching our every move, and in the Phoenix airport, where we had a layover, we binged on all kinds of junk food. I smoked a few cigarettes. For a few hours, it was as if we weren't in the army.

Fort Huachuca, where we arrived late that night, had been a training base for intelligence personnel for decades. Instead of the limestone and greenery of the Missouri Ozarks, the town of Sierra Vista is mountainous desert, near Tombstone. I have heard people compare the land to Afghanistan. The cinder block buildings of the base had grown up around the original wooden structures of a cavalry outpost, with an old cannon and a general aesthetic resemblance to a spaghetti western soundstage. Arriving there was like an exhalation from "Yes, Drill Sergeant" mode. When I asked what time to set my alarm for the next day, the answer was: "Whenever you want. It's Saturday." I could barely remember what that kind of latitude felt like. Waking up naturally, because the sun was out, and looking out the windows to see mountains in the west, clear and vivid like a postcard, felt like a shock to my system. The air smelled dewy in the mornings and early evenings, when it rained for an hour every single day in July. Every Monday through Friday at dawn, for our physical training, we'd run onto a barren desert road, with hundreds of us teeming along, in our vests and lime-green chest ribbons to keep us visible in the dark. I ran with the "alpha" group—the fast runners. Daylight broke slowly and unevenly over the mountains, painting the desert just as the runner's high hit.

I began to learn what it really meant to be an intelligence analyst. We spent long hours in the boxy air-conditioned buildings studying slides of tactical locations, learning to map, and learning how to understand signal intelligence reports. The training material still involved historical scenarios from the Soviet Union's fight against the mujahideen, and the Iraq-Iran war, which were the closest historical analogues to the Afghanistan and Iraq engagements. I learned to call the satellite imagery "the birds," which came in different types: overhead, isometric, infrared, black and white, ground-penetrating radar. There was an enormous amount of material—over twenty-four weeks, we worked fifty hours a week memorizing everything on the two thousand "smart card" slides we studied: I could rattle off the specifications of French aircraft, of Russian tanks, what weapons the Syrians had. I learned that the Soviet Union did not allow its pilots to make decisions, and that the mujahideen in Afghanistan often fought from higher ground.

But intelligence analysis is not just the memorization of facts. We learned how to cobble together all these sources to build a cohesive patchwork picture of what was going on: we learned to give a "scientific wild-ass guess," or "SWAG." You have to understand how to take all the context you're given and make sense of it in a useful way, to look at a battlefield and understand not only what's happening in the moment, but what that tank column is going to do next. It's a little like detective work—and I turned out to be really good at that kind of problem-solving.

The two big ongoing wars, in Iraq and Afghanistan, seemed intractable. They required a different kind of thinking than conventional warfare. A lot of people don't realize that having more technology doesn't mean that you have more capacity in every way. And that's the story of those wars: Eight guys with a bazooka can fuck shit up and cause massive chaos. Thirty guys, in an urban environment, can easily tie down an entire battalion in combat for days. We had to learn to think like the insurgents, to learn that anything could happen. We had to know what guerrilla fighters could do, and how to use conventional disadvantages as unconventional advantages. I loved the actual craft of analysis. It was high-level abstraction, detached from emotions—at least at that point in time.

I made friends more easily within this group than I had in basic training. Classed as we were by skills and interests, we had more natural affinities, which made for a more collegial atmosphere. I found a group of Dungeons & Dragons players right away; we spent our off-hours playing D&D, or video games on PlayStation and Xbox. We were nerdy—as an extrovert, I was an outlier—and at least as far as I could tell, we had a higher than usual percentage of queer people for the army. It also seemed like many in the group were overqualified or overeducated to be enlisted persons. Often, people had ended up in the military because they found themselves in their thirties and unable, despite their natural abilities and even a college degree, to lift themselves out of poverty.

The army was a lifeline of last resort for many of my colleagues, as it had been for me. The feeling of just surviving from chow to chow went away. But that meant there was time for my dysphoria to creep back, too. We could wear our own clothes on the weekend, and I gravitated toward a bright pink shirt, as if trying to stake out who I was, for me and for everyone else. I just wanted to feel more at home. People noticed. People made comments.

The first weekend at Fort Huachuca, I bought a Lenovo laptop at the post exchange—the shopping center for the military base, which has roughly the feel of a giant Walmart Supercenter. I began to spend my nights and weekends back online—connected to my world again. I spent much of my post-curfew time on YouTube, Facebook, and this strange new corner of the internet known as 4chan: the land of memes, "Caturday" night festivals, trolling, irony, and outright "lulz." In chan culture, there were no moderates. Striking a careful compromise or looking carefully at "both sides" wasn't going to get any attention there. Everyone was an extreme version of themselves, whether a socialist, an anarchist, a communist, or the sort of baby neofascist that now dominates that part of the internet. Atheism was my personal creed, the thing that shaped the rest of my views. It was deeply satisfying to cue up a vlogger who could elegantly articulate the harm done by a misguided belief in God. *Kitzmiller v. Dover*—the 2005 Pennsylvania case addressing a school district policy that required the teaching of intelligent design—had sparked my interest in atheism during my libertarian phase in high school. Like many young people at the time, I was briefly captivated by the outsize voices of the four horsemen of atheism: Richard Dawkins, Christopher Hitchens, Daniel Dennett, and Sam Harris. I even tried to write like them on the forums, certain and logical and artfully cruel to the Christian right. (Now I understand them to be misogynistic, classist, and often xenophobic.)

My chan buddies and I were baby edgelords. The term for this kind of cynical, juvenile, and often insincere internet troll hadn't been invented yet, but you could see the seeds of some of what's devolved into the modern internet. We created new terms to describe our new concepts, like *memes*, *clapbacks*, *firin muh lazer*, *downvote brigades*, and *doxxing*. We were technically proficient misfits, ganging together in a garbage-fire glob of shattered egos. A new community of more militant atheists formed around early YouTube stars: Zinnia Jones, Thunderf00t, and the Amazing Atheist.

A lot of the people I watched back then on YouTube or chatted with on 4chan slipped uncritically into the anti-Muslim bigotry I came to recognize, but did not take seriously enough, in Hitchens and Dawkins. I didn't have that kind of anger. I had no interest in being pejorative toward "our enemies." Every interaction I'd had with Muslims was inconsistent with that worldview. I'd grown up in Oklahoma and probably said, and definitely heard, things that I now understand to be wrong, both ethically and factually. But what I saw on those forums had a real tinge of hate to it that I instantly recognized as being different in kind from the urge to say something transgressive to push social buttons or be provocative.

But still, I wanted to fuck things up. I became a troll on Christian evangelical websites and creationist discussion forums. I'd sign up, spend a while talking like them and integrating myself in their community. I'd share Christian memes. Sometimes I'd even copy and paste comments from other sites, so I got the tone just right, all fire and brimstone and moralizing. Then, once I was in—sometimes so in I was given moderator status—I'd drop an opinion like "Actually, I think evolution is legit," and a flame war would start. I'd get kicked off within a couple of days, and the forum would probably close ranks and go right back to their version of normal, but I got hours of amusement out of it.

The risk of my participation, as a soldier, was part of the turn-on; it was like a whiff of freedom. Trolling gives you a human connection. Even though it's a negative response, it's still a connection. You're yelling angrily into the void, but instead of hearing an echo, someone yells back. It's acknowledgment of your existence, your humanity.

Not to mention that I was getting community, solidarity, and support from the chat rooms—everything I felt like I wasn't getting at work, where I felt lonely, alienated from military culture and its regimented masculinity, even in this looser, friendlier environment. There were a few other people I had bonded with, but mostly, I looked to the world outside the base. My sex life was nonexistent: I was so afraid of losing my career. I loved my job, loved the intellectual work of being an analyst. The Bush administration had continued to enforce the Don't Ask, Don't Tell policy. They'd kicked out so many linguists at an intelligence training base in Monterey, California, that there was a crucial shortage of people who could speak the languages we needed in order to effectively go to war.

At the end of our Fort Huachuca training, we did a field exercise meant to simulate combat. It was a wartime simulation, full of firing ranges and bombing ranges. They handed us rifles filled with blanks and sent us off to work—it was like an incredibly high-tech version of paintball. We spent most of our time in a trailer. We did real-time analysis, based on actual combat operations in Iraq from 2006, for five days and five nights, the closest thing yet to the actual job. Graduation day felt a lot less special than it had for basic training. We didn't even wear dress uniforms. But I received two awards—one for academic performance and another for physical fitness—that I hadn't expected. My father had showed up for this ceremony, too, and he practically jumped with joy. I changed into my civilian clothes in a restaurant bathroom, and Dad drove me in his rental car to the Tucson airport. But the farther we got from the structure of the graduation ceremony, the more his happiness with me was already turning back to indifference.

It wasn't until I went back to Maryland that I realized how much I'd changed in those months of training, how the army had rewired my brain as much as it had my muscle mass. I spent a few nights of my leave back in the clubs. I wanted—needed!—to get laid before I went on to my next stop. But everything felt different now. Instead of stand-ing back, waiting for someone to approach me, I chased. I was strong, confident. It helped, somehow, to know that I could fight someone and win if I needed to. I had a new kind of power. I was ready to take risks. I was ready to take responsibility.

6.

Zinnia Jones was even younger than I was, just nineteen. She was a web designer and activist with a YouTube channel—where she called herself the Queen of Atheism—who wore bright red lipstick that set off her long, shiny hair. I'd come across her randomly one night, sitting alone in my room clicking around idly in the dark, bouncing from one anti-religion rant to the next. Zinnia stopped me in my tracks, though. She fascinated me not just because of what she said, but because of who she was. She was openly trans—unlike anyone who felt at all accessible to me. And she had her instant messenger screen name on her profile. I started typing.

"You don't know me, i apologize, i got this [address] from your youtube channel."

"No problem, there's a reason I put it on there :P," she replied.

I began to explain. "I saw your more personal stuff and figured you were on the same page . . . as me. You remind me of . . . well . . . me." I began to type my life story to her. "My plan is pretty simple but vague," I concluded. "Get credentials, nice ones . . . ones that make it difficult for really creepy conservative people to attack . . . then jump into politics."

Since August 2008, I had been working for the Tenth Mountain Division, a light infantry unit, as an intelligence analyst at Fort Drum, near Lake Ontario in northern New York State. This was about as far away from Arizona as you could get, a long drive along Interstate 81 from Syracuse toward the Canadian border, on a long, densely forested plain stretching out toward the Adirondacks. It was a frigid winter in one of the snowiest places in America, with subzero temperatures; for our physical training, we rode the elliptical or did calisthenics inside a storage unit, or laps on an indoor track—no more transcendent sunrise runs. Instead, I watched the same cinder blocks go round and round. Even though I was sleeping in upstate New York, I was really living in Afghanistan, providing support to brigades deployed overseas. There were no more imagined situations, no more training based on wars that had been fought while I was in preschool. This was real information that I was dealing with; I was taking huge pieces of data and making granular predictions that were useful for the officers thinking through strategy. The decisions I was making had real-life consequences for people on the other side of the world. As I told Zinnia, when she told me to stay safe during deployment, "I'm more concerned about making sure that everyone, soldiers, marines, contractors, even the local nationals, get home to their families. I feel a great responsibility and duty to people . . . its strange, i know."

The Second Brigade combat team had a storied history across the U.S. military, starting with the Persian Gulf War. Its Second Battalion, Fourteenth Infantry Regiment, a battalion known as the Golden Dragons, was the one involved in the now-infamous incident described in the book and movie *Black Hawk Down*. My boss, Master Sergeant Paul Adkins, had been involved; he had seen his first combat in 1993 and served in Operation Gothic Serpent in Somalia, part of a relief effort for a country torn apart by our Cold War–era foreign policies, when two Black Hawk helicopters were shot down during the Battle of Mogadishu. It was an experienced group, and I was one of just a small handful of new soldiers. The brigade had, by the time I joined, seen the most combat of any non–Special Forces unit since 9/11, and had sustained more losses than any other unit. In August 2006, the brigade was deployed to a sparse area of farmland south of Baghdad, at the bottom of the "Triangle of Death" in Iraq. It was bordered to the southwest by the Euphrates River and was crisscrossed by a massive network of irrigation canals. The road by the river, "Route Malibu," became the site of numerous IED attacks and battles, and as a result, the brigade stayed three months longer than originally intended. They wore the pain and loss of those battles.

The unit was on a two-year-long furlough of sorts in New York as a way of giving the team a break, before we were scheduled to deploy to Logar and Wardak Provinces, in eastern Afghanistan, in December 2009. These soldiers knew their shit in a way you can't learn in a textbook. Everyone talks a big game in the army, but many of those people mouthing off haven't actually seen real combat. The soldiers I was serving alongside understood that it wasn't some big macho LARPing game, that combat isn't something to be glorified. They knew, and they made it clear to me, that the goal, more than anything, is to minimize the amount of time that you, and the people you're fighting with, spend being shot at. They understood the tough decision-making you face on the ground.

Many of them had also learned, through that experience of watching repeated and sustained casualties, that we could do nothing to "win" the war. We were there to hold territory. We might make an advance here or there, but it was whack-a-mole. The insurgency comes back here, there, over there. After years, this had become numbing. There was no end in sight, and so a lot of vets I was meeting had decided that the only attitude to take was: I'm going to tune everything out, pull a paycheck, and own this territory until I can go home and see my wife. This was a job, one to be done effectively, but at the end of the day, it was mostly about protecting one another and keeping one another alive while the politicians peacocked. My brigade-mates' mindset affected my mindset. I learned quickly: our job wasn't to win, it was to come back home, to keep as many of our people and innocent civilians alive as possible. *There is no such thing as winning in a war.*

I didn't fit in at Fort Drum. Partly because of who I was, but also because I was military intelligence, caught between two worlds professionally. We didn't quite have the mentality of enlisted soldiers, but we also didn't fit in well with the wider intelligence community, which was dominated by civilians and senior joint military staff in the "alphabet agencies," as we called them.

Rank mattered a lot less in my role than it did elsewhere in the army, which suited me well. I was never great at performing as a subordinate in a situation where I felt I had useful information or insight to offer. Commanders expected us to provide actionable intelligence they could use in making, or at least considering, different decisions. We gave them options, and I could ask questions, be skeptical, treat officers like peers. They needed to be able to think of me that way, too, to trust my advice. There were fewer than twenty other people doing analyst work in our brigade of three thousand soldiers, and part of my job was providing analysis to the brigade command, the highest-ranking officers. The first time I briefed the brigade command, one of the officers asked how old I was, to haze me a bit. I had to show him ID, because he refused to believe that I was actually only twenty years old. I sometimes felt more like an officer than an enlisted person, swimming more in their office politics than those of the privates who were technically my peers.

At Fort Drum, we could video-conference with our colleagues

overseas, but we didn't yet have the internet bandwidth to watch real-time videos of the combat zones, or even to download them. We reviewed screen grabs from unpiloted aircraft—grainy black-and-white videos that still seep into my dreams. They were incorporated into the interminable-seeming PowerPoint presentations we watched every twelve hours, with operations updates about significant actions and discussions of the weather and whether the parts were delivered for whatever equipment to whatever distant base. The video feeds were one data set among many pieces of information that I loved to fit together: the price of bread in a village, which crops were diseased or burned. What the local government was doing that day, who they'd arrested and why, and what they really meant by "dissident" in that particular situation. (I quickly learned that calling someone a dissident was sometimes just a way for the government to court a bribe, or punish someone who disagreed with a government policy.) Even which team won an international soccer game could be valuable data that affected what the streets of a city might be like. Road closings, landlord disputes, traffic jams, dust storms, flooding, kidnapping reports, robbery reports. Anything could be a source. We saw everything. Our eyes were everywhere.

And then there were our specific targets. Anyone of interest—defined very broadly—to the United States could be a target. With the more sensitive methods that the government availed itself of, we could learn everything about a person. *Everything.* Relationship patterns, who they were talking to, who their friends were talking to, what they were buying, their secrets, their sexuality, their infidelities. The depth and expanse of the available information was breathtaking. We had access to every aspect of our targets' lives, their strengths, flaws, lies, and hopes. Learning someone's brain the way we did is so much more invasive than a strip search. People believe their thoughts, at least, are private, but they're not. Browser history, for instance, can tell a lot about someone's private inclinations. Humans are absurdly predictable, and any step a person takes outside their pattern, or even just our knowing what is important within that pattern, can potentially become a tool for coercion. I was supposed to take all of that, the most intimate knowledge of a human being it was possible to gather without being in their brain, and make a dispassionate military assessment, to notify higher-ups of my clinical evaluation, to predict how a person or a group might behave.

I wanted to know everything about what it was like to be deployed. My first primary supervisor at Fort Drum, Staff Sergeant Anica, ran our physical training exercises and managed our administrative matters while awaiting his transfer to a plush job at the Pentagon. He was from Mexico originally, and even shorter than me, stocky and approachable, with a deep and warm sense of humor, tinged with some darkness that seemed to stem from his last deployment. I used to ask him about what he had done in Iraq, eager to get details. Usually he'd talk about anything, but not this. "It was a job," he'd deflect. Or he'd tell me a funny story meant to distract. I kept pressing.

The thing Anica didn't want to talk about was the traumatic DUSTWUN incident. Everyone who'd stayed over from the previous deployment talked about it in hushed tones. Even the acronym *DUSTWUN,* for "Duty Status Whereabouts Unknown," seemed to cast a dark cloud. On May 12, 2007, a group with rifles and explosives had ambushed a U.S. squad in a temporary observation post along Route Malibu, called Crater Overwatch, killing five U.S. soldiers and one Iraqi soldier, and capturing three others, Byron Fouty, Alex Jimenez, and Joseph Anzack.

The entire brigade reacted within minutes, aggressively searching a thirty-mile radius of their area of operations. The search lasted for weeks, and hundreds of Iraqis were rounded up for questioning in the process. Finally, soldiers found Anzack's body in the Euphrates River.

He'd been shot in the head, execution-style, with a single bullet. The Islamic State of Iraq, a precursor to ISIS, posted a video taking responsibility, and asking the United States to back off from its search for the other two soldiers. One afternoon, not long after I'd arrived at Fort Drum, the section chief, Major Murphy, walked silently from a common area into his office. He was a big guy, usually calm and playful, like a big teddy bear. Not that day. He slammed the door so hard, pictures fell off the walls. We could hear him tearing up the office from top to bottom, throwing things.

"What the fuck is going on?" I mouthed to Sergeant Anica and another analyst.

"Don't worry about it," Anica told me. "We'll clean the mess up later."

A few weeks earlier, the bodies of Fouty and Jimenez had been recovered by a different brigade. That day, the brigade was holding a memorial service with their families. It turned out that Major Murphy felt personally responsible for failing to find the bodies—especially since they were recovered in a place where the brigade had already searched. Outside the command offices, the brigade staff framed one of the captured black-and-white Islamic State of Iraq flags as a daily reminder of what had happened. I watched quietly. What had happened to Fouty and Jimenez could happen to any of us. Pessimism and disillusionment snaked through the brigade.

At night, in the single-soldier barracks, I burrowed deeper into my wide online world. The internet as we now know it was starting to emerge, and a lot of the most interesting changes were happening in the IRC rooms where I was spending sleepless nights.

An Internet Relay Chat server contains a stream of user-created and -moderated channels, often called "rooms." Any particular IRC server will contain as few as a hundred or as many as a hundred thousand or more channels, with anywhere between two and a few hundred people in each room, looking at the stream of messages. Participants can also use a private messaging system, or "whispers," to speak directly to one another. They were like private clubs for the Extremely Online.

I'd usually have five or ten channels open at a time, my screen swirling with messages, full of crude ASCII art and memes. IRC servers require an invitation to enter, like a digital speakeasy, with a moderator who serves as a kind of bouncer, keeping out the trolls and cops who might want to disrupt things. Back then, the most intense ones were operation-based: a place for 4channers to plan out cyber-actions against Scientologists or Mormons or whoever the target was at that time. I was a part of Anonymous, a collective that had targeted Scientologists with doxxing (exposing an individual's private information) and swatting (getting SWAT teams to respond to reports of a violent crime in progress at a target's home). (Such operations were dubbed "OpChanology," a portmanteau of operation, 4chan, and Scientology.) Research was my thing: I'd spend hours combing legal databases like LexisNexis or PACER for tiny bits of useful information, things that could lead you to vulnerabilities; the Church of Scientology, which had sued just about everyone it could for just about anything it could, ended up leaving quite a trail of useful intel about itself in the public records as a result.

Other channels were tech-focused and pragmatic: they might be a place to pool lists of best security practices and methods. You'd have to prove your facility with operational security in order to be allowed in. It was a method of both cultural vetting and skill-set testing. When I entered I got a private message, asking me to prove that I deserved to be there, asking who I was and what I was doing. For the purposes of those channels, I was a programmer in the UK, and I was "just there to talk," which was more or less true. As my test, an admin gave me a server address and asked me to get the hash code of a specific file name on it. (Cryptographic hashes are random and usually coded in hexadecimal, so you're never going to just randomly guess at one: you have to get access to the document and to the system.)

My target was an IP address in the Golden Triangle, in Southeast Asia. I did a port scan with Nmap, an operation that let me look for any ways into the system. There was one port that was deliberately left just open enough for me to get in, like the digital equivalent of having a door locked but the key still in it. It was the kind of thing an inexperienced person would never see, but if you knew what you were doing even moderately, it was a piece of cake. I found a way in, found the key, then deleted the logs showing that I had entered the box. It was absolutely harmless, but it was proof of my social worth, as measured by my technical skill.

I made some friendships from the message boards, but they were fleeting ones: the whole point of that part of the internet is that you don't know who you're talking to. Anonymity is both a feature and a bug. Disembodied, it was easier to be my truest self, and I suspect I wasn't the only one who felt more alive, more real, in the various alter egos I created and destroyed at will. I used not only a pseudonym but also a special browser and VPN so that my IP address couldn't be tracked. Even then, it was clear to me that taking measures to protect privacy was a worthy end in itself, whether or not you had "something to hide."

On weekends off, I traveled back to D.C., for a brief return to my old life. I'd go out to house parties near Dupont Circle, or to clubs. One night, wearing a three-piece suit with a purple vest, I attended a fundraiser at a queer bar on Seventeenth and R Streets for Gavin Newsom, then the mayor of San Francisco, who was running for the Democratic nomination for governor of California. He'd made a big, bold move on behalf of gay people's right to marry, and had been generally support-ive of our community. More important, this was an open-bar event for which the whole D.C. queer scene was showing up. It was my kind of crowd.

Lucas—not his real name—worked at the *Washington Blade*, the D.C. area's gay-issues newspaper, but when I first met him, I didn't know he was a journalist. I did know he was a cute guy and that he was hitting on me. He was interesting, a little older, and easy to talk to. We left the event together and went to another bar. I talked to him for hours about my life. At some point, I figured out he was a reporter, and he quickly discovered I was in the military—living under Don't Ask, Don't Tell. He had a lot of questions for me, about what life was like under the policy, how my colleagues treated me, how I could have re-lationships and a sex life. I trusted him, and I told him the truth. We kept texting after that night, and I became a background source for his writing.

In 2009, the Joint Chiefs of Staff informally commissioned their respective judge advocates general to conduct policy reviews to deter-mine how a repeal of Don't Ask, Don't Tell might affect units in each of the services. There was no reporting yet on the substance of the re-view; it was still an internal draft policy document. But I had access to it, because it was on the JAG servers, and I was interested, so I searched. The document that was produced to summarize the findings was one of the most upsetting misunderstandings about queer people I had ever seen, with comically uninformed comments and questions posed in the margins. It lacked any basic understanding of gay people, or of sexual relationships in general. It relied on an old police review from the 1990s that was filled with outdated, offensive stereotypes about queer people—would a repeal mean the army would have to accom-modate increased HIV care? What if the domestic partnerships of gay soldiers change rapidly because they relationship-hop?—rendered by lawyers, in detail, in an official document. They were grasping at straws to find ways to continue to justify the ban, despite Obama's promise to end it.

I was disturbed. I started to think that other people might want to know about it: after all, this document was going to be presented to the secretary of defense, and it would become a political football that allowed people to say that a Don't Ask, Don't Tell repeal would harm unit readiness—which I knew, from my own life, from common sense, and from data, just wasn't true. It also showed that even the military was a little baffled by the ancient justifications for the rule. It was too potentially harmful to keep bottled up. I texted Lucas about it. He asked for a copy, so I printed it off at work, rescanned it at the barracks, and emailed it to him. I wasn't worried: it was an unclassified document. A few weeks later, he texted me—alongside some flirtation—to tell me how much the report informed his reporting on the subject when he'd approached official sources with questions. I took some pride in influencing the public discourse.

I never developed any relationships with national reporters, though I would have loved to (why would they talk to a junior enlisted person out in the boonies in Fort Drum when they could talk to someone who worked for the secretary of defense?), but there was a local journalist I'd met through the upstate New York gay scene. She covered military affairs, and I'd give her small bits of inside information. I'd become friends with a smart, savvy army press officer, and she encouraged me, once I suggested it, to talk to the reporter as a kind of unofficial channel. I liked having influence, helping make things happen. I helped gin up feel-good positive media coverage for Fort Drum during the usual Memorial Day, Veterans Day, deployment homecoming, and Christmas return periods. And in exchange, I gave the journalist gossip about command staff frictions and departures, and leaked tidbits about the impact of various policies on the morale of rank-and-file soldiers—such as a highly controversial policy of publishing the photos of all arrestees at Fort Drum as a deterrent to drunk driving.

I got something more tangible out of my relationships with the journalists, too: actual information, which I in turn could trade to my friend in the base press office. The questions the reporters would ask, the kinds of things they were interested in, often told me something important that I didn't already know about the base. It helped me anticipate when there might be friction between the fort and the local community—all of which would be of interest to my press officer and her colleagues. Meanwhile, the press officers saw things happening at the command level that intel officers and enlisted people didn't have access to; my press officer friend shared this information with me sometimes. There was utility in that kind of information. It made me a better analyst. The way secrets are kept in the military makes you realize just how valuable any kind of carefully guarded knowledge is.

Part of my job was making sure that safes and armories filled with guns and classified information had the right physical security measures in place. I quickly realized that the army was full of incredible security risks. For instance, the safe that held the firearms vault on the base—full of rifles and a massive cache of ammunition—still had its lock set to the factory default settings. But that was nothing compared to the lax digital security you saw in the army in the 2000s; an enormous amount of energy was spent ensuring the physical security of electronics, but on the electronics themselves the security was paltry. I picked up on that the very first day I interacted with the military: they were using a standard Windows-running computer. Windows, back then, *was* your security vulnerability, the most popular operating system in the world, and therefore extremely easy to exploit. It takes me about three minutes to get into a box like that. But the government had a contract with Microsoft, dating back to the early nineties, worth billions of dollars, for that shitty software, which left the entire digital backbone and infrastructure of the Department of Defense helpless.

I had begun, by then, to get a modest reputation in my unit for being good with computers. Once, during an exercise, I built a private file server for the office using an old laptop. People appreciated that we could bypass the slow, complicated central system and just use something local.

My computer skills got me noticed—in both good and bad ways. The Joint Readiness Training Center in swampy Fort Polk, Louisiana, houses one of the military's three combat training centers for brigades to train in "the sandbox," with emphasis on realism for Iraq or Afghanistan; the training scenario shifts based on each participating unit's mission needs. Each exercise is a huge affair, an elaborate simulation of the actions of civilian officials and citizens of an occupied country, re-creating networks of insurgencies and criminal organizations, news media coverage, and humanitarian and nongovernmental organizations. In October 2008, our unit simulated a deployment to Fort Polk for a month-long training exercise. We set up shop, with training officers monitoring and overseeing our every move. During the live exercises they stood over our shoulders and monitored us like schoolteachers, continually increasing the difficulty of the challenges and exercises.

Between the exercises, the intelligence analysts took software classes; in one, we learned a new tool for link analysis diagrams. I started playing around with the back end of the database, to see how it fit in with our existing workstation. I decided to download the entire database, including the parts of it that the trainers kept away from us until later stages of the exercise. Having it, I decided, would give our group an edge going into the next stage—which would make our office look really good. I used a command line terminal to get in through the back door; to get administrator privileges, I simply logged in as "Administrator," with the password "admin." It was far too easy to access this database.

I had done this kind of thing before, with the tacit approval of my bosses: if there was a piece of information somewhere on the network that had been deemed "mission-critical," but which wasn't technically available to us, often because of high turnover and the complicated nature of the permissions structure, I'd just go get it. It was like being asked to reach a book from the top shelf; more accurately, it was like being asked to bring someone a stepladder so that they could reach the book. I used the back end of a Microsoft SharePoint server to access slides for a meeting the officers couldn't attend. They didn't care how it got done, they just wanted the information. Commanding officers turned a blind eye when it made them look good. I assume that when you're expected to advance in your career based on politics, and you take responsibility for the lives of junior soldiers, you stop seeing rules as rigid lines not to be crossed, but rather as blurry obstacles to be surmounted in order to accomplish a greater goal. The only rule was: don't get caught. Soon, this turned into a productive habit.

But this time when I executed the command to export the database, intending to use a router as a "demilitarized zone" for the transfer of the large file, disaster struck. I'd made a typo somewhere along the line. I'd fucked up the router, and it turned out that it wasn't a local one: this was the router that ran the military's classified networks for the entire southeastern region. Several thousand people, and a few of the ongoing training exercises, immediately lost access to the network. The video feeds from unpiloted aircraft, and information from line units transferred from radio into the text feeds of the commands—all gone. Poof, disappeared. I heard dozens of people yelling about their connections being out. It took me a minute to realize that I might have been the cause.

"All right—who did it?" one of the training officers asked, sarcastically. I knew he was joking, but I raised my hand, slowly. I knew they would figure it out eventually, and if I didn't own up, things would get a lot worse for me. A short, balding white man, the major who oversaw the brigade's network, pulled me aside. His response surprised me a bit. He didn't care what I'd done; he only wanted to know the details, so they could fix the situation. Almost immediately, the network came back up. It ran smoothly. The major and two other officers gave me a halfhearted lecture about not doing things like this in the future. The exercise continued as normal, we returned home, and I forgot about it.

But a few months later, as I was working at my computer, my boss, Master Sergeant Adkins, came to talk to me. "Some people are here to speak with you from *D.C.* They're in suits," he said, scratching his head, a signature Adkins gesture of uncertainty. My stomach started to go funny. Was I in trouble for something? We walked out of the office and into a conference room, where a man and a woman not much older than me were already sitting. I sat across from them. They looked like federal agents, though they didn't carry badges or guns. The woman started to talk. "We hear you're pretty good at computers," she said with a genuine smile.

The situation became clear. I wasn't in trouble. I'd been referred for a new unit the military was creating: the Army Network Warfare Battalion, which would operate out of Fort Meade. It was for "offensive computer network operations," or in plain English, it was to be the military's new cybersecurity team.

It was an exciting idea. I could live in Maryland—my home—and do intellectually challenging work that used all the skills I'd spent so many late nights and bored teenage days honing. Not only that, but the hours would be better. Rather than the punishing, breakless twelve-hours-on, twelve-hours-off days that were already starting to wear on me, these would be staggered shifts, with regular two-day-off intervals to recover and recharge your brain.

But there was a catch. I was fenced in: by this point, my unit was scheduled for its deployment, and I was to be, I believed, an important part of that deployment.

The recruiters offered to pull rank. This was a mandate that had been categorized as a "national priority," which meant it was coming from the secretary of defense's office. I wanted a deployment under my belt, though. I wanted to build a career in the army, and to look good coming out of my enlistment, too. There's a huge difference between people who have done a tour in a war zone and people who haven't. It's more than rank; it's respect. I asked if we could restart the conversation when I was back stateside after my deployment. They told me it was a onetime offer, but I sensed that this was a negotiation tactic. "Cyberwarfare" was the future, and this unit, just in its infancy, would only get bigger and more important.

So I turned the recruiters down, and said to stay in touch. They did; later, after I'd deployed, I got email after email from them asking if I was still interested. We scheduled a time for an aptitude test.

This is another one of those points I look back on and wonder about. It would have been so much easier for me to work on tactical things at a desk. I could have done meaningful work that didn't shred me to pieces inside. It would have offered job security and a connection to my community, and it was a permanent position, with a ladder I could climb.

But once our unit deployed, I couldn't leave. I couldn't try to get out, and so I didn't even consider it. That wasn't a string that could be pulled, no matter how much of a national priority cyberwarfare might be. By the time I was back and available for the cyber unit, I'd have been near the end of my four years, and ready to reenlist. For an opportunity like that one, I would have.

Things didn't work out that way.

7.

While I was at Fort Drum, I wasn't just learning how to be an intelligence analyst. I was also figuring out how I wanted to live as a gay person. The night that President Barack Obama was elected, I sat alone in the top bunk of my barracks room at Fort Drum staring at the ceiling. My phone lay beside me. Once I'd seen that Obama was elected, I'd tossed it aside and stopped paying attention to the celebration in the streets and the self-important news anchors' analysis. It felt redundant: extra verification of an event that was finished. I zoned out, exhausted from the day.

For a lot of people my age, that November was a hopeful, earnest moment like none they'd ever experienced before. They bought into the ideas of "hope" and "change" following the two terms of President George W. Bush. Not me. I was disengaged from American politics, and thought of myself as a bureaucrat, doing my job within a system that would continue to be more or less the same no matter who was in the Oval Office. Obama was just another president, a careful lawyer, who relied on memoranda and processes to make any decision. From a practical, military perspective, he didn't look all that different from his opponent, Senator John McCain, the highest-ranking Republican on the Senate Armed Services Committee.

Ping. Ping. Ping ping ping. As I slipped into sleep, there was an insistent flood of text alerts, out of nowhere and all at once. What could possibly be going on now, when the election was over?

I rolled over and grabbed my phone. I saw the messages, and a wave of nausea flooded over me. In a fog I dropped from my bunk and stumbled to the bathroom, gasping and heaving.

Proposition 8, the California ballot initiative to define marriage as between only "a man and a woman," had passed by a narrow but definitive margin. I felt overwhelmed in a way I didn't recognize. This was my worldview shattering. My whole life, I'd been told that things were always going to get better, that the system was set up with checks and balances ensuring this was the case, that liberal society meant slow but steady "progress" toward democratic inclusion. This idea was in all the philosophy I'd read, in all the lessons I'd gotten in school. Prop 8 wasn't just a repudiation of that promise, or that vision of our system. It wasn't even just a national tragedy. It was a personal rejection of me, and millions of other queer people, as human beings. I felt the horror of the moment in my body. My head pounded, my legs were gone. I stared at the grimy linoleum floor, the white porcelain under my damp cheek. I dragged myself up and to the barracks shower, but I was too shaky to stand. My body was reacting as if my literal foundations had crumbled. I sat on the shower floor and let the water run over me for two hours, weeping. I didn't care if anyone heard.

I woke up late, still raw, my eyes swollen. I barely made it to morning formation, where everyone was talking about the election while they stretched outside on what was an unseasonably warm day for November. Master Sergeant Adkins asked me what I thought of the Obama result. I didn't answer for a moment. "I really don't want to talk about politics at work," I said, copping out. He backed off. Politics is a "hands-off" subject in the military, by regulation. I wanted to howl with pain and rejection. But I couldn't have explained myself or my anger without admitting on the record that I was gay.

I was alone at Fort Drum, but everyone I knew outside of work, everyone posting online, seemed to share my sorrow over Prop 8. For lots of people my age, it was a crucial moment. It made us unified. It gave us the sense that we were embroiled together in a battle. A lot of my friends believed that this would be okay, that the courts would sort it out eventually. I didn't buy that. That wasn't what I wanted. It wasn't what I believed would happen. Nor did I have the patience to wait. I was too furious.

I felt overwhelmed, and I wanted to take direct action. This was my first inkling that the moral arc of the universe doesn't necessarily bend toward justice. That instead, there is a constant and active struggle. And regardless of my changing understanding of how history happens, for the first time I truly understood that the fundamental promises of this society—liberty and justice for all—are just words, unless they are supported by meaningful values and concrete actions.

My intellectual and political life can be divided into pre– and post–Proposition 8. It made me think long and hard about my blind faith in nationalism. I wanted to know more about why it had happened, where the hate and the money had come from. I didn't believe that a majority of people in California necessarily supported what Proposition 8 stood for. Wealthy religious conservatives from all over the country had funded the effort to get the referendum passed. I began to read deeply, pulling on the threads, getting more and more furious at a system that allowed people to leverage money directly into influence and power—to basically manipulate the population into making a decision. The more I read, the more radical I became.

I found Howard Zinn's *A People's History of the United States*. I wanted more. I burrowed deeply into queer history, into protest. (I hid the books in my locker.) I read *Stonewall: The Riots That Sparked the Gay Revolution*, by David Carter; articles about Sylvia Rivera, Marsha P. Johnson; websites on the Compton's Cafeteria uprising; *Transgender History*, by Susan Stryker. I watched *The Times of Harvey Milk*, Rob Epstein's documentary about the life of the assassinated San Francisco supervisor, and the subsequent White Night uprisings following the acquittal of his confessed assassin. I learned the mantra "Queers, don't be quiet, Stonewall was a riot." There was all this history that no one had ever taught me, that didn't fit neatly into the liberal-establishment version of gay rights.

Meanwhile, the financial crisis deepened. It gripped everyone I knew. I watched my family's retirement accounts evaporate. The small mutual fund where I had deposited my twenty-thousand-dollar enlistment bonus—my literal investment in the system—plummeted in value. I was looking for explanations.

On a rainy afternoon, days after the election, I took a Trailways bus to Syracuse for my first-ever protest. (It's legal for soldiers to attend protests out of uniform.) Join the Impact had planned events in four hundred cities that day, with an estimated million people in worldwide attendance. I'd read about the protest on Facebook and reached out to the local organizers—a lesbian student and an older gay man—to see what I could do to help. Even with the nasty weather, nearly two hundred people showed up at city hall—mostly younger queers, but a few older couples too. We had rainbow flags and posters that read NO H8 and MARRIED WITH PRIDE. I carried a sign that said, in rainbow lettering, EQUALITY @ THE HOUSE, @ THE WORKPLACE, @ THE BATTLEFIELD. Seeing other people feeling just as hurt as I did restored my sense of being recognized as fully human.

But as I counted the crowd, I suddenly thought of the insurgency

and counterinsurgency tactics I spent all day studying. Peaceful protest got the Iraqis nowhere. Our soldiers would more or less laugh at
the Iraqis who tried civil disobedience. The people with the signs could
just be mowed down; they were docile. It was the people who fought
back, who refused to move, who even pushed the crowd out of the way
as a way of taking a stand and showing political agency—those were
the ones who concerned the military. As one major (who worked in
operations, not intelligence) had succinctly explained at the base: "We
don't negotiate with protesters—but we sure as hell negotiate with
mobs."

I felt a glow of solidarity from the protest, but I didn't think we'd
gotten real attention from the people in power: there were one or two
news vans, but no police. The previous summer, I'd visited D.C. for
Pride weekend, and stood in the hot summer night among the crowds
at the Dupont Circle Saturday parade. Someone tall, dressed in all
black, with a pink bandanna wrapped around their neck, singing and
laughing, had approached and handed me a pamphlet, then said something I didn't quite catch. I put the pamphlet in my bag, alongside the
rainbow belts and pins and beads I'd collected that day, and later stuck
it in a little box where I saved my gay-rights memorabilia. Months
later, preparing for the Syracuse protest, I opened the box and finally
read the pamphlet. It came from a group called Bash Back!—an anarchist queer collective focused on direct action and influenced by
Stonewall and the White Night riots. *Question everything*—the message of the pamphlet—seemed like the right attitude. Bash Back! had a
Myspace page, which I promptly visited. I yearned to riot, but working
in the military limited my ability to attend direct street actions. An
arrest could mean administrative punishment, a discharge, or even
court-martial.

So for me, direct action meant showing up online, late at night, by
myself, using the skills I'd learned through my involvement with

Anonymous. We doxxed the Family Research Council, a right-wing evangelical political organization that is so antigay that the Southern Poverty Law Center has labeled it a hate group. We wanted to show who funded them and where they were sending their resources. This was the first time that I ever embraced the idea of being part of a radical queer community. This collective gave full voice to the anger I felt at the way queer people were excluded from a society that expected us to participate without respecting us at all.

Despite this newfound camaraderie, I was overwhelmed by work stress and my obsessive thinking about injustice and oppression. Exercise wasn't cutting it; drugs and drinking were not options in the military. I longed for even a single night of human companionship. There wasn't exactly a hot gay club scene in upstate New York, so I turned to internet dating. I didn't know what I wanted, so mostly I waited for people to message me first. Things were extremely direct on the web: age/sex/location was basically all you needed, unless you were inclined to share more intimate stats, statuses, and preferences. In the days before location-based apps made getting laid almost as easy as hailing a cab, most people, including me, went on sites like Adam4Adam and Gay.com. I sifted through profile after profile, messaged a few people. The first guy I went out with was cute but flaky, less interested in me than in testing my sexual boundaries.

But Dylan—not his real name—interested me more. He was tall, with green eyes, long unkempt brown hair, and a bit of a beard. We met on a dating site, then soon started texting and chatting on AIM and Yahoo Messenger; I'd lose hours flirting with him, talking to him about everything that crossed our minds. It was late fall, just when it starts to get frigid and dark in New York State, and our flirtation became the most exciting part of my day. He was a softhearted liberal who cared deeply about the environment. I was a soldier, in the process of getting even more alienated from government. But I fell hard for him. Everything about him was attractive. But he lived near Ithaca—two and a half hours away.

The first time I met Dylan, he picked me up from the airport in Syracuse. (I'd flown in from a two-week leave in D.C.) Upstate New York in January was as advertised: snow as far as the eye could see. It was windy, and the white billows overwhelmed the whole landscape. Dylan met me at baggage claim, and even though I'd arranged the whole thing and was expecting to see him, I felt surprised that he'd actually showed up. I reached up to hug him, awkwardly. We walked outside to his car, an old nineties Subaru, and when he turned the ignition, folk music from his stereo filled the car. I was nervous, on edge, chatting about the snow. I gave short answers to his questions, thinking about how strange the situation was, whether the road was safe. Finally, about an hour into our drive to Ithaca, I looked over and processed it. *That's Dylan. This is the person I've been talking to all this time.* We walked around Ithaca, and the winter sun reflecting from the white-blanketed streets was so sharp I needed sunglasses. We went to his place and immediately went to bed, and stayed there. Our date lasted fourteen hours.

At first, Dylan was more invested in us having a clearly defined relationship than I was. We'd spend our rare days together alternating between sex, food, and video games. He was eighteen, just finishing high school and getting ready to head to Brandeis for college. I felt like a veteran by comparison. I'd just turned twenty-one, and I'd celebrated by throwing myself a small party in the barracks room at Fort Drum, with cookies and pizza and a bottle of Moët & Chandon. Mostly women showed up, until the men in the barracks noticed that I'd managed to gather a crowd of women.

Dylan's naïveté helped me feel more worldly, more self-assured. I was starting to fall in love with him, even if I didn't know exactly what that was yet. For Valentine's Day, he bought me a dozen roses, and I bought us matching bracelets, with equal signs symbolizing equality, both within the relationship and as queer people in the world. I began to spend my weekends and my three-day passes going to Boston to visit him once he'd moved there for college. But I could also feel him pulling away as school closed in around him. Once, we took an online quiz together to find out our compatibility; one of the questions asked who the most important person in your life was. I answered that it was Dylan; he, a committed Catholic, answered that it was God.

In Boston, Dylan and I started to go to meetups for the local tech security scene. This was a window into a whole new world, one that felt both familiar and revelatory. He was majoring in neuroscience, and many of the people we met went to MIT, Harvard, Tufts, or BU, studying physics or computer science. I met literal experts in rocket science, something I'd never dreamed of. These were my people; I felt an instant affinity, a shared set of interests and references. We'd do trajectory physics problems for fun, or spend hours drinking beer and arguing with different versions of that one college guy who really wants to talk about Nietzsche. The in-jokes, the posters, the T-shirts, the discussions imagining the structures of a more utopian internet—it all felt like my IRC channels had come to life.

That life couldn't have been more different from my work life. I spent my weeks thinking about life on the ground in Logar and Wardak Provinces in eastern Afghanistan, where we were slated to fly soon. The region was mountainous, populated by a variety of tribal and ethnic groups, and it was virtually impossible to convince any of them to recognize the authority of President Hamid Karzai's NATO-supported government. It was a massive mess, which was why the United States planned to send an influx of forces, including my unit. Over the year from the moment when I set foot in Fort Drum to the moment when I would deploy there, I studied Wardak-Logar down to each village, learning about intra-Pashtun political dynamics and Tajik society.

But political decisions forced me to throw away my work. Helmand Province, in the south, had become the epicenter of the Taliban insurgency during the runup to a national election. The U.S. military establishment was concerned that the situation threatened its ability to credibly project power throughout the region, and spent the spring of 2009 pushing the war-skeptical Obama—still green in his new role— to send more troops. (It had recently become the conventional wisdom that agile counterinsurgency worked, and the 2007 "surge" of troops to Iraq was considered an example of the new approach's effectiveness.) The White House announced an aggressive Afghanistan strategy, and they needed a unit that had experience on the ground there and would be ready to go sooner than us.

All this reshuffling of unit deployments meant that army command was sending us to Iraq instead of Afghanistan, and the timeline rapidly accelerated. Months and months of pre-deployment work was instantly worthless. We'd prepared for a rural mountainous region, and now we were going to an urban environment in the high desert, in a different country, on a silty floodplain. I had to develop a brand-new set of maps and imagery, build new data sets and entirely new professional relationships, grasp a whole new set of knowledge. The political geography was also new—eastern Afghanistan lies in the shadow of Pakistan, while the drive from Baghdad to the Iranian border is shorter than the drive from New York City to Washington, D.C. These were long, long days, and sometimes weekends. Morale was an even bigger challenge than overwork for the soldiers in my unit. Most people in my brigade had already been to Iraq a couple of times, and no one wanted to go back to that familiar hell.

To deal with the stress, I self-medicated with coffee, energy drinks, cigarettes—and sex. Dylan and I had kept our relationship open, and he lived hours away. I hooked up with a few guys near Fort Drum—though I avoided guys in the military as much as possible. It was an everybody-knows-everybody gay scene, which could get complicated quickly. There was one gay bar, Clueless, within driving distance, in Watertown, but everyone there worked on the base. I went just once, on a Saturday night, and met the whole gay community of Fort Drum. It felt territorial, claustrophobic—and risky. If any minor incident had drawn attention to the bar, and all the gay soldiers in it, we all would have been discharged.

Early spring in upstate New York feels like a continuation of winter. It was a Sunday in late March 2009, one of those cloudy days when there's still snow piled in patches on the ground. I had the day off, so I spent it in civvies, browsing at the post exchange. I was at the food court, eating a Subway sandwich, when I saw a cute guy, maybe five or ten years older than me, staring at me. His eyes on me felt good. The man stood up and did exactly what I hoped for: walked across the room. "Hi there," he said. "How's your sandwich?" I blushed.

I loved this kind of attention. His eyes stayed on me; he wanted me; he listened to everything I said. I began to unspool everything. Oklahoma, my parents, Chicago, why I'd joined the army. I moved on to my frustrations at work, to how tired I was, to how alone I felt. I told him how much I wanted to be able to go out, like I did in D.C. He was Southern, and didn't say much about himself, but he kept asking me questions. I loved his curiosity, was flattered by it. I didn't know for sure that he was military, nor was I thinking about it too hard. We just sat in the artificial light, surrounded by plastic trays and ketchup dispensers and military men looking vaguely uncomfortable in their off-duty khakis, and I still thought it was romantic.

When he offered to drive me to the Starbucks a few miles away for a coffee, I agreed. We got in his SUV and went to the tiny Salmon Run Mall, just outside Watertown. We wandered around until we were hungry enough for Taco Bell, in the food court, for dinner. I asked him to drive me back to Fort Drum, and on the way, he stopped the car in a parking lot. He pulled over to a dark corner, behind leftover mounds of snow from the fading winter. Finally, in the front seat of his SUV, he made his move. I was into him, but I was tired, and just didn't feel like doing anything that night, I explained.

He looked frustrated. He came on to me harder, which at first felt like playful flirting. He just wanted a shot. He kept grabbing me, trying to kiss me. So I pushed away, playfully at first, and then it started to get more aggressive. He grabbed at my belt buckle, his hands wandering under my shirt, pushing harder. I started to reach for my knife. Ever since Chicago, I'd kept a weapon on me as protection. He could see me reaching, and, still holding on to me, he told me that I shouldn't try to pull anything. That he was an officer, and that it would be an enlisted person assaulting an officer, and it would be my word against his. He knew that as an intelligence analyst, my career depended almost entirely on my security clearance. We both knew that an accusation didn't need substantiation to trigger the revocation of a clearance. The mere accusation alone would sink my career, especially under Don't Ask, Don't Tell. There would have been all kinds of questions about what I was doing with him parked in the car. I'd have been discharged. I had to choose, in that split second, between career and safety.

He grabbed me by the waist and pushed me into the back seat. He climbed over, and I stopped fighting. Going on autopilot may have saved me from losing my job, but it made me feel somehow responsible for what was happening to me. I remember him whispering in my ear, "I knew you'd like it." The most profound betrayal, I believed back then, was not his transgression, but my own complicity.

I didn't say a word to him. Afterward, I sat in the passenger seat. I looked outside the window. I rolled it down and lit a cigarette without asking for permission to smoke. Back at Fort Drum, we stopped at the checkpoint. He rolled down his window and the gate guard scanned his ID card. I glanced at his ID, and I'm fairly certain I saw his rank. I don't remember his name. To protect myself, I gave him directions to the wrong barracks. I called a taxi once he left.

The military issues every soldier a card with instructions on how to report a sexual assault. Everything I did contradicted those instructions. I didn't want to report it, I didn't want any evidence. Because of Don't Ask, Don't Tell, the mere accusation would have been problematic. Back in my tiny room, the first thing I did was strip from top to bottom and throw all my clothes in the laundry. Then I took the longest, hottest shower of my life.

For most of the night, I barely slept. I huddled under the covers, dazed. And then I woke up to someone banging on my door, and all my alarm clocks going off. It was seven twenty, and I'd missed formation. "Let me get dressed," I yelled. The pounding on the door and screaming continued. It was the Admin, as I will call her. She did not outrank me, but her bureaucratic role gave her an informal sort of power over me. She was nosy, a busybody, and she hated my guts. I put on my uniform, opened the door, and walked right past her. She tried to catch up, still angry and scolding me. I didn't give a fuck about her, or about life just then.

I headed to physical training, and I found the section sergeant, Master Sergeant Adkins, to talk to him about being late. But the Admin followed me and wouldn't shut up. She kept talking about what I'd done, and escalated to yelling. I couldn't take it. I yelled back at the top of my lungs. The primal scream brought some relief, but I could still feel the discomfort of the night before in my body. And now I was at war with this ridiculous person. There were write-ups and punishments—no one offered help or asked questions. The Admin suggested that I not deploy with the group. Adkins disagreed; we needed my skill set.

Numbness. Dissociation. I tuned out of work, stopped listening to the world around me, just went into the darkest, deepest corners of my mind. I could barely talk to Dylan anymore. That night had changed me, my appetites, and my feelings about myself. I desired nothing. I felt only gross. I became a much heavier smoker, up from three cigarettes a day to more than a pack. I started spending more and more time online or playing video games, late at night, drinking coffee and Red Bull at 2:00 a.m. I drank tons and tons of caffeine to get me through the day. I either barely slept, or slept for fourteen hours straight. My personality broke.

The drama with the Admin continued. I tried to ignore her—she felt like the least of my problems—but she had always gone after me, for no real reason. We were both enlisted soldiers from Oklahoma, but she seemed to care so much more than I did about the surface-level hierarchies of the military. She cared deeply about how the uniforms looked, and whether a memorandum was formatted in the right way—so much more than she cared about any of the more substantial aspects of the job. She did paperwork on security clearance, and other projects like that. She used administrative bullshit to bully me.

I sniped back at her. She was easy to irritate and undermine, so I made her life miserable. She did the same to me, leveraging her supposed authority. She'd do the pettiest things, like monitor how much soda I was drinking and report it up the chain. I think there was an element of jealousy: I had an easy, friendly relationship with the officers she so desperately wanted to impress, and I was doing more interesting work than she was. I wasn't her only target, but I'd kick back at her more than most people, which she wasn't used to. I wanted to grind her gears in any way that I could.

In May 2009, the army sent me to northern Virginia for a two-week-long training on geospatial databases. I took the opportunity, visiting home, to unwind and relax a little, even though it was becoming apparent that the front-page news about Afghanistan and Iraq was going to affect our unit. The Admin called me to tell me that she knew I was sleeping with guys, and that while she didn't *want* to ruin my career, that would depend on whether I was willing to play by her rules. She wanted credit for my work, to advance her own career. She also wanted me to treat her like a boss. I was furious.

By now, there wasn't very much aggressive enforcement of Don't Ask, Don't Tell—in fact, our unit had an unofficial policy of avoiding investigations, and I knew that I wouldn't be discharged at her suggestion—but the Admin was the kind of person who would at least try to go to the installation general or to command in D.C. And the more paperwork there is on that kind of thing, the more risk there is. "Go fuck yourself!" I yelled, risk be damned, and hung up.

Sometimes at Fort Drum it felt as if my life didn't start until I had taken off my uniform and opened my computer. Sitting at a desk at work, I felt like a robot, acting in a prescribed role. Work that had once fascinated me was now boring, methodical. But online, at home, I was alive, a pioneer. There were whole deep universes to be shaped.

The more time I spent online, as I withdrew further from life at Fort Drum, the more time I had in this new world. Often when I was at the computer, in my room alone, I'd dress as a woman. It made me feel better, more relaxed, like a deeper version of myself. I had a stash of clothes, Goth stuff. I began researching what it would actually take, in practical terms, to transition. Above all, it would mean leaving the military. YouTube, only a couple of years old, was filled with videos of people undergoing transitions. I was obsessed.

Before I got into those videos, my exploration was all abstract, dry medical reading about gender-affirming surgeries or the best cocktail of hormones to use. Now, seeing someone—an actual human being—living life as a trans person made it concrete. I saw people who felt the way I thought. They spoke like me, with all the hopes and dreams and pains and fears that I felt. They were a reflection of myself—some future me, or some version of myself in a parallel universe. I grabbed tightly on to this sudden realization that trans people were just like me. Despite having enlisted in the military, despite going through this intense training and preparing to deploy overseas and making myself into a soldier, there still existed a kernel of something else, something more real about me. Underneath all my walls and defenses and bullshit—underneath all these layers of false pretenses and lies—existed the simple, basic truth. I am trans.

But this wasn't some easy breakthrough movie moment where the clouds parted and everything got instantly easier once I acknowledged that. In fact, things got more complicated. I asked Dylan what he would think if I started taking hormones, growing breasts. Would he still like me? He wasn't enthusiastic; he was confused. He was turned on by masculinity. But still, he said, "I guess I would." I got the sense he was just saying what he felt he had to say. Dylan did drag shows sometimes, and I didn't think he fully understood the difference between doing drag and being trans. I wanted reassurance that he loved me for who I was; he wanted me to talk about something else.

The closer I got to deploying—to slipping away from my dreams ever actually coming true—the deeper I dove into my dreamworld. I fantasized about settling down. Dylan was the longest relationship that I'd ever had, and I liked to imagine that he'd wait for me through the whole yearlong deployment. I wanted to do all the things that would help make that a reality. I suggested over and over that we get an apartment in Massachusetts, near his school, to move in together when I returned. I wanted a real home, a safe place. I wanted a piece of paper that said if something happened to me in Iraq, Dylan would be the person who would get the benefits, that he would be the one to take care of me. He said no, that it was way too early, that he wasn't ready. I was suddenly insecure in my primary anchor, my relationship. I was crushed.

I buried myself in work to fill the emotional void. I felt that my job was important, and I took my obligations seriously. By then I had expertise, deep knowledge. Transitioning would mean quitting. Keeping a secret—a concept that went against everything I believed about information freedom, about openness online—was the only way that I could get to Iraq and do my job. But I was worried. "I have this increasingly awful feeling," I instant-messaged a friend one night. "It comes from the realization that I am a trusted government employee with the highest security clearance. I know too much . . . I don't know if you can imagine the pressure."

8.

People sometimes say the floodplain of the Tigris looks like the moon, covered in silty, fine sand. But to me, it looked like Oklahoma, all empty plains and dun-colored palette and dust clouds that touched everything.

My arrival in Iraq in that fall of 2009 was jarring. A gradual descent would make a U.S. military plane an easy target for anyone in Baghdad with an interest in shooting at American soldiers—which is a whole lot of people. And so our unpressurized military transport plane nose-dived down. My inner ear blossomed with almost unimaginable pain, my stomach took a wrong turn into my chest. It was like a roller coaster, if the roller coaster were designed by a sadistic clown and if, rather than an amusement park, it deposited you into a war-ravaged country.

Baghdad was one of the world's great cities, a metropolis of more than six million, but instead of ruins or monuments dotting the city-scape, it was freckled with aerostats—large blimps with cameras and surveillance equipment—and saturated by military outposts. The whole landscape of Iraq had been shaped around service members and the business of war—of killing and protecting. People went about their days as normally as possible under a military occupation, carrying shopping bags and fast food past heavily armed soldiers. Occupying dense Baghdad was a bit like occupying Brooklyn and Queens. Residents didn't like us being there, but they had to get their children off to school, go to work, see their friends. I watched little kids in tidy uniforms play soccer in parks only a mile or so from active helicopter fire. They could see and hear the battle zone, but they were still little kids, just having fun. I imagine they knew it wasn't ideal, but it was normal.

My first stop in the Middle East had been at Camp Buehring, in Kuwait, which, even in October, was hot as fuck, filled with thousands of soldiers just passing time, waiting for their flights into Iraq, bored and watching DVDs of classic American movies under paintings of Kuwait's nobility. I IM'ed my friend Louis—not his real name—to update him on my trip. "Starbucks Internet hotspot. It's how America fights its wars these days." Louis and I had met through mutual friends, including Dylan, in Boston, after spending time chatting online. We were both interested in tech stuff. I gave him my address in Iraq, and told him, "Spread it around. Care packages welcome (especially Cambridge/Harvard/MIT items) . . . Send me stuff, preferably small tidbits, reminders of those who support me, etc. The weirder, wilder, or harder to find the better." We talked tech specs—was there good open-source video chat software we could use? Did we need to encrypt, he wondered, since I would be talking about my sexuality and Don't Ask, Don't Tell was still the law of the land? "Not at all," I typed. "Monitoring systems is technically infeasible. It's just military/government scare tactics. There's very little monitoring in place. That which is in place, is in place on those who are deemed a credible threat already."

I was supposed to spend two weeks in Kuwait, acclimating, but less than a week in, I woke up ready to spend another day playing real-time strategy games on my personal MacBook, only to hear a voice yell, "Manning, pack out, you're heading out." I was the only private among the senior command staff on the C-130 Hercules transport plane taking us on the short flight to Baghdad. The inside of the plane was Spartan, with only the most utilitarian features—ropes, nets, and basic seats—and it was stuffed full of crew and equipment. There was no air-conditioning, and the fuselage felt like an oven, baking us in the darkness.

I was exhausted and hungry. We lugged our sixty-five-pound rucksacks to the base. The very first thing we did was eat. My whole time in Iraq was like that: I lived chow to chow, the same way I had in basic training. Camp Liberty, where we stayed temporarily after landing, was part of a sprawling U.S. military complex near Baghdad International Airport. It was filled with burger joints, lattes, trinkets, buy-one-get-one-free sales, as if we'd been deployed to a shopping mall. The message was clear: American freedom—the thing we're exporting to the Middle East—is defined by the ability to buy things.

The next morning, in a loud twin-rotor Chinook helicopter, we headed to Forward Operating Base Hammer, a new base east of Baghdad. The twenty-five miles of landscape between the airport and the base was barren, as if it had been abandoned by all living things. We got there at midnight, and the trailers—glowing in the artificial light of dozens of portable lanterns—became my new universe.

FOB Hammer was a city. It even had a mayor, who was responsible for things as excruciatingly mundane as zoning. Yes, there were Black Hawk helicopters and chain-link fences topped with razor wire, sandbags and concrete and Hesco barriers outside of every building. But there was also a fire department and a Green Beans coffee shop. I remember listening to the radio in a Ford F-350 truck while waiting to pick up a lieutenant. I got bored with whatever American pop song was playing and clicked to the next station. The Baghdadi pop shocked me back into recognizing my surroundings. It was so easy to forget that I wasn't in the United States. The lines between places blurred.

And yet, there was no mistaking *what* we were: ground command for a war. The tactical operations center was located in a disused basketball gym and set up like a lecture hall, with desks overlooking three giant screens that showed, at all times, a giant map of the area of operations and live drone footage from the region. On their laptops, analysts played (whether for work or their own amusement) an intermittent loop of videos that were highlight reels of war: explosions and vehicles dissolving into shrapnel and flame.

FOB Hammer had an acrid, synthetic smell. Every morning, a pollution fog of diesel gas and car exhaust snaked its way through the base and cut through the loamy smell of the floodplain. Incinerated trash from the burn pit at the southern end of the base met the brick-factory fumes from a town outside the northern end of the base. When it rained, the ground turned to peanut butter, a sludgy, muddy mess that coated our boots. Winter introduced itself as a misty fifty degrees. Instead of snowstorms Iraq had dust storms. It was bleak and beige and above all boring, a region at the tail end of a decade-long drought.

FOB Hammer was huge. It had been expanded for the American surge in the spring of 2007. Its presence was intended as a show of strength against the large, organized militia groups that had grown in the densely populated neighborhoods of southeastern Baghdad and that wanted to overthrow the Iraqi government. And it worked, according to the army, which claimed that FOB Hammer was the linchpin in transforming the political dynamics of the Sunni Triangle. The story went that U.S. forces had worked in concert with the locals to make that happen. Still, even at its most active, the vast majority of counterinsurgency work is just about following people as they live their lives.

Our energy seemed entirely focused on patting ourselves on the back for bringing "democracy" to the region, even though there were increasing signs of a long-term political spiral. It's true that things were less violent than they'd been at the peak in 2007, when FOB Hammer was a regular target for attacks. But by the time my unit arrived, in October 2009, the gains from the surge had begun to fragment. For the first time, the Islamic State of Iraq—now widely known as ISIS—was making its presence known. That month, there were coordinated bombings that targeted a meeting for national reconciliation in western Iraq. Two simultaneous suicide bombings in Baghdad killed more than 150 and wounded 700. It was the deadliest attack since 2007. The news in America was all about the impending dawn of democracy, and free elections.

These attacks coincided with my arrival in Iraq, so I had to go to work for my first shift immediately, on about five hours of sleep. I met the people I'd been emailing with for months, ever since it had become clear we were going to Iraq; now, we briefed in person.

I crashed the minute that first shift was over. My room in the barracks was in a trailer, divided into three units that held two people each, with a locker and a bunk bed for each occupant. The trailer was entirely unadorned. At the local store, run by regional immigrants and Iraqi nationals, I bought a little table and a small refrigerator for a pittance. I had my MacBook Pro, some reference books on statistics and programming, and an iPod Touch loaded with Nirvana, Rage Against the Machine, DMX, the operas of Philip Glass, Beyoncé, and lots of electronic dance music. The only sentimental object in my room was an original Game Boy that Louis had sent me as a gag gift before I deployed.

Every night, I'd walk down a muddy path to the basketball court, past the massive, constantly roaring power-generator trailer and a group of parked MRAPs (mine-resistant ambush-protected vehicles), towering over us like All Terrain Walkers on Tatooine. Our SCIF (sensitive compartmented information facility)—an office into which you could not set foot without a security clearance—was dark and windowless, a tangle of cords and computers, each hooked up to the vast repositories of the American classified network.

We were crammed cheek by jowl. It was hard to even move around without bumping into someone. Early on in my time in Iraq, I was promoted from private to specialist, to signify the nature of the work that I did, but "specialist" didn't mean much to the kind of person only obsessed with officer's stripes on a uniform. One of the officers was the kind of guy who wanted you to say "sir" at the end of every single sentence, which had not been the norm in my unit at Fort Drum. I hadn't encountered much of this. I worked mostly with intelligence officers, who want analysts to speak freely about what they see, and throwing a "sir" onto every recommendation didn't exactly encourage that mindset. They were less obsessed with hierarchy than officers in operations and the rest of the military tend to be. This was a flashback to boot camp, to lessons about power and leverage and control.

My workstation was at the free-throw line of the basketball court. You could still see the lines on the court, although the paint was chipped, and my chair was broken. I spent my shifts toggling among three computers: one for top-secret material, one for classified, and one for unclassified. The constant, often bloody video feed, coming to us in real time from mere miles away, haunted my dreams and waking hours.

At Fort Drum, the connection had been too slow for live footage, but here, the war was in the room. No more screenshots, no more physical distance, no more time lag. There was the huge screen, looming over us constantly, and then our own monitors, where we could zoom in to almost helmet-camera levels. This was as close to constant, endless combat as you could get without being in it.

I soon began to feel disconnected from my body, as if I were living in a simulation. I'd dissociate, look for solace in the numbness and sameness of my routine. I seemed to be in two places at once. But how could I not be? That was literally what was required of me. I was on the basketball court, typing assessments and dealing with the stultifying bureaucracy of office life—but I was also on the front lines, seeing the world through the eyes of a soldier who might be in the act of killing, and who was always at risk of being killed. There was no more intellectualizing of problems, no more analytical distance. The video feed was an in-your-face reminder of the stakes.

Back at Fort Drum, I had experienced a moment of shock when I saw exactly how much incredibly detailed, invasively intimate information I was getting about the people we were tracking. It was an unreal amount of information, but it quickly became second nature to work with it as a tool. I didn't have time to process what it meant, on a philosophical level, that we had this kind of access to people's lives. I just took it in as it came, sorting it for utility: Did this add up to someone we could exploit? Was this person a potential source? Or were they a threat, someone we should try to capture or even kill?

In upstate New York, my brain could turn off the feed when the day was over. I could leave work. Now, the job was my life, my universe.

The human right to privacy, the right to not be manipulated or coerced or actively destroyed by a government, wasn't something I considered on a deep level, not at first. Nor did I linger longer than I needed to on the ethical implications of what we were doing, on the big picture and my role in it.

But once I began to see the results, it hit me in full—the way that my daily tasks connected to this bigger, troubling picture of the role that America was playing in the region. The brutal results of what we were doing on the ground were unavoidable for me. Anything that gave us an extra edge became so valuable, so important, it rose above the importance of the Iraqis I thought we were supposed to protect— and since I worked as an intelligence analyst, getting that extra edge was my job, my *life*.

It didn't matter how many episodes of *Metalocalypse* I binge-watched, I was still in Iraq, and I was still part of an apparatus that was dehumanizing people at every moment. I couldn't compartmentalize anymore. Day in, day out, for twelve or fourteen or even eighteen hours a day, we watched real-time surveillance feed of the destruction all around us. We read about endless death in our reports, and then looked at U.S news outlets, where it wasn't anywhere to be seen. I was living in a horror movie mash-up of *Office Space* and *Groundhog Day*.

Iraq is blurry. Most of what I remember is how hard everything felt. How difficult it was to do something as simple as laundry. I had to walk a mile there and a mile back. We only had four uniforms, so I made that walk a lot.

It was the same thing every day. I put on my uniform, top to bottom, and hated it every time. Unless you were trying to hide in a 1970s lounge chair, the camouflage was effective only at erasing any trace of personal identity among other similarly dressed soldiers.

Since I was on the night shift, I had dinner for breakfast every day. Our shifts were long, twelve hours on, twelve off, 10:00 p.m. to 10:00 a.m.—and that was on a good day, when we didn't have a heavy load. I slept during the daytime, and slept terribly. People came in and out of the housing unit all the time. The cardboard I put up to cover the windows did little to soften the glare. Slowly, and then quickly, my emotional health began to decay.

But my performance improved just from being on the ground. My assessments got sharper, less canned. I had more situational awareness. Most people spent any free time they had just zoning out with video games, but I'm an extrovert. I'd make the rounds, chatting up anyone from an officer to the guy in the armory who I paid twenty bucks a month to clean my M9 carbine rifle. I built an especially close relationship with the indirect-fire team, who were tasked with shooting down incoming rockets and mortars. We struck up a deal: I'd help them refine their gun turret trajectories using a custom predictive analyst program—a load of complicated math—and in exchange I'd get their raw data directly from them, within seconds, rather than waiting for hours until it was released.

Office politics were complicated. The intel community draws in people who tend to be different in some way or another, and at least in our group, this meant a slightly larger population of (closeted, isolated) queer people, and women, who I'd estimate made up something like 60 percent of my office, as opposed to just 14 percent in the military at large. There was a lot of fear-driven interoffice sex, and all of this led to a certain amount of disproportionately intense intrigue. In the middle of some soap opera or another, I put a sign on my desk that read STOP THE DRAMA.

I still felt in love with Dylan, and too tired and overworked to pursue anything sexual with anyone. Dylan and I were in a messy breakup; he'd pull me in and push me away, telling me he needed space one day, and the next day posting photos on Facebook of himself at a Don't Ask, Don't Tell demonstration, wearing a pin that read ARMY WIFE. Technically, it was an open relationship, but I'd changed my Facebook status to single before I'd left the country. We talked just enough to make me crave him, but not enough to make me feel he was still mine.

But I couldn't say a word about my private life because of Don't Ask, Don't Tell; I couldn't bitch to coworkers about the relationship, or get solace from their reassurances. In effect, I was structurally obligated to be emotionally isolated.

Coworkers knew I was gay. I kept a fairy wand on my desk, for one thing. Once, I was at breakfast with a woman I worked with closely, and she pointed with a meaningful grin to the big bowl of Lucky Charms I'd poured myself and said, "Boy, those *rainbows* look good." I couldn't do anything but blush and laugh. She was a lesbian in a marriage of mutual convenience with a gay man who was also in the military; together they'd decided that this would be good for their careers. For all its cutting-edge tech, the military was like living in another century.

People could be manipulative, too, using what they knew about you to extort favors or simply to entertain themselves at your expense. Several times, my supervising captain stood over me while I was at my computer, began to knead my shoulders, and then placed her breast firmly on the back of my head and rubbed it around. There were other people in the room, and I was stunned by her bizarre behavior. Other times, she'd grab me and say dirty things in my ear. I assumed other people could see what was happening. This wasn't about sex; it was about shaming me.

But the closer my colleagues were to me, the less they cared about my sexuality. Besides, I was good at my job. I felt like a freak, but at least I was an indispensable freak.

As for my gender, there was simply no room for me to think clearly about it. But that did not stop me from feeling. As the days passed, my anxiety and depression worsened. I was always on an irregular schedule, sometimes getting only two or three hours of sleep. Exhaustion shifted from being an occasional physical state to the only feeling I had room for. I figured that if I could pour myself into work, everything else would fade away.

The military is stressful enough. You're never alone, never given time to think. The added factor of being in an active war made it that much harder to address myself to my own inner world, and yet, or perhaps as a result, the insistent pain of my unresolved dysphoria got harder to ignore.

So I sublimated every anxiety into work. Even in my few off-hours I'd go down Google rabbit holes that were related in some way to my job. I became obsessed with doing research that I couldn't access on the classified network, the kind of information that would take several weeks to wend its way through State Department channels. I'd look up translations of local news articles, blog reports that I'd run through Google Translate. There was a lot of useful information floating around locally that didn't get talked about in the English-language press, where the only things that got coverage were catastrophes and terror threats. I was interested in water treatment plants, the jockeying between political parties—the stuff that's actually going on in a country on a lived, daily basis.

My best work was rarely used, though. What officers liked were briefings with lots of slides and lots of pictures, anything pointing to exactly where the "bad guy" was. I became skilled at telling operations people what they needed to hear in order to justify a decision they had already made. But I also had to be objective, to do what I thought was my duty, to perform the real analysis, even when that meant pointing out that what we were doing in certain places was creating the chaos, that *we* were the violence, *we* were the aggressor. The "bad guys" were only reacting to what we did. When we went into a neighborhood and shook it down, flushing people out and leaving death and destruction in our wake, we caused the whole area to unravel. War was being built on unreliable binaries of "good" and "bad." And we ignored what we didn't want to see. The officers often didn't listen when I brought them inconvenient information.

The work was occasionally intensely rapid, demanding fast turnaround: an incident or threat required an immediate analysis to be delivered to the operations side. But more often, it was a sustained march, long, draining, plodding: editing or finishing the work of the day shift, crossing t's for the bureaucracy. As I wrote to my friend Louis back in Cambridge, "Leaves a computer savvy guy a lot of time to pry around."

That exploration was sanctioned: we were supposed to be laser-focused on the mission at hand, but as intelligence analysts, we were also supposed to creatively look beyond our immediate sources of information and take in the bigger picture. Cultivating an operational understanding of the whole engagement—taking into account the significant actions of the war at large—was encouraged.

During my early weeks in Iraq, the whole base was focused on the upcoming parliamentary elections, which were set to take place in March 2010. My job—as an all-source analyst in what was known as the S-2 fusion team—was to monitor a specific Shia group. It was one of the hardest problems you could have as an analyst.

I used Bayesian statistical analysis to look for patterns in their behavior, but this particular target group often defied my priors and predictions. They operated by throwing their support and expertise behind local groups operating in east Baghdad, and as a result I spent a lot of time covering religious and political leaders and community basement militia groups of varying alliances. This target group was very good at what they wanted to do—and that was to kill Americans. They were good at everything they did, in fact. They kept me awake at night with how good they were. They were ghosts. It was staggering, and the consequences were bloody.

Tracking this group made it clear to me that our engagement in Iraq and Afghanistan had surprisingly little to do with those actual countries. Our involvement was about a bigger picture. It was about trying to project American hegemony to other powers in the region. You could look at the accumulation of death, after years, on all sides, and think that this war was unwinnable. Or you could consider whether pouring enormous resources into a never-ending war was actually the point.

If that's what it was, then this war was dick-waving by people who were half a world away from the conflict. Meanwhile, on the ground, it was about survival. We were dying over posturing, over bullshit.

I began seeing a therapist again. Not by choice. The command referred me. Nearly everyone in the intelligence shop saw one, of course. I'd received a litany of misdiagnoses over the years, generalized anxiety disorder being the most common. Of course, it was gender dysphoria that caused the anxiety and depression spirals, but I wasn't ready to face that yet. I'd first gone to see someone when I had panic attacks as a teenager in Oklahoma. But in Iraq, depression, anxiety, anger, and extreme stress were logical reactions to what we were seeing. How could I watch people die and not be affected?

The therapist, a kind older guy, seemed helpless. I couldn't really say much to him—he didn't have a high-enough security clearance for me to discuss my actual work. We were stuck. I'd tell him I was exhausted by my job, and then he'd ask for specifics. I'd have to shut down the entire conversation: everything that most frightened and stressed me out was—and remains—highly classified. I could feel his frustration; it mirrored my own. Antidepressants like SSRIs were out. I'd experienced awful side effects from them in the past—nausea, nosebleeds, urinary retention, and other kidney problems.

But the biggest obstacle to my therapy was Don't Ask, Don't Tell. A therapist wasn't required to report homosexual activity to a commander, but, erring on the side of caution, or sometimes just outright prejudice, some of them did. Same thing with clergy. Every potential resource represented a risk.

I couldn't tell my counselor about my personal life; it felt too hazardous. I couldn't explain how much I ached to see Dylan and how much it hurt me when he was slow to reply to my IMs. Even with colleagues, I had to play the pronoun game. Dylan turned into a girlfriend, not a boyfriend. Sometimes with a knowing wink, sometimes not, depending on the context—but we were all legally required to obfuscate. It was one more artificial wall that I had to put up, one that, no matter how hard I tried, kept me from opening up and getting close to people in the military. That loneliness only exacerbated every bit of depression, worry, and alienation I was feeling.

And I certainly couldn't say to anyone that I was not interested in being a man, or even that I felt deeply uncomfortable with the gender I was expected to play. Between my own inability to find words that resonated or described my experience and the repressive rigidity of the military, I couldn't even articulate it to myself.

9.

IRAQ

DECEMBER 2009 TO JANUARY 2010

I live with the fact that people died because of my team's work. And I didn't struggle with that in the beginning—it was the job. I loved seeing that I'd changed the battlefield. There was pride in dismantling an enemy group. At first.

But the loss of life—not "our" lives, just *life*—added up. One set of deaths eats me up—precisely because I *wasn't* there. One night that winter, I was taking a break for midnight chow when we got word that operators from the Joint Special Operations Task Force wanted to capture one of their high-value targets, a man I'd been tracking carefully. I'd worked my ass off on him for weeks, painstakingly developing up-to-date information about his involvement in planning potential operations in eastern Baghdad. I knew not just where he lived, but where he ate lunch, when he met for assignations with lovers, and how he obtained alcohol in a legally dry country.

The operators were exquisitely skilled at coming and going quickly and quietly. That night, our office got just forty-five minutes' notice that they were going to take him out. They'd gotten a "fix"—one of the three *f*'s in the "find, fix, and finish" formula—which meant that, via targeted monitoring, they'd figured out his location.

The "finish" part was their specialty. But this time, they screwed up. I'd recently created an updated target package (a dossier and map of essential information). But instead they used an ancient one from 2007. The target had moved three blocks away from his 2007 address, a fact that I, and everyone else in my group, knew. The operators relied on this bad information and went to the wrong building, where they killed everyone in the house who resisted capture, all the witnesses, and, finally, even the fucking dog.

I came back from lunch to news of about a dozen presumably innocent people who were now all dead. We had to pretend it had never happened. Special Ops went back to Qatar for their next mission. We stayed. We lived with the bodies. We were left to deal with the anger in a neighborhood where that many human lives were lost to a clerical error—to laziness and arrogance.

In the wake of the night raid, the intended target disappeared. Trying to rebuild a package on him seemed pointless. I don't think Special Operations notified the local infantry unit, who were deliberately left out of the loop, so no one ever knew what really happened beyond a few of us in the intel shop. There was no record. I had never been so angry.

Lots of people wonder whether my later disclosures were an unforeseeable event, or whether the real surprise is that many other people didn't *also* make these kinds of disclosures. I wonder, too.

All the conditions that would contribute to such an action were certainly present. The intelligence community had changed dramatically as a reaction to 9/11; there was an institutional sense that the bureaucratic machinery, and the turf wars among different departments and agencies, had fatally hindered intelligence sharing in the lead-up to that day. By the time I enlisted, the idea of a strict chain of command in the intelligence community had—in practice if not on paper—largely been abandoned. Instead of the rigid insistence on hierarchy that existed elsewhere in the military, intel was a relatively flat environment. While wearing my analyst hat, I could give my frank personal opinions, ask questions, criticize certain decisions—and the command considered that vital to the healthy functioning of the shop. (Of course, this meant we occasionally clashed with people from operations, who liked to pull rank above all else. We threw the refrain "intel drives ops—not the other way around" right back at them, and at the end of the day, they knew we were right.)

In the last decade, the American government had radically altered its approach to collecting and regulating information, and our little basketball court was operating downstream of that. The number of classified documents had expanded exponentially after 9/11. Before that day, there had been around eight million documents per year marked as classified. By the time we deployed in Iraq, the number of classified documents was reported to be more than fifty million. Meanwhile, ProPublica reported that the government had begun to intercept several billion phone calls and emails a day. And more people than ever—four million, or roughly the population of Los Angeles, many of whom were contractors—had the necessary clearance for access to classified information, which was bouncing around between government agencies and the military more than ever thanks to the new mandate for intel-sharing.

Meanwhile, the on-the-ground operational security was far from airtight. In our supposedly high-security office, people kept the passwords to laptops containing government secrets stuck to those same laptops, written on Post-its. People flagrantly disregarded the strict regulations against having any personal material inside either room of the SCIF, and we all used DVD-RWs to trade and download to the shared hard drive the media we consumed to keep ourselves entertained—copyrighted music, serial-code-broken computer games, bootlegged movies.

I was frustrated by the jarring dissonance between what those of us deployed to combat zones knew to be true and what the rest of America believed was happening. It was all-consuming. People needed more information to understand what was happening. I even saw it on my own Facebook account. My friends—fairly liberal people—posted links to op-eds that reflected a deep misunderstanding of what was actually going on. They seemed to believe that simply having a Democratic president instead of a Republican one could solve something. Liberal, Obama-voting Democrats appeared to think our involvement in Iraq was suddenly working out just fine, at least since their guy had taken the oath of office.

The drawdown plan that Obama's administration was following had, in fact, been cooked up by the George W. Bush team, and the Obama team more or less rubber-stamped it. We could have started it earlier. We had the logistics and the capability and the impetus to do it, if not the political will. The reasons for staying at all seemed to be more about optics than strategy. Things were going to fall apart if we were there, and things were going to fall apart if we left.

Part of my job was putting together long-term assessments about what would happen if we followed the drawdown plan, based on previous trends and how the Iraqi population might respond. But I had two different bosses, and Captain Martin, the officer asking me for those assessments, had different priorities than Captain Lim, who was asking me for ops work, the more day-to-day assessments. They'd argue over who'd get more of my time, and the compromise result was that I'd get called in for extra shifts by both of them.

Fifteen-hour days became common for me. I'd end up losing my days off, working for a week straight. I put up a kitschy demotivational poster near my desk. People in my office loved it. IRAQ IS A TREADMILL, it said, overlaid on a map that showed all of Iraq as our brigade's area of operation. RUNNING AS FAST AS YOU CAN, AS HARD AS YOU CAN, GOING NOWHERE.

In mid-December, during my free time, I reached out to my friend Louis on IM.

"Sanity-o-meter doing okay?" he asked.

"I think sanity has dwindled drastically," I replied.

I showed up forty-five minutes late to work that night. I'd fallen down a rabbit hole of video games and the internet. Specialist Smith—not his real name—who was the same rank as me but in charge of the night shift, tried to rip me a new one for tardiness. Later that week, it happened again. This time, Smith was prepared: he'd asked Adkins, the master sergeant and the highest-ranking soldier in our intel shop, for special permission to discipline me, and informed me that I had to show up to work early, at nine fifteen each evening, in uniform, at Smith's sleeping quarters, so he could escort me to my shift. It was infantilizing, and it wasn't the only punishment; Smith was also taking away my day off.

I was overwhelmed. I felt on the brink of . . . well, everything. All I did was work or think about work. And this wasn't enough. They wanted to treat me like a child. I lost it. In a blind rage, I flipped over the table near me. Smith tried to restrain me, which only made me feel more targeted; another soldier came in and they both held me back.

The anger was swift to come and swift to leave. I finished that shift with no other incidents. But the damage had been done: the Admin, who already hated me, had been one of the people to hear the fight and had come to watch. It was like an early Christmas present for her, a chance to tell on me. She reported it to Sergeant Adkins. But Adkins thought my work was valuable, and my performance level was high enough that he didn't want to take disciplinary action. If he had, I would have lost access to classified information, and I would have been a lot less useful to him. He needed personnel.

Louis had begun to worry about me. He sent me a care package: a paperback copy of Richard Stallman's *Free Software, Free Society*, with a personal inscription from the author directing me to "fight for freedom"; a few volumes of Neil Gaiman's *Sandman* epic; a book called *The Relaxation Response*; and others on managing PTSD.

On Christmas Eve, 2009, I had to work, as on any other night. It was a month until my leave, and I was counting down the days. Part of my job was to weigh in on route clearance packages, the army term for a routine operation we'd perform at night to make sure that a particular road was safe for our infantry to travel. I had to evaluate whether there were likely to be any improvised explosive devices (IEDs), land mines, or potential ambush locations.

I was part of the counter-IED working group. That night, I strongly recommended against what was called Route Aeros, a proposed path that wasn't part of our normal movement pattern. It was obvious from the moment I looked at it that it was dangerous. There was a very good reason we didn't normally use it: a massive cache of weapons was right nearby, which I knew because of the intel on the threat group I was monitoring. But I didn't have any authority. It was the way the tacticians in the Brigade Special Troops Battalion wanted to go, so they did.

There's a specialized military vehicle called a Buffalo that checks and clears the routes in advance of the infantry. The one we sent out that night was attacked by an explosive. It's likely that it was set up quickly, as soon as the threat group that built it—probably the one I was analyzing—realized that we were, for some stupid reason, moving very slowly down this road that they had easy access to.

The vehicle was damaged, but a civilian car that had pulled off to the side of the road to let us through took the brunt of the explosion. Its position had prevented anything worse from happening to the soldiers. But one Iraqi civilian in the car was killed on contact, while another four were severely injured.

The reaction inside my unit gutted me. Instead of being upset at the random death of an onlooker, my fellow soldiers were elated: *Thank goodness OUR people weren't killed. And hey, look, even our vehicle was minimally damaged!* The dead and injured Iraqis, who had nothing to do with this battle, weren't even spoken about as collateral damage. They were talked about as human armor for us. *It's a good thing those civilians were in the way*, they said—except they casually used a slur to refer to Iraqis. *We should just surround our vehicle convoys with them all the time.*

I didn't care if it was some kind of dark expression of relief. I was horrified. I couldn't stop thinking about the near-universal belief among soldiers that those human lives, in comparison to ours, were utterly expendable. I watched civilian deaths on a screen all day, every day. Sometimes it was the result of mistaken identity. But reporting by *The Washington Post* has also confirmed that certain units used a technique called "baiting," in which something as innocuous as wire or as blatant as a Kalashnikov-style rifle was left on the ground. Any Iraqi who picked it up was now holding a weapon, in the sights of American snipers.

Sunni extremist groups, such as al-Qaeda and the Islamic State of Iraq (which would later merge into ISIS), also killed many, many people who were unarmed and unaffiliated. The attacks were aimed at us, at the Americans, but that's not who ended up dead. We had T-walls, big walls that can be moved around like barricades; we had Hesco barriers. We were fortified. Vehicle-borne IED (VBEID) attacks were the most common: the extremist groups would fill a large car with explosives and just drive it into a target to kill as many people as possible. Simultaneous attacks would be coordinated all over the city. It's the kind of incident that grabs front-page headlines when it happens in the West, but when it happened in Baghdad, to Iraqis, it was a blip. Death was everywhere, and everyone who had picked a side was responsible.

But this set of death and injury was one I couldn't get out of my brain. It had been *my* unit; *I* had weighed in; *we* had celebrated. Every unit had stories like this. As hard as they try to conceal it with clinical shorthand, every significant action that we carefully cataloged in the proper language for the official channels was a tragedy. Every tallying up of injury, of death, was so much more complicated and deeper-reaching than the carefully coded acronyms and euphemisms allowed it to be.

I woke up on Christmas Day pissed off about Route Aeros. I couldn't believe someone had signed off on it despite all the warnings against using those routes. That violence had been preventable. I felt powerless.

I didn't celebrate the holiday; I missed the Christmas meal because I was briefing people on the Route Aeros incident. There was no one at home for me to call to mark the day. My aunt was away, Dylan had stopped answering my phone calls most of the time, and I had nothing to say to either of my parents.

At the end of December, a few days after Christmas, I wrote to the *Blade* reporter I'd dated back in D.C. Part of the letter was complaint, and part seemed to be me dangling information at him—though of course this letter, like everything I wrote, had to go through a censor before it made it to him. "It seems (to me at least) that my chain of command is basically fucking me over," I wrote. "They have a tendency to place high expectations on me—then they work me like a mule. But when it comes to discussing my future career, all of a sudden, they become deaf." I wanted to explore options with the government intelligence community, I told him, but my direct supervisors wouldn't let me.

There were intellectual silver linings, I wrote him, to my job. "There are some very intelligent and meaningful people I work with. But, they mostly work in the room next door with all of the super secret spy stuff, and all the crypto-support stuff." And, I added, I was very taken by "the sheer breadth and scope of some of the document repositories I work with. It's absolutely amazing how much historical data we've collected over the past six or so years. There are hundreds of thousands, if not millions, of these reports that, when taken as a whole, comprise what must be one of the most important document collections in our history. It encompasses all the different types of data points in one complete story. From the quantifiable: dates, times, to the unquantifiable: emotions, basic lives, from the mundane and banal minor incident reports finding weapons caches, to the horrifying and brutal, violent attacks, death, night missions gone wrong. And yet it's stamped with all these quite ridiculous and often unnecessary classification markings. It's not like this stuff is our intelligence reports gleaned from human sources or our disturbingly vast and complex communications surveillance system. They're historical. I wish this stuff were in the public domain. I mean, it wouldn't end the wars any sooner. But, maybe having a detailed account of what a counter-insurgency actually is, in detail, it could prevent us from thinking about it the next time around, twenty years from now? Makes me wonder."

I ended with a few questions for him about his life and apologized for rambling—I'd been up for twenty hours straight, I wrote, and told him I didn't have anyone there I could vent to. "Happy Holz!" I signed off, and drew a little cartoon face of me smiling at him. The censors let everything sail on through. He didn't pick up on what I was hinting at; after all, he wrote mostly about issues of gay social justice, not military engagements and the national security apparatus.

On New Year's Eve, I was alone again. I sat outside at a smoking pit, near the IT center, where all of our internet was piped in. You can see the stars in Iraq, clear and bright, the way you can in Oklahoma. I lit one cigarette after another and decided that *this* was going to be my decade. It was 2010, I was twenty-two, and I was ready to *do* some shit. I didn't want to be stuck any longer. I didn't want to be dysphoric for the rest of my life. I wanted to figure out if I was ready to transition. I wanted to start making the things happen that I believed in. Cheesy as it sounds, I looked up at the stars and decided that I wanted to see if I could change the world, instead of feeling overwhelmed by the things I found awful about it.

Within the week, I decided I was going to act. I was going to show the world what I was seeing. I had already downloaded onto a DVD-RW the four hundred thousand SIGACT records, as well as HUMINT and CIED reports, that would become known as the Iraq War logs, as a backup for my work. (I always tried to have backup for relevant data in case there was slow connectivity or a computer crashed.) I never needed to hide what I was doing—the discs were labeled and stored out in the open.

But now I was ready to share these databases. I added the files from Afghanistan. On January 8, I began the process of moving the DVD-RWs that I stored at work to my personal laptop. I transferred them to my MacBook Pro, and then to the SD card that I intended to take home with me on leave. We all burned so many things onto DVD-RWs daily—and took them out of the SCIF, whether for personal use or training—that no one even gave me a second glance.

My leave was coming up soon, and I was steady in my decision to release this information. But there was no way I was going to be able to do this on paper—picture being behind me in line at Kinko's!—so, imagining a journalist opening a file, I wrote a text file with the tagline "Readme." I wanted to be clear about the file's technical and historical utility. I'd been well trained in the art of writing a précis, of directing action and encouraging caution. This was exactly the kind of assessment, analysis, and report that the army had built me to write.

> Items of the historical significance of two wars Iraq and Afghanistan Significant Activity, SigActs, between 0001 January 2004 and 2359 31 Dec 2009 extracts from CSV documents from Department of Defense and CDNE database. It's already been sanitized of any source identifying information. You might need to sit on this information, perhaps 90–180 days, to figure out how to best release such a large amount of data, and to protect source. This is possibly one of the more significant documents of our time, removing the fog of war, and revealing the true nature of 21st century asymmetric warfare. Have a good day.

The decision to bring those files to America and upload them was one decision among many others. I made life-and-death decisions every day. I always had the responsibility of other people's lives in my hands. This felt, in some sense, like just another choice, where I was weighing the costs and benefits and deciding that this was the best way to save lives.

It would be weeks until I could hand it over, and things only got worse. The internet was, as always, where I sought solace, where I signaled that I was in pain. I messaged Louis, late at night his time, with no response. So I turned to Facebook: "[Manning] feels so alone," was my status update. The next morning, Louis saw the message. I didn't waste time on small talk. "I'm lost," I wrote.

He thought I was being playful. "In Iraq? That's not good :-(I thought you were supposed to find people!"

"Figuratively," I replied. "I don't know who I am, where I am, what I want . . . I'm tired. And alone . . . And hopeless."

Louis tried to comfort me, reminding me that I had "what, one year and nine months?" left in my service, that when I was back in the States I would have people to talk to, "a ton of time to post-process it." He had an uncle who had been a doctor in Iraq, he reminded me, and so he'd heard it all.

It didn't matter, I told him. That seemed so far away. "I'm finally drowning," I typed. "I have a bank account and social security number, nothing more . . . I've seen too much, figured out too much. I can't seem to wriggle out, even just to breathe. No one has enough time to understand, and I can't find enough time to take a breath of fresh air." I told him that I'd lost hope in humanity, felt like "a pawn in this game, like everyone else."

He told me not to lose faith in all mankind "based on a war zone," and suggested that sharing might help. He even suggested that I try writing an anonymous blog, as therapy. "There's no such thing as anonymity," I told him, which turned out to be more true than even I realized then.

I ached about Dylan, I told Louis, and was inconsolable when he told me that things would get better once I left the military, that having a stable location would make it easier to find a nice boyfriend "who respects you." I didn't want hope. I wanted to sink deeper into my profound sense of alienation and precariousness. "I'm incredibly lost," I replied. "People want to help me, but they don't know how. And those who do try and intervene push me closer off the edge. I can't find stability. I'm about to crash right now and I don't know how bad it's going to be . . . I don't even know what I want anymore. I'm not suicidal but I've certainly thought about putting my hands up and refusing to be someone's bitch, say exactly what's on my mind."

I summed up how trapped I felt. "I'm fed up with everything: personality differences getting in the way of the job at the micro level; living under a policy that leaves me unable to talk about my problems, and effectively being punished for not saying anything at the micro level; keeping important information out of the public sphere at the macro level; being betrayed by congress, the public and the president at the macro level over freedom I'm supposedly fighting for at the macro level; being completely unable to know who I am, and being so psychologically compartmentalized for survival at the personal level. The pressure builds and builds and builds, and I'm surrounded by it 24/7."

"I guess if it really gets to be completely unbearable you do have an out—purposefully getting discharged," typed Louis, before suggesting that I look into "orgs that help people in your situation."

"They suck," I replied. "They're just as bad, and getting discharged is damaging. Especially how I would do it. I wouldn't keep it under the rug. No matter how hard they tried to keep it quiet. I've kept in contact with journalists."

Louis understood what I meant, and suggested that being a source might even *help* get me admitted to certain colleges, or employed in certain jobs. I dismissed his idealistic thinking—I'd still have to spend several more months in Iraq, and I'd face a disciplinary board. That, I thought, was the worst that might happen to me.

Just a few days later, in the Baghdad airport, on my way back home to America for leave, I opened a chat window. This time, when I messaged Louis, I was in a much better mood. I told him that my commander wanted to help me get into West Point, onto a career track as an officer. Maybe, I said, I could even use Don't Ask, Don't Tell to my career advantage, like Dan Choi, the soldier who'd come out on MSNBC to protest the policy, then, following his discharge, become a famous military gay-rights activist. "He was basically given free college, an easy job during an infamous unit deployment—my unit, 2007—and great national publicity. Bastard. You want to know what he actually DID?" I typed.

"Maybe not over insecure channels (?)," Louis replied.

"Sat in a bunker all day, signing paperwork. Hey, I do that. Except, inside of a tin and plywood building. If a rocket makes a direct hit, I'd be shredded to pieces by wooden shrapnel. Everyone knows what he did at his unit, but god he was smart. Yet, not bright like me. I'm beyond sinister. I'm after the presidency. End DADT? Fuck that. I want to live in the most bumpin' house in DC."

And then I went back to what was really on my mind.

"I think we're going to be ok, me and Dylan. I think we'll be ok =)."

10.

My leave started on January 23. I flew in to stay with my aunt Debbie in Potomac, but as soon as I could, I went up to Boston to see Dylan. I'd been longing for this, but it didn't feel like he had. He was distant. He didn't want to make concrete plans for our relationship. I tried to ask him what he thought I should do about releasing the SIGACTs by using coy hypotheticals about what he might do if he had secret documents that he thought the public should see. He was confused; I was vague. When I tried to give more context, he asked too many questions. There was stuff I couldn't tell him. I freaked out, and I dropped the whole thing. After a few unsatisfying days in Boston with Dylan, I went back to my aunt's. I felt more alone than ever, and torn up about how to act.

But after the blizzard hit, after I went to that Barnes & Noble, after I took the long trip back to Iraq on February 11, I finally felt some relief. Just the act of uploading the SIGACTs—*months* before it was published—made me feel like I'd done something, that I'd relieved my conscience a little. I felt a duty to my fellow humans to do this, to make the world understand more about what I knew was happening in Iraq and Afghanistan every day, to understand what the true casualty numbers were. I hoped and waited for WLO (the WikiLeaks Organization) to find the SIGACTs.

But I wasn't just a random intel analyst uploading information to a dead drop. I had my other online life. And since early January, one of the IRC chat rooms I checked had included X-chat, an open room filled with people I was pretty sure were associated in some way with WikiLeaks. I'd followed the room partly because I was lonely, but mostly out of interest and curiosity. In late November 2009, WikiLeaks had released a collection of 570,000 pager messages that were sent on September 11, 2001, from both government officials and American civilians. The only thing that WLO had said publicly about their provenance was: "It is clear that the information comes from an organization which has been intercepting and archiving US national telecommunications since prior to 9/11." I wanted more information on how and why they'd obtained the messages. I dabbled around the website and I found documents about weapons trafficking between two nations that affected my daily work. This was actually quite useful for my job, and I integrated the information into my work product.

The IRC group felt like a true collective at that time, a loose affiliation rather than something formal. The chat room was mostly technical talk—how to troubleshoot, how to work on the practical apparatus itself. (The tool I'd uploaded the SIGACTs with was a JavaScript-based web page, proxied through multiple jurisdictions so that any information uploaded would have various and conflicting levels of legal protections.) It was, in some ways, like any other chat room for technical and network security types, except I knew that this chat room was sitting on a potentially explosive, history-altering leak—that no one seemed to have looked at. Were they checking their submissions form, I wondered? Was there a snag?

———

That winter, the chat room was preoccupied with the bailout of Iceland—which was meant to solve the financial collapse of the country's banks. At the time, WikiLeaks appeared to be operating out of Iceland, which was still in the throes of the financial crisis, one of the hardest-hit countries in the world. Iceland's government had negotiated a complicated bailout for its banks, setting in motion populist anger. The United Kingdom intended to use "antiterrorism legislation" to give its creditors power to freeze Icelandic assets in case of nonpayment.

In late 2009, one of my bosses sent a section-wide email to all the analysts and officers suggesting that we take a look at a State Department Net-Centric Diplomacy portal, which contained a trove of diplomatic cables. He thought the information they contained could be useful to us in our analytical work. I read every single one that related to Iraq, and then began to poke around in the rest of the database, which was full of fascinating stuff. Intrigued by the Iceland bailout discussion in the chat room, I searched the State Department portal for cables that might be related, and on Valentine's Day I found one, called 10REYKJAVIK13. It was short, just two pages long, but its content seemed to signal that Iceland felt bullied by the UK and the Netherlands, another creditor, and was asking the United States for help. But according to this cable, the United States didn't appear to see any strategic benefit to getting in the middle of that fight.

I decided to upload the cable. The Icelandic people were getting screwed, and even worse, they didn't even know what was going on. But I worried that the submission form didn't work; after all, no one had mentioned the SIGACT files that I had uploaded. Still, it seemed worth trying. I transferred the cable to my personal computer and uploaded it. This time, the message was a text file, so it would be immediately legible. Hours later, they published it. My trial balloon proved that WikiLeaks must have gotten the SIGACTs. The cable's publication also made immediate news, which was a satisfying feeling.

But the cable wouldn't end up being the main thing that I'd up-loaded that month. On February 21, I sent what would become known as the "Collateral Murder" tape, which showed grainy aerial footage from July 2007 of an Apache helicopter air strike gone horribly wrong. It depicted the deaths of innocent Iraqi civilians and Reuters journalists in the suburb of New Baghdad.

I'd first seen the video back in December. A colleague from my shop had found the video on the shared drive, where it was in a JAG file. At first, I thought it was just another piece of war porn, another light-'em-up video, something we could pass to one another and say "Watch these fucking guys get wiped out." People in combat love watching war-porn videos: shit blowing up, mostly. YouTube is full of them, but those were nothing compared to the ones we had on our shared drive in Iraq. They'd play on a loop in Windows Media Player, like a long movie that was all action and no plot, or a video game with amazing graphics. It was there, it was entertaining, we were bored. But this one was different. Other analysts debated whether the incident had violated the rules of engagement. In fact, in the JAG file it was la-beled as legal training material for how to defend soldiers accused of rules-of-engagement violations—messy situations in which they needed to pretend the lines had been clear. Instead of joining the debate, I decided to look for more context, searching Google using the date-time grid and the geographic coordinates.

The video shows an incident that killed eleven people—two of whom were Reuters journalists. Two U.S. helicopters approach a group of Iraqis. You can hear the American soldiers say that the group is shooting at them, though the visual evidence contradicts that. What they've mistaken for an RPG is in fact a Reuters photographer's camera lens, poking around the corner of a building, photographing the scene. The lead helicopter begins shooting at what the soldiers think to be a threat. They hit the Iraqis, nine of whom will die. "Oh, yeah, look at those dead bastards," one person says. One man, wounded, starts trying to crawl away. A soldier says, "All you gotta do is pick up a weapon." (In other words, give the soldier cause to shoot.) When a van full of Iraqis—simply Good Samaritans trying to help—pulls up and attempts to move the man to safety, the American helicopter starts to shoot, this time with shells that can pierce armor. They repeatedly fire through the windshield of the van, hurting two children who are sitting in back. "Well, it's their fault for bringing kids into a battle," says a soldier later, after a ground crew comes by to assess the damage. "That's right," another person replies. Later, the crew appears to enjoy the sight of a vehicle driving over the dead bodies strewn on the ground.

I discovered that Reuters had used the Freedom of Information Act to ask for the full video; the news organization had been privately shown a three-minute clip but wanted to know more about how its journalists, Namir Noor-Eldeen and Saeed Chmagh, had died. The military's first statement claimed that the American soldiers had killed nine insurgents plus a mere two civilians (the journalists). Then they claimed that there had been fighting on the ground (a "firefight") that they were responding to. In reply to the FOIA request, CENTCOM had told Reuters that they couldn't give a time frame for when the request might be fulfilled and that the video might no longer exist. This response troubled me; they didn't want Reuters to see what had really happened. So did the bloodlust of the American soldiers, the dehumanizing way they reacted, especially to the children and to the wounded man crawling to safety. It reminded me of the cruel detachment of a kid torturing ants with a magnifying glass.

I also discovered that a *Washington Post* journalist, David Finkel, had written about that specific event in his book *The Good Soldiers*. It was clear to me that he'd seen the video. I felt that his account, which was primarily from the perspective of the soldiers, did not really capture the full brutality of the event. The soldiers, in the excerpt I found on Google Books, seemed to justify it as payback. Eastern Baghdad had, several days before, been ambushed by Sadrist militiamen detonating bombs. (Muqtada al-Sadr was a Shia Iraqi cleric and nationalist who first emerged in 2003 as the leader of a political movement with a powerful military wing. He was from a famous lineage; his father-in-law had openly supported the revolution in Iran, and was killed by Saddam Hussein in 1980.) Everyone was on high alert, and there was still fighting going on the night of the Apache incident. The military explained privately to a Reuters editor seeking answers that the men had been "military-aged" and that because they appeared to be holding weapons, the engagement was justified. (Photographs taken after the incident showed that an RPG launcher and several AK-47s had been collected from the scene.)

I was troubled by what I saw and read. But the most shocking thing about this video, in which innocent people are killed simply for being in the wrong place, is that everything about it was perfectly legal under the Geneva Conventions and our own rules of engagement. The army's internal investigation determined that the soldiers had ultimately acted properly, under the circumstances. That was why the lawyers were teaching it.

I quickly realized that this wasn't "cool" footage of an Apache killing people; it was a much more complex incident than even military people realized. This was probably one of the few moments that captured, within its brief time frame, the entirety of what warfare is about. Within that video you can see the power afforded by air superiority. You can see the confusion created by unidentified markings on vehicles and people, the harm and chaos that happens when people don't know what's going on but feel the pressure to act. You can see the room for error that's introduced when multiple air and ground units are trying to coordinate, through different jurisdictions, and finding it difficult to communicate. The men, the camera, the van—none of it was exactly what the soldiers believed it to be. The misidentification of targets is one of the most difficult, deep, tangled aspects of war.

But when a war is presented to the American public, it looks like a finished product: cleaned and edited, funneled through embedded reporters who have their own complicated relationships with the military to manage. Or it's flashed briefly across CNN, simplified into the kind of takeaway you can fit across a chyron. In that fairy-tale version, there are only surgical strikes. Trucks—filled only with bad guys, because in this make-believe version who the bad guys are is always clear—are blown up cleanly, from the front of a cruise missile.

This footage of the Apache incident showed exactly what had been keeping me sleepless, the murkiness of the whole project. It contained all the elements of complex asymmetric warfare, the same ones I wanted to highlight with the SIGACTs disclosure. I didn't have an overarching ideological agenda, but I had a clear objective: I wanted to complicate the retrofitted, sanitized version of the war that was spreading like wildfire back home, where any questioning of a clear narrative was perceived as disloyal.

When I first saved the video, it was with the intent of finding a way to get it to the Reuters office in London when I redeployed later that summer. But after WikiLeaks published the Reykjavik cable, I saw another way of getting Reuters the answers it sought, and sooner. A week later, I uploaded the Apache video to the WLO submission form. I included the army's internal investigation, so there would be the proper context on what the footage was showing, what the rules of engagement were at that time, and how the army had dealt with it. I wanted the world to understand that nothing was cut-and-dried here.

I told the chat to expect an important submission. Someone who went by the handle "office" responded; later, this person would change their handle to "preassociation." We eventually began to talk on another encrypted chat client, Jabber, and I saved the person in my contacts as "Nathaniel Frank," a decoy that was an homage to the author of a book I'd read the previous year (*Unfriendly Fire: How the Gay Ban Undermines the Military and Weakens America*).

I never knew for sure who the real person was behind the "Nathaniel Frank" handles. Over time, and from the role he played in the chat room, I came to understand this was an important person in the group. I guessed it was likely Julian Assange, or maybe Daniel Schmitt (now known as Daniel Domscheit-Berg), another central figure in WLO. Or else it was someone representing them. To this day, I can't say with absolute certainty who it was; that's the point of having a handle online, of course. There are no driver's licenses presented in the hacking world. (I used a random name generator to get my handle: DawgNetwork.)

At first, my conversations with "Nathaniel Frank" were general. We had similar interests—politics, information technology—and I had no one at work I could talk to about those things on the level I wanted to discuss them at. Soon, we were talking almost every day, sometimes for almost an hour at a time, about a range of topics, not just whatever publications WikiLeaks was preparing. I felt freer to be myself thanks to the cloak of anonymity the encrypted chat provided, and that was a lifeline to me then. It was an escape from the pressure and anxiety of the deployment. The chat room was also a place where my interests didn't make me strange, they made me interesting. In retrospect, I realize that this meant more to me than it did to "Nathaniel Frank," and that our closeness was an artificial, circumstantial one. But I so badly needed an escape valve, and some semblance of friendship and trust.

The video of the Apache incident that I uploaded was the raw footage, thirty-eight minutes long. Among Assange and other WikiLeaks volunteers, how to best handle the footage was hotly debated, as I would later learn from reporting in *The New Yorker*. In some ways, that debate and the task of getting the video out into the world is what pushed WikiLeaks into becoming an actual organization rather than simply an affinity group. There were arguments, and a jockeying of personalities and priorities. The video introduced a certain amount of stress into the collective, and exposed—or created—factions. Some people, including Assange, were more interested in making a splash than in presenting a complex situation in all its subtleties.

At the time, an Icelandic member of parliament named Birgitta Jonsdottir was involved with WikiLeaks. (She would later cut ties with the group over concerns about Assange.) Someone in the chat room—who I guessed might be her but didn't know for certain—suggested making this part of a news report. Journalists from RUV, an Icelandic television station, would travel to Baghdad within a week of the video's release. The journalists discovered, by talking to people there, that the children from the van had survived, but their parents had died. It was a strange feeling, lurking in the chat rooms alongside my work channels, and knowing that the Icelandic TV crew whose arrival in Baghdad I was reading about in the official public affairs officer's reporting at work was the same one I was reading about in the IRC. And it was even stranger to know exactly why they had come there.

It took two months for the video to be edited down, mostly by the journalists, to a crisp, horrific eighteen minutes; the group gave it the memorable title "Collateral Murder," which helped it go viral. (The full tape was also available on a website that WikiLeaks had made.) The eighteen-minute version contained editorial touches like a quote from George Orwell—"Political language . . . is designed to make lies sound truthful and murder respectable, and to give the appearance of solidity to pure wind"—and an introduction that clarified just who you were about to see killed and wounded (children, among others). The edited version shortened the time between the soldiers' most callous comments, making them appear perhaps more cruel than they'd been. The tape doesn't show that the men walking with the Reuters journalists had AK-47s and an RPG launcher. But what was most chilling about the video was how instantly clear it was to the viewer that this was the truth, and optimistic headlines about low civilian casualties were the propaganda.

WikiLeaks was becoming a subject of great curiosity, and Assange was beginning to position himself as the figurehead, rather than a comrade among equals. During the editing of the video, a *New Yorker* reporter who was writing a profile of Assange was embedded with the collective. For the release of "Collateral Murder," Assange arranged a press conference, held at the National Press Club in D.C., where he wore a tie. He had made himself synonymous with WikiLeaks, and with that visibility came a certain amount of power, enabling the more troll-y, nihilist contingent (Assange first among them, but also Daniel Domscheit-Berg) to dominate the internal discussion. The more serious, responsible-minded faction—the tech-minded journalists, the politically connected—stepped back.

I was nervous about how Americans would respond to the Apache footage. Would they see what I had seen in it? Would they understand what it revealed about the pressure-cooker environment of war, and how it shaped the behavior of the people struggling to live within it? It turned out that many who saw it were just as troubled, if not more so, than I was. I felt encouraged by this response.

The Department of Defense and CENTCOM didn't just hate the video, though. They put out statements saying they couldn't confirm the video's authenticity, which was clearly meant to undermine the footage's credibility. Even Captain Martin, one of my supervisors, said she didn't believe it was authentic. This frustrated me. I emailed her a link to the video from our drive, and a link to what WikiLeaks had published, so she could look at them side by side for herself.

That winter and spring, I continued getting more and more disillusioned. I began to indulge my habit of trolling comments sections. In January, at the State of the Union, President Obama announced his intention to work with Congress to end Don't Ask, Don't Tell. But I didn't think the repeal was going fast or far enough, and so, in the comments section of articles covering the effort, I'd make the case for more aggressive progress. I used guest accounts and Tor, an anonymizing browser that I'd previously installed on my computer to safely monitor the social media websites of militia groups operating within central Iraq. I moved on from that to commenting on what I saw as underinformed articles about the war I was fighting. I hated reading people like Thomas Friedman spouting off smugly and simplistically about how patriotism and the "rule of law" had "overcome sectarian disputes," when it was obvious to anyone on the ground that sectarian disputes were only getting more complicated. I thought maybe my comments could spark some small current of people thinking a little harder about the whole thing. *The media is glossing this over*, I'd write. Of course, I never identified myself as a soldier, let alone an intel analyst.

I wanted the world to understand the Thing, the seeing-the-Matrix feeling that I'd been experiencing ever since I got there. The Thing was chaos that was unsurprising, almost organized in its entropy. I saw the Thing when I read the news, and I saw the Thing even more clearly when I analyzed the algorithms that were meant to make me better at predictive analysis for the army. It was as if the tragedies and battles were a pattern in nature, shocking and yet entirely predictable, like the tides or the tilt of the sun or the growth of plants. But the chaos was coming from us, the agents of destruction.

One night in early March, an officer in the Tactical Operations Center sent me a packet of raw photos and documents, explaining to me that the Iraqi Federal Police (IFP) had rolled up fifteen people for printing "anti-Iraqi literature." He asked me to find out who "the bad guys" were and figure out the significance of the arrests for the IFP. I researched. None of these people had ties to militias or terrorist groups, so that wasn't it. An officer on a different team had accidentally been forwarded photos from the arrest, which she passed on to me. The literature in question was a sort of zine-like, scholarly critique of Nouri al-Maliki, who was the Iraqi prime minister at the time, and of the impact his cabinet's corruption had on the people of the country. Our interpreter, a Turkish woman, agreed with me that it seemed like a basically benign document. I told the officer who'd assigned me the task that there was a discrepancy between what the IFP had described and the facts on the ground. This was just political stuff, relatively tame opposition material. I was surprised by the officer's response: he told me to "drop it." This wasn't the kind of information they needed. He then wanted me to find out where the material was being printed. I assumed this meant his priority was maintaining a good relationship with the IFP. But I believed that if I followed that direction, I'd essentially be helping the IFP find more of Maliki's political opponents to arrest. Simply for expressing their political views, they'd be in the custody of a special unit, and would probably be tortured. A long imprisonment would be the best-case outcome. Their families might never see them again.

The officer told me to just go back to work, as if the preservation of innocent people's freedom was outside my line of duty, not the entire reason we were supposedly there.

I was furious, and he was, too. Our body language changed. This was no longer junior enlisted person and senior officer. I repeated what was obvious: the police were being used as a tool to silence dissidents, and we were enabling that. He was furious at my reaction, my aggression. The officer hated my guts after that. But what were we doing in Iraq, while saying that we were there to protect the local populace? Our stated mission didn't mean *shit* if that was how we behaved.

They transferred me to the day shift so he wouldn't have to deal with me, although the official reason they gave was so I could be better supervised. I couldn't stomach the idea of enabling a crackdown on people for simply publishing a critique of the ruling elite. I decided that I would disclose the information via WLO, before the March 7 Iraqi elections, in the hopes that it might get enough press that the IFP couldn't continue targeting political opponents. I burned the photos and the report to a DVD-RW, and uploaded it to a dead-drop remote server that WikiLeaks operated, rather than through the general submission form. I told "Nathaniel Frank" directly over chat what he'd find in the upload. He said there wasn't enough information or specifics for the international media to get interested in it. I tried to give him more, but WikiLeaks decided it wasn't worth publishing.

I kept turning over the fate of the people who'd published the anti-Maliki literature. Could they be turned back over to U.S. custody and end up in our Guantánamo Bay detention facility? I knew it was unlikely, but I was in a headspace for worst-case scenarios. Guantánamo was on my mind, and I started searching through what we had on the server about it. I soon came across the detainee assessment briefs (DABs). These were the short summary memos about each person who either was or had been held in custody at Guantánamo.

I had always thought Guantánamo raised interesting issues of moral efficacy, but reading the DABs clarified what I believed. Yes, I understood that the United States needed to interrogate people who might be trying to do harm to it or its allies. But the more I read, the more it seemed that the people we were holding were low-level foot soldiers who had little if any useful intelligence. If we'd arrested them in the theater of operations of a war, they'd have long since been released. Guantánamo had been a huge flashpoint during the Bush administration, and President Obama, early in his administration, had said that he intended to close the facility, and that he believed that keeping it open harmed our "moral authority" in the world. Reading through the briefs, I agreed with his assessment.

These DABs, I realized, weren't detailed analytical products. They didn't have the names of sources, and they didn't quote from interrogation reports. They were several years old, and often, the intelligence that they summarized was unclassified. In other words, I knew that keeping them secret didn't have much intelligence or national security importance, but I thought that publishing them could help the public understand what was happening at Guantánamo, as reading them had for me.

I asked "Nathaniel Frank"—on March 7, the day of the Iraqi elections—what he thought. Were they worth publishing? He told me that it probably wouldn't change much politically, but that perhaps they could be of use to the individual detainees in their legal battles, and that they seemed important for filling out the general historical record of the Guantánamo detainments. This seemed right to me. I downloaded the DABs using a program called Wget (an extremely common tool that the government would later try to portray as nefarious and esoteric). Then I copied them onto my personal laptop. Once more, I put the files on the dead drop; I now had a directory within it that was assigned just for me, labeled "x." I told "Nathaniel Frank" that it was there, and decided to also upload an internal report from the army's Criminal Investigation Command: it was their analysis of the potential threat posed by WikiLeaks. WLO published it. I told "Nathaniel Frank" that in *The New York Times* an army spokesman had confirmed the authenticity of the document. "Hilarious," I typed to "Nathaniel Frank."

In late March, searching through the CENTCOM directory for information I needed for my job, I discovered a video of a 2009 air strike in Garani, Afghanistan. More than one hundred Afghani civilians, mostly women and children, were accidentally killed, and the air strike had been covered all over the world. But seeing something like that was different from reading about it, as the U.S. government knew, especially in the wake of the awful images from Abu Ghraib, which had become, effectively, a recruitment tool for al-Qaeda.

It was chilling to see death on that scale, and the conclusions of the report that accompanied it were even more disturbing to me than the ones for the video that became known as "Collateral Murder." I sent it to the drop. The video was never published, either by the U.S. government or WikiLeaks, and the report I read remains highly classified. But what I saw was indelible and awful: graphic footage of women, children, and old people dying the most painful kind of death, a result of munitions containing white phosphorus hitting an extremely flammable structure.

This was the last thing I uploaded. Soon, at long last, the SIGACTs, the first thing I'd sent to WikiLeaks, would be published, and would change everything.

11.

A military tradition: When a soldier is killed, everyone in their unit forms a line. Roll is called, and the name of the fallen soldier is repeated, again and again, into a silence broken only by quiet weeping. It's nearly unbearable. By the time I learned this firsthand, I'd been in Iraq for nine months, and thought I'd been through every possible kind of psychological horror. I was so wrong. I'll never forget what happened on March 18, 2010. I'm still in therapy over what I saw in Iraq, and this was one of the worst things I've ever seen.

That night, just as guard tower shift duty switched over, someone inside the residential towers across from the military base used a rocket launcher to shoot a grenade at the base. The rocket fell short of its target and hit Specialist Robert Rieckhoff, the soldier who had just come on guard duty in the tower. He died immediately. Rieckhoff, and all his relationships, memories, and plans, was gone, just like that.

The whole base went on alert. I went into work about three and a half minutes after his death, and within twenty-five minutes I was looking at photos of the bloody scene and his body and reading the written statements of witnesses. There was no time to process what had happened, or to grieve a human life. We had to go into work mode immediately. For the next three hours, I tried to ID which building the missile had come from. Meanwhile, the Fifteenth Field Artillery Regiment, Second Battalion, went to every single house in that neighborhood, breaking down doors to try to find the attacker.

The status of forces agreement (SOFA), the United States' formal promise to the Iraqi government about how our troops would treat the country and its citizens, didn't mean a thing in that moment. We ripped that neighborhood inside out, less to find the responsible party than to punish. We got angry, because there was no time to be sad. Beating down doors might have been a rational way to search for the shooter; tearing apart rooms and crushing people's possessions beyond repair was our way of ensuring that this neighborhood would suffer for the entirety of what was Rieckhoff's last shift. For twelve hours, we went beyond a quest for justice and crossed over into collective punishment. In the military, the concept of mass punishment is among the first things you learn. If one person out of thirty messes up, all thirty do push-ups. This understanding, that an individual's actions affect the group, gets ingrained in soldiers so deeply that they don't even realize they've internalized it. It becomes the collective responsibility to make sure that an individual doesn't make a mistake, doesn't get left behind or killed. And it also means we learned to feel that inflicting mass punishment on others is normal. If one person attacks us, the whole fucking community can go to hell. When you're mad enough, this feels necessary. Everything in those moments is dealt with in the reptile part of your brain that processes stress and trauma, and the only thing a human being wants is revenge, absolute and indiscriminate. "I'm part of an *us*," thinks a soldier, "and out there is a *them*." I didn't have a job in that moment, but a mission: to take out my anger and pain and frustration on *them*.

In Iraq, I went mad like that four or five times a week. I didn't know

Rieckhoff. I had seen him once or twice. Just like everyone else, though, I was blind with rage. He was one of *ours*. But our anger did little to mask the fact that we were all scared.

We worked for twenty-five hours straight, and the best we could do was narrow the suspect list down to three people. We tracked the shit out of those guys, using every tool at our disposal. To this day I have no idea which one of them did it, or if any of them did. I am still quietly gutted by the idea that I could have prevented it, that the missile was launched by someone I'd already been tracking.

We captured and detained these men, then gave them to the Iraqi government. We didn't keep track of people once we got them "off the battlefield," as the phrase went. Kill or capture, and the problem is solved. Whether that was the right thing to do or not didn't matter to me then. With enough grief and adrenaline and fear, we can all become amoral, even malevolent.

By spring, it had grown unbearably hot, a hundred degrees at times. The end of our deployment was in sight. We'd even begun a countdown of the days left on a big board, but everyone was still tense. We'd been there too long, frayed to the breaking point too many times. Fights became commonplace over relationships gone bad, cheating, work, and the stress of war looming over everything. By April, we'd push people into side rooms, relieve them of their weapons, and let them literally just duke it out without an officer watching.

The Admin's hatred toward me had calcified. She regularly called me a faggot, undermined me with officers, tried to turn people against me. While I was on leave, someone had stapled an eight-and-a-half-by-eleven-inch sheet of paper above my workstation with a drawing of two birds printed on it. The caption read RETARDS: WE ALL KNOW ONE. Meanwhile, the Admin had taped up a similar sheet by her workstation, titled TARGETING OFFICE RULES, with a list of targets that included "shitbags" and "sissies." I began to catalog the insults—not just against me, and not just homophobic: In one meeting with three colleagues, they implied that President Obama was unable to be a good leader because of his race and his supposed non-American national origin. Someone said the country was increasingly run by "blacks and foreigners," which all three agreed was a problem.

A young woman of Asian descent who had joined our unit just before we'd shipped out was an even bigger target than I was. The minute she arrived, people started fucking with this private. They pretended it was because she was new and inexperienced, but I'd never seen someone in the workplace treated with such obvious racism and sexism.

I have an instant affinity with anybody who is getting harassed, humiliated, or tortured for just being different. I've dealt with that kind of treatment my whole life. I tried to informally complain; in late February, I went to the Second Brigade Combat Team's Equal Employment Opportunity office to quietly try to stop the bullying. But instead of things getting better, they got worse: the bullies—who were directly chastised by an officer—began to sarcastically, showily pretend to be kind to this woman and to me, praising our work in mocking tones. It was clearly a kind of reprisal—they believed that the private had been the one to file the complaint, and things got even worse for her.

The private went to a sergeant and tearfully told him that she felt humiliated and helpless, targeted for something she hadn't even done. He asked me to make it clear that I'd been the one who'd gone to the Equal Employment Opportunity office. I wrote up a formal memo that included a conversation I'd overheard: the bullies talking about a plan to write about the private's "unmilitary bearing and conduct." They explicitly believed that bearing was connected to her ever-lowering self-esteem, and spoke about wanting to destroy her career as revenge.

They also said that "certain individuals" were "butt hurt"—but then one of them mockingly corrected the use of "butt hurt" as a phrase someone overly sensitive might find offensive. In the end, I decided not to file my complaint—the reprisals had stopped.

My mind was elsewhere at work, and people started to notice. Later, in my official file, they'd write about the blank stares I started to give sometimes that spring when asked a question. Instead of seeing this as a mental health crisis, my superiors described "an impression of disrespect and disinterest." I was preoccupied with the worry that my leaks weren't making the impact I wanted, that they had been for nothing, that no one's eyes had been opened. That there wouldn't be enough of an outcry to hold anyone accountable.

I messaged friends a link to the "Collateral Murder" video, and asked Dylan over instant message if people were talking about it. I Facebook-friended Ethan McCord, one of the soldiers in the video, a man who had acted honorably to rescue children after the violence. He'd come forward in the press to say that the incident—and even more so, the subsequent cover-up—had utterly disillusioned him. "From my experiences in Iraq, we shouldn't even be in these countries fighting wars. This is a war of aggression, of occupation. There is nothing justifiable to me about this war," he told *The Nation* later that summer. "And this isn't someone sitting back saying 'I think' or 'I believe.' This is from someone who was there." McCord had been sent home early. IED attacks had left him with a shattered lower spine and traumatic brain injury, but instead of giving him a medical discharge, the army claimed that he was being discharged because of a preexisting personality disorder. This meant he didn't get veterans' disability benefits. I felt linked to him, and wanted the connection to be codified somehow, even if just on Facebook. McCord confirmed my request, but I was just a random to him. He had no idea that I had risked everything to get the evidence of what he'd experienced out into the world.

I couldn't see my way to the end of deployment, let alone further into the future, but I knew I didn't want to live the way I was anymore. I didn't want anything in my life to be the same. I started to resent people who got to go home from the office every day, who could disengage from their work, people who weren't in Iraq. A thought ran through my mind on repeat: I can't wait to leave so I can sleep for days. All I wanted was for everything to somehow work out, for me to somehow be happy, and I had no clue how that could ever happen.

The leaks' release broke a dam inside of me. I wanted the era of secrets to be over in my life. In April, just a few days after "Collateral Murder" had been published, I sent an email to Master Sergeant Adkins, attaching the selfie I'd taken in February at Tysons Corner Center, of me in a blond wig and lipstick. I labeled it "Breanna.jpg." "This is my problem," I wrote. "I've had signs of it for a very long time. It's caused problems within my family. I thought a career in the military would get rid of it. It's not something I seek out for attention, and I've been trying very, very hard to get rid of it by placing myself in situations where it would be impossible. But, it's not going away; it's haunting me more and more as I get older. Now, the consequences of it are dire, at a time when it's causing me great pain in itself." I told him that my entire life felt "like a bad dream that won't end." I tried to delete it after I'd sent it—regret closed in and overwhelmed me instantly—but by then it was too late.

My superiors, from both the intelligence and operations sides of the unit, effectively ignored the picture and the email. I was too useful to the unit. Instead of giving me the treatment I needed, or a discharge for violating policy, the command sent me to a chaplain. Once again, it was someone I couldn't speak to honestly.

Dylan was still on my mind, always. He toyed with me—"Thinking of you dear," he wrote on my Facebook wall in March, a public declaration of affection—but he rarely answered my chats or calls. I posted on Facebook about the debilitating stress caused by how he'd "left me with this ambiguity for months on end." I kept trying, kept making myself vulnerable to him—but he had moved on. At the end of April, he decided to make that clear to me once and for all. "It's over," he messaged me. "Not open. Over."

I ached. "With closure, there's at least some peace in this rotten world," I wrote on Facebook, after the final breakup. "What do I have left at home—the answer is clearly Nothing."

I craved confession. Someone *had* to listen to me. I Facebook-messaged Jonathan Odell, a novelist whose writing I admired—he'd written about growing up gay in a conservative southern town—and asked to speak in confidence. I had, I told him, been involved in "some very high-profile events, albeit as a nameless individual thus far." Odell read my Facebook page, full of Dylan heartbreak and alienation from my work, and an article I'd sent him, an anonymous interview that I'd given to Lucas at the *Washington Blade* about life under Don't Ask, Don't Tell. Odell wrote that he thought he understood what I was saying. "Facebook doesn't even touch the surface," I told him. But our conversation didn't go anywhere.

Louis's messages remained a regular source of emotional support, but other people in my life had become more distant. I tried calling people I'd met in Boston. No one picked up. It got even hotter in eastern Baghdad. The world felt like it was boiling over.

On my Facebook page, I wrote, "I am not a piece of equipment." I wanted my humanity to be recognized, *remembered*. Back then, with so much testosterone in my system, I never cried, I just got *angry*. One afternoon, I couldn't take it, so I went to a storage room where I sometimes hid to punch things, throw some shit around, let off steam in private. "I WANT TO GO HOME," I tried to scratch into the room's single vinyl chair with my Gerber army knife. I got as far as "I WAN" before I realized I felt more exhausted than rageful. I curled up in the fetal position next to the chair. After an hour, someone realized I'd gone missing. Adkins came to talk to me. He listened as I told him about the pain I was in. He was sympathetic, but I was past the point where sympathy mattered. He sent me back to work.

Adkins wrote a memo about me in late April. I reported having no sense of time, and had the dissociated feeling of watching myself on a screen. I would stop midsentence in conversation, and I'd stare blankly when talked to, he chronicled.

The Admin and I finally had it out. She'd been coercing me to do her bidding for a year at that point, reminding me with every little "faggot" that she had power over me. And now she'd gone through my phone and found out I was trans. This was fresh material for her. *Why don't you just neuter yourself?* she asked. I lost it. It was as if she'd found an open wound and pressed a finger into it as hard as she could. I swung at her. She was bigger, but I was faster and stronger. She body-slammed me, but I thumped on her, inflicting real pain. The retribution—and release—felt good. Until someone separated us, and the hammer came down on me, not her. Hard.

As punishment, I was temporarily demoted from specialist back to private first class, and taken out of the SCIF in early May. Adkins ordered the bolt removed from my weapon. The FOB Hammer psychiatrist diagnosed me with an "occupational problem and adjustment disorder with mixed disturbance of emotions and conduct," and recommended my discharge. They temporarily assigned me to work in the supply closet. It was the worst kind of brainless busywork. I felt useless, bored, with nothing to think about but my own pain and loneliness. At night, in the darkness, trying and failing to sleep, I worried about government retribution for my disclosures, about what an investigation would entail, about just how forensic it could get. I knew that investigators would certainly be able to determine that our eastern Baghdad office was ground zero. I started to think that a witch hunt might ensue, that my colleagues would be caught up in it, tainted by association, their private lives combed through. I didn't want that on my hands.

I had an idea. Adrian Lamo, a well-known hacker who appeared on a list of WikiLeaks financial supporters, was a queer activist: he was bi, and he had an ex who was transgender, from male to female—and another ex who was a counterintelligence agent. At one point, the government had placed him on house arrest after he hacked *The New York Times*; there has since been speculation that he'd cut a deal with the FBI to work as an informant.

Those common identity politics gave me a way to approach him, to talk about what was going on. I knew about his likely ties with the FBI, that our encrypted communications would certainly be monitored, and that anything we discussed would be recorded forever. It was time for someone to listen to me. On May 21, we began to chat.

Two days after we started talking, Lamo contacted the feds via a friend, and they started feeding him questions to ask me. A *Forbes* investigation has since alleged that he was working for something called Project Vigilant, a semisecret government contractor that monitors internet service providers and provides the information it harvests from that to the government. According to that narrative, Lamo first told his boss about me, and Lamo's supervisor told *Forbes* that he'd pressured Lamo to turn me in at the behest of the intelligence community. This isn't a claim that I've been able to verify, and I have my doubts about whether this is exactly how it happened. (The hacker community hated Lamo for what he did. His life had a tragic end. He had a history of addiction and died unexpectedly in 2018.)

Not even a week after I'd started talking to Lamo, I was summoned to a conference room. Two agents from the Army Criminal Investigation Division waited there to question me and to take me away, accompanied by civilians from the State Department and the FBI.

But I was ready for them. I'd had about a six-hour heads-up. I happened to be standing near a flight-ops person making conversation, who mentioned a VIP flight coming from the embassy. The last time that happened, it had been the Criminal Investigation Department, for a sexual assault case: I guessed this meant that someone was about to be court-martialed. I knew the feds were probably coming for me. I mostly remember feeling hungry and chain-smoking cigarettes as the plane got closer, thinking about what would happen next. This was the end; I was going home in shame, but I was going home.

They were easy to spot. Guys in suits—even carrying Glocks and M9s—stick out on a base. They had fresh-shined shoes in the dusty desert, and I remember looking at those shoes and thinking, You're wasting your time. They gave me a waiver to sign, and I asked for a lawyer, but I wasn't physically restrained in any way. We all went together to the dining facility for a meal, one that felt normal, even calm, full of ordinary small talk. It would be my last meal in Iraq ever, and my last one outside of custody for years.

12.

The first time I was actually cuffed was on the flight from Baghdad International Airport to Kuwait. That was my first jail, I suppose. But the plastic flex cuffs felt cosmetic. The whole procedure seemed like just more unceremonious military bureaucracy, an anticlimactic episode that did nothing to herald what would become the most harrowing period of my life. The guards—soldiers I knew from the smoke pit at FOB Hammer—joked around with me to cut the tension. We quoted movies at each other—the kind of nineties comedies that bros use to break the ice or avoid meaningful interactions in just about any situation.

These guys didn't even know what I was detained for. It had been a secret investigation; even my crime was classified, and they'd been told not to ask me anything. I didn't ask questions of them, either. I hadn't slept in many hours, and had barely eaten. My immediate bodily needs trumped any bigger-picture thinking. I needed to go to the bathroom. And I needed a cigarette. The ache of withdrawal had kicked in hard and fast.

Ali Al Salem Air Base, where we landed in Kuwait, is a huge base, used as a temporary holding area for soldiers going in and out of Iraq and Afghanistan. It's filled with consumer comforts, like a McDonald's, intended to feel familiar to U.S. soldiers. Upon arrival, the soldiers took me to a side area, where a chaplain came by to see me. "Do you need spiritual help?" he asked. I couldn't think of anything I desired less in that moment. What I really wanted was a cheeseburger, which someone brought me. They were nice enough to ask what I wanted on the side, but no one offered me a cigarette.

Going to the bathroom as a detainee turned out to be a complicated operation. Dignity is important to the military. Even a detained soldier wears the same uniform as everyone else. I wasn't paraded or made an example of; they seemed resolved to minimize my exposure, whether for my privacy or military secrecy I do not know. But bathrooms are communal, which presented a challenge. Eventually, the guards decided I could go without the handcuffs, but with an escort. They knew me and thought I was a pain in the ass—but not a flight risk.

That night, they allowed me a couple of hours' sleep, inside a tent with my two escorts. There was nothing comfortable about that nap, but it was desperately needed. The next morning, we took a bus to the next stop, Camp Arifjan.

Kuwait in the spring was 120 degrees. It felt like walking through sludge—slowly, into hell. My escorts handed me over to naval masters-at-arms (MAs, the naval military police) at the Theater Field Confinement Facility—which sounds dramatic, but was just two barbed-wire chain-link fences surrounding a group of tents. After three hours of processing—a physical examination, another chaplain to brush off, a cursory mental health check-in, some indeterminate paperwork—I was now officially in the custody of the navy, which ran the facility.

They took away the Velcro patches denoting my rank. During the intake, I didn't even think to mention my gender dysphoria, which had been so acute just a few days ago. I was in a dissociated haze, checked out, and back to military basics: just following orders.

At first, the navy treated me like a regular inmate in the general jail. I was held in a tent with two other detainees. We weren't restrained, and we had access to a shower and a television. We read pulpy novels, played cards and board games, watched VHS tapes. We complained about the food and talked about everything but what had landed us in that tent. I existed in the perpetual present, feeling only my needs for food, for sleep, for a cool space, for the cigarettes I still wasn't getting. I had no connection to the future, no capacity to even imagine what was looming.

That changed when I spoke on the phone with the assigned military lawyer. The call wasn't clarifying, exactly—he told me that he didn't have a lot of information, that he couldn't talk to me too much, and that in order to protect myself, I shouldn't talk to him too much over the phone. But he also referred to my access to weapons and classified material; he mentioned prison. I began to consider consequences beyond dishonorable discharge. But with so much uncertainty, I continued to exist in a kind of suspended animation.

After almost a week, several masters-at-arms arrived at my tent and told me to pack out. I could only assume someone higher up had changed their mind about the threat I posed. The officers handed me a plastic container in which to place my few belongings. They confiscated it, and marched me over to the solitary confinement area.

It was like no prison cell I'd ever imagined. Inside the tent was an iron cage, sized for a large animal.

The officers put me in the cage and walked away, the door clanging shut behind them. "Why?" I asked. "What has happened? What has changed?" "Can't tell you," they replied. How long was I going to be there? No answer. Two hours later, when someone came into the tent, I harbored a brief hope that I'd be moved back to my previous tent, with the other prisoners. Instead, they took my bootlaces. They took my belt.

I have never felt so close to suffocating as I did in that steel cage. The tent was meant to block out the sun's heat, but the effect was claustrophobic. There were two air conditioners, but neither functioned consistently. It was the hottest season of the year, in the hottest part of the world, and I would be trapped there for fifty-nine days.

I was no longer numbly vacant. I boiled over with catastrophic terror and animal loneliness.

At the same time, my sense of reality narrowed. I couldn't see, remember, or imagine anything beyond the cage. My world had shrunk to an eight-by-eight-foot metal jaw clenching around me. The MAs delivered food three times a day. The arrival of breakfast—egg and sausage biscuits, plain pancakes with a little plastic syrup packet—was the only way I could tell time. I studied the water bottle I'd been given. It was from a Kuwaiti bottling company, Rawdatain, labeled in Arabic. I stared at it so long it became funny: the only thing I had from the outside world, and I couldn't even read it. I counted the number of things in my cell, and counted them again. I counted the number of holes in the wire cage. The cage said MADE IN FORT WAYNE, INDIANA. It was the only thing I had to look at, to read, to think about. The ways in which I was alone were deep and complex, creating an ever-evolving sense of isolation. There was no internet offering escape into a world beyond my own circumstances, no anonymous people beyond the screen and the keyboard who might offer human contact. I was trapped like an animal, and eventually, I was reduced to caring only about my animal needs.

This was like nothing I'd ever known or imagined. I thought I might have been disappeared. I thought that they could do anything to me—

and no one would ever know. Guards would pass by, leaving casual remarks in their wake: *You're going to be here for a very long time. Maybe they'll send you to Cuba, or Camp Lemonnier in Djibouti. We do bad things there.* I imagined I would be quietly ruined. I thought I was going to die in there, and I thought that was the goal.

In my mind, my confinement wasn't tied to the disclosures or any of the consequences that might have flowed from them. At some point the disclosures stopped being a daily concern, then I forgot about them entirely. The part of my brain that understands if-then statements, that considers the relationship between the past and the future, had withered away. All my memories of that time are trauma memories—unclear, difficult to think about.

Most of the cage was taken up by a bunk, or "rack," as it's called in the navy. There was a toilet, and a shelf, and very little room to walk around, but I moved as much as possible to calm my mind. I'd do the basic drills I'd learned all the way back in training: push-ups, sit-ups, side straddle hop, mountain climber, cherry picker. I'd repeat the names to myself, count out the repetitions. There was no darkness. The artificial light, beamed in with a generator, illuminated the tent day and night. At first sleep was hard, but soon it was almost all I wanted to do. Eventually, they'd let me read what was lying around—Tom Clancy, John Grisham, Danielle Steel—but concentration felt almost impossible.

It's hard to say when Stockholm Syndrome set in. The guards, as cruelly as they treated me, were the best friends that I had, because they gave me food. They gave me water. They even let me have orange juice sometimes. One guard was particularly aggressive. He would begin to hand me the food tray, and then pull it back the moment I reached for it. It cracked him up. Inundated by mockery, I lost all perspective. I perversely imagined those guards who weren't gleefully cruel to me as champions of kindness and integrity.

Two or three times a day, the guards would take me out of the cell, then tear apart everything inside. The rationale was that they needed to make sure I hadn't acquired contraband or disclosed secrets—but really, it was meant to destabilize me. None of the guards would tell me what was happening in the world. But about a month in, a therapist and another chaplain came to check on me. I had no sense of what kind of charges I was facing, nor what had happened as a result of what I had done, and they wouldn't answer any of my questions about that. So instead, I decided to ask who was winning in the World Cup, and I got an update on the *Deepwater Horizon* oil spill off the coast of Louisiana, which had happened shortly before I'd been taken into custody. It was strange to go from being hyperaware of the news, every second of every day, to having virtually no inputs from the outside world.

Every so often I left the tent, in shackles, for a shower. It was more like a birdbath because the chains stayed on, as did my underwear: I'd wet a washcloth and wipe myself down with it, but could never go under the showerhead.

By the end of June, I was a stranger to myself. As in basic training, I had been deconstructed, taken apart, and reconstituted, this time as someone unable to function. One day, I started to babble, to scream, to bang my head against the wall. Doctors had to intervene. I remember that this happened. I do not recognize the person in those memories.

I believed I would be left in the cage forever. I would never see the sky when I wanted to, or see birds, or see my family ever again. I spent all day and all night thinking about regrets, things I hadn't understood were important. I had neglected my relationship with my sister. I had said the wrong things to Dylan, had pushed him away. I should never have quit Starbucks and gone into the military. I should have kept seeing the therapist in D.C.; I should have transitioned. I hadn't appreciated freedom.

I wanted it all to end because I thought my life was already over. I would die without acknowledging or living a life consistent with my gender. A picture representing someone who was not quite me would be splashed all over the news. I would be universally deadnamed in the press. My heart was breaking, along with every other part of me. My conviction that I could not carry on without transitioning was matched only by my certainty that I would never leave the cage.

A few weeks after that, I began to believe I was already dead, and that this cage was my afterlife. I was no longer afraid that they would kill me; I was sure they already had. Almost as an experiment, I made a noose from my bedclothes.

Looking back, it would have been physically impossible for it to work. It was a primal scream. When the guards came by for my fifteen-minute checkup, they realized what I'd tried to do. They put me on suicide watch and diagnosed me with depression, anxiety, and gender dysphoria. The officials told me that I should reach out if I had thoughts like this again—which was a little hard to accept as an honest expression of help and solace, given that I was to remain imprisoned in a small cage for an indeterminate time.

Things got worse for me after that. I was no longer allowed clothes; instead, I had to wear a smock. I was given only finger foods: hot dogs, potato chips. The chips were served on a paper plate; I wasn't even trusted with a cellophane bag anymore. There were no more showers. For the next month, I didn't get to leave the cage once. I was under constant observation. There was a camera outside the cage, so that both the guards and I could be monitored. Superior officers even began searching the officers who were watching over me, in case they'd smuggled something in or out. They held me down to restrain me while they searched my cell, wearing latex gloves. They went to every nook and cranny, and photographed it.

A psychiatrist prescribed me Celexa, but my body reacts to SSRIs like I'm being poisoned. The antidepressants helped quiet my brain, but they were causing me kidney problems. I had nosebleeds. I was too nauseous to eat, and I couldn't urinate; when I did, I pissed blood. Still, in consultation with my doctors, we decided this was the right choice.

With the antidepressants, I stopped feeling resigned to death. I wanted desperately to get out of the tent. I was able to occasionally pull myself back from the complete psychological disintegration I had felt before. I complained about my treatment. Nothing changed. One of the psychologists who came by told me that no matter what happened to me, he was limited in how he could help. And then things took on a stranger tone, and he began to tell me that no matter what happened, I was a good person, that he respected me and who I was. I didn't know what he was talking about. I was in a fucking cage. I didn't know what my action had set in motion, what had been on the news. I thought that everything had failed, that I hadn't succeeded in bringing anything to light. I remembered the writ of habeas corpus: one of the oldest principles in the common law system, which allows a citizen to protest an unlawful imprisonment, to petition a judge and require the government to show its justification for detaining them. I tried to get a piece of paper to write one, but the guards said no. A pen was off-limits, too, after the suicide attempt.

I was certain I had been in that cage for months and months and months—maybe even a year. And then, I began to get vague hints from the guards that something was going to change, intimations that my time in the cage was coming to an end. One navy official got more explicit: "Either you're going to Guantánamo, or you're going to the USS *Boxer*," a cruiser that, after Obama had moved to stop sending terror detainees to Guantánamo, had served as the floating brig for at least one Somalian linked to al-Qaeda. He told me I had been designated as an unlawful enemy combatant—the shadowy legal classification the Bush administration had used against detainees, including U.S. citizens, in the "war" on terror. The classification robbed them of their rights to due process, a lawyer, bail, and a fair and speedy trial. It was a tactic that the courts had struck down—he was just fucking with me—and some part of me knew it wasn't legal, but those guards were the only source of information that I had. I became convinced he was telling the truth, that the military had found a way to rob me of my rights. It was comforting to have confirmation of anything—even my worst fears.

At the end of July, WLO had uploaded seventy-five thousand records from what became known as the Afghan war logs to its site, and *The Guardian*, *The New York Times*, and *Der Spiegel* copublished them. (The Iraq documents would be published later.) Public sentiment, already turning against the war, dipped still more with facts revealed in the documents—

The fallout from the release of the Afghan SIGACTs was instant and intense. The documents proved, unambiguously and unimpeachably, just how disastrous the war still was. Once revealed, the truth could not be denied or unseen: this horror, this constellation of petty vendettas with an undertow of corruption—*this* was the truth of the war.

The disclosures became a flashpoint for a larger argument about how the United States should engage internationally, and how much the public deserved to know about how their government was acting in their name. I had changed the terms of the debate, pulled back the curtain.

But while all that was happening, I knew nothing about it. I remained in a cage.

13.

The publication of the disclosures changed the government's calculus on how to treat me. Within four days of the Afghanistan SIGACTs' appearance in the media—after two months in a cage at Camp Arifjan, with almost no sensory input apart from stifling heat and intermittent air-conditioning—I was moved from my tent. Around dinnertime, without warning or explanation, half a dozen masters-at-arms appeared before my cage. They had my duffel bag, which they inventoried silently in front of me. I was then given a thorough medical examination. After so long without meaningful human interaction, the sudden activity threw me into panicked confusion. "What is going on?" I asked each new person. "We can't tell you," each of them responded.

I was packed into one of a convoy of SUVs, which had been driven through a sally port (an exit point for vehicles) all the way into the jail. There I sat, in the center seat, sandwiched between two MAs, in leg irons and a "body cuff," a chain around my waist to which my handcuffs were attached. We drove out after sundown, lights flashing. This motorcade on steroids came to a halt, after only about two hundred meters, at a helicopter pad. I was bundled out of the SUV and lifted into an embassy helicopter. A short ride later, again crowded among a heavily armed military guard, we landed at Ali Al Salem Air Base. They took me into a small hangar and placed me in what appeared to be a break room. Two men guarded the door from within, two from without, and two stayed by my side.

I still had no idea what was going on, or why I was in Kuwait. Around midnight, someone brought me a bottle of Coke and a meatball sub. I slept briefly, upright at the table in a tiny room, in a hangar, at an airport in Kuwait. Then I was jolted from sleep. The guards woke me up, hustled me to my feet, and dragged me to a waiting SUV that took us to a 747 military charter. My armed entourage and I had the entire top deck to ourselves. A flight crew came around for beverage service, indifferent to my shackles.

We landed in Germany, where yet another SUV dropped us at an airport terminal. It was empty and silent, all the kiosks unstaffed, the waiting areas vacant. I could see into the next terminal. The archway was guarded by a dozen or so fully armed air force police, in full tactical SWAT gear—but there was nobody beyond that threshold, either. We waited there for a silent hour, until I was led down the jetway to the tarmac, packed back into the SUV, and driven back to the same plane. I had no idea where we were heading until we landed in Baltimore.

"Do you have anything to declare?" asked the agent in the emptied customs antechamber. I couldn't believe the question in this context.

"No?" I replied. We drove to Quantico, the Marine Corps base in northern Virginia.

Despite my shackles, I was relieved to be back in America. I thought my treatment would have to be aboveboard on our own soil. But the rules were changing all the time.

My first day at Quantico, a Marine Corps gunnery sergeant giddily informed me that I was his first "celebrity."

"You're all over Fox News!" he said, as though I already knew. While I'd been caged, in utter solitude, the world had been talking about me, about what I'd done. The things I'd wanted exposed were no longer buried. They were out there, being discussed and debated. But at that moment, I was too stunned by my circumstances to understand or care. There was no triumphant flash of recognition for me. I was trying to survive, minute to minute, trying to understand my immediate needs and the risks I faced.

I was moved into isolation immediately. The marines referred to it as "administrative segregation," a euphemism I would hear again in jails and prisons, but everyone from the guards to the UN investigators recognized it as solitary confinement. It came to feel as though I had always been in solitary, and would remain isolated forever. My enforced solitude in the United States felt more permanent than it had in Kuwait. Things were somewhat better, theoretically. On continental U.S. soil, there was air-conditioning, plumbing. My cell was eight feet by six feet. It held a bed, a drinking fountain, a toilet. If I angled my head just right, I could see the glint of a skylight through a small gap in the cell door. I was in that room for more than twenty-three hours a day—an improvement over the twenty-four hours a day of containment in Kuwait.

But marines watched me every single moment. Every five minutes the guards would come in and officially check on me. *Are you okay?* they'd ask, an obligatory rote recitation. I had to reply out loud with an affirmative yes; I couldn't just nod my head. The rules were laughable— but they were taken deadly seriously. Every weekday morning, the marines woke me up at five sharp (on weekends, I got to sleep until seven). I was not allowed to sleep—or even *lean* on anything—until after nightfall, at eight. The guards ordered me to stand up if they saw me sitting down. The marines took explicit notes on everything I did. I was allowed no personal belongings in my cell. If I needed my toothbrush, my glasses, even toilet paper, I had to ask for it. A marine would hand it to me, and I was required to return it the moment I finished using it.

The guards organized my life by imagining all the ways I might be a threat to myself, and then eliminating those possibilities. At night, if they couldn't see me while I was sleeping—if there was a blanket covering my head, or even if my back was just turned to them—the marines would shake me awake to check that I was alive. Once again, I was allowed only a suicide smock, bulky, uncomfortable, and constricting, with boxer shorts underneath. After a few days, I asked for new underwear. No matter how many times they had been washed, I could still smell Iraq on them.

The marines removed the smock at night, leaving me in just shorts. I wasn't even allowed to have my glasses close by while I slept. Blankets were carted in every night and removed in the morning. For a while, I was forbidden to have a pillow. Finally, the marines decided to give me a mattress that had one sewn on, so there was no risk of my smothering myself with it.

This carried on despite the fact that only a few days after my arrival, in August, a psychiatrist had declared me safe from myself. I was taken off suicide watch, my status downgraded to "Prevention of Injury"—and although this meant these punitive, restrictive policies were optional, the marines chose to maintain every one of them. The brig's officer in charge had been asked explicitly to run all decisions about my treatment up the chain of command—which meant the Pentagon was paying close attention to my pretrial confinement.

My isolation was total. A United Nations report that followed a fourteen-month investigation later characterized my treatment as "cruel, inhuman and degrading treatment in violation of article 16 of the convention against torture." I couldn't see or talk to any of the other prisoners; most of them weren't locked up anywhere near me. But every once in a while, I could hear them through the walls, hear the chatting, hear the normal human interactions. I could imagine that I was part of a group of people.

My days in Quantico were closely regimented. I could watch television, by myself, outside my cell, the basic local stations, for one hour a day. Each night, I got two and a half hours of correspondence time, when I could write to family and friends and supporters. But I could communicate only with certain people, who were all on an approved list. And if I wanted to take a shower—fifteen minutes maximum—that was subtracted from my letter-writing time.

A guard offered to get me a copy of my preferred scripture. I couldn't even think of how to respond. Eventually, my lawyer managed to help me access books beyond the pulp that was on offer at the Quantico library, and even then, I had to request them by name. Once the prison approved them, they had to be sent directly from the publisher. Only one book or magazine was allowed in my cell at a time. Like everything else, it was removed before I went to bed and returned in the morning.

I wasn't allowed to exercise in my cell. If the marines saw me doing push-ups or sit-ups, they'd force me to stop. I was near catatonic, dulled by lethargy; I knew if I was to survive, I needed to move, to inhabit my body. To get around the "no exercise" rule, I began to dance, alone, to imaginary music, for hours. The most entertaining thing in my cell was the plastic mirror. I'd make faces into it, imagine the way other people saw me when I talked. Or I'd play one-sided peek-a-boo with the marines. The guards thought I was crazy, but I was coping.

I got one official hour of "exercise" a day, in a different, slightly larger empty room, where I was allowed to walk. I'd pace in endless figure eights. If I got bored—and I often did—and said I wanted to stop, the marines would happily take me back to the cell early. My body turned softer, pudgier. My fierce muscle went away.

Publicly, the government justified my isolation by claiming it was to protect me from self-harm, which they connected to gender dysphoria. Privately, a Marine Corps general made that decision based on reasons of "national security." I was alone, indefinitely detained in a windowless cell. I had all the time in the world to consider who I was, to define who I wanted to be. I had none of the resources to make it happen. My depression deepened. I coped by dissociating, and it is difficult for me to describe emotions from that time. I can recall details of what happened to me, but not how they made me feel. The experience is blank—that is the horror and torture of solitary confinement.

During the first several months I was at Quantico, the publication of the disclosures continued, drawing international media attention to their substance, and to me, as well. But I was too disconnected to notice, too preoccupied with surviving with my faculties intact. What I now know is that in late October, a larger group of journalistic outlets— *The New York Times*, *The Guardian*, Al Jazeera, *Le Monde*, the Bureau of Investigative Journalism, the Iraq Body Count project, and *Der Spiegel*—partnered with one another and with WikiLeaks to publish the next round of disclosures: what became known as the Iraq war logs, more than 390,000 documents.

People from the libertarian right and the far left defended me: academics, journalists, and even the former whistleblower Daniel Ellsberg. The nationalist right, however, hated me. That fall, at a book signing for his Christmas-themed children's book, the former Arkansas governor Mike Huckabee declared that I ought to be executed. Representative Mike Rogers echoed Huckabee's wish for the death penalty. Moderates and centrists predictably argued for the status quo: I had exposed important information, but I should have done it differently; I had divulged too much, and done it improperly. The media seemed mostly to be covering the case from the government's point of view. Isolated as I was, I was barely aware of the response to my disclosures, let alone to me in particular. I wouldn't have had the energy to care, in any case.

Still, for some Americans on the left, the most significant effect of the documents' publication was the disenchanting revelation that Obama's administration was, in certain concrete ways, at least as violent and secretive as the Bush administration had been. My disclosures brought to light Obama's use of drone strikes in Yemen and the increasing restriction of the press's access to information. For many, it became difficult to justify the government's many sins, and it was difficult not to count my prosecution among them. For my part, I had no time to notice or care, even as the news cycle raged around me.

In November 2010, there was a third round of disclosures. A month after the Iraq SIGACTs made headlines, the 250,000 U.S. State Department cables I'd sent to WikiLeaks months before were published, with some details redacted. It was a stunning look behind the curtain, and showed just how frankly our officials talked in private about other countries and the way the United States threw its weight around on the international stage. Journalists immediately started using the cables to fact-check, to get a deeper understanding of the powerful institutions they covered, and to uncover new truths. ████████████

██
██
██
██
██
██
██
██
██
██
██
██
██
██
██
██
██
████████

The government got even more furious at me. Secretary of State Hillary Clinton had strong words on the matter. The publication "puts people's lives in danger, threatens our national security, and undermines our efforts to work with other countries to solve shared problems," she said in an official statement. "Now, I am aware that some may mistakenly applaud those responsible, so I want to set the record straight," she added. "There is nothing laudable about endangering innocent people, and there is nothing brave about sabotaging the peaceful relations between nations on which our common security depends."

But privately, according to subsequent reporting, she spent hours on the phone with diplomats all over the world telling them that, in fact, no one was in danger because of the disclosures, despite the painful news cycle. And internal government reports, including one commissioned by the White House and one by the State Department, showed that none of the revelations had, as a practical matter, hurt our place in the world. The media, for its part, continued to benefit hugely from the disclosures, writing ever-juicier exposés; and at the same time reporters more or less continued to accept the government line about my actions. I was both the most important source they'd had in years and the biggest threat to American interests abroad.

Even though I could not devote any energy to following the storm of reportage, the storm gained fury. My treatment at the hands of the U.S. military became its own news story. The German parliament's human rights commission wrote to President Obama in protest. More than two hundred professors—including Obama's former constitutional law professor and friend Laurence Tribe—signed a letter by Harvard Law School's Yochai Benkler and Yale Law School's Bruce Ackerman condemning the conditions under which I was held. "The sum of the treatment that has been widely reported is a violation of the Eighth Amendment's prohibition of cruel and unusual punishment and the Fifth Amendment's guarantee against punishment without trial . . . President Obama was once a professor of constitutional law, and entered the national stage as an eloquent moral leader. The question now, however, is whether his conduct as commander in chief meets fundamental standards of decency." Even the right-wing *Na-*

tional Review wrote that while my treatment might well have been *legal*, "that doesn't make it right."

Some high-ranking government officials were shocked. In early 2011, P. J. Crowley, the top spokesman for the State Department and a twenty-six-year veteran of the air force, was giving a talk at MIT's Center for Future Civic Media when someone asked about me. Crowley said that while he thought I was "in the right place"—jail—I was, given the punitive conditions of my confinement, being gravely mistreated by the DOD. He went on to call my treatment "ridiculous and counterproductive and stupid." When a journalist asked if that was a statement on the record, he said yes, only later clarifying that this was his personal opinion. Three days after his MIT talk, Crowley resigned under pressure, and issued a statement standing by what he had said. Crowley, at least, understood that my treatment harmed America's ability to maintain a moral high ground in our negotiations with hostile actors. Indeed, around the same time, the Iranian government's treatment of three captured American backpackers who had been taken near the Iraq border made news: our government correctly described their captivity as torture, but the conditions under which the DOD was detaining me were worse.

That same week, the journalist Jake Tapper asked President Obama in a press conference about Crowley's comments. "I have actually asked the Pentagon whether or not the procedures that have been taken in terms of [Manning's] confinement are appropriate and are meeting our basic standards," he replied. "They assure me that they are. I can't go into details about some of their concerns, but some of this has to do with Manning's safety as well," he continued, echoing the patently irrational official stance that my isolation was, in some inexplicable way, intended to keep me safe.

It wasn't the only time Obama had to answer questions about me.

During an expensive fundraiser at the St. Regis Hotel in San Francisco, an organization called Courage to Resist seeded the audience with activists, who got up and sang a song about me as a form of protest. Obama, in response, said he understood their position, but that I had broken the law. And he was clearly furious about the leaked diplomatic cables. "I can't conduct diplomacy on open source," he said. Every time President Obama spoke about me, he made it sound as if I had already been convicted, when, in fact, my defense team had barely received any evidence from the government, let alone gone through a court-martial.

One major exception to the generally hostile government response to me came from a surprising quarter: Secretary of Defense Robert Gates. He had been critical of the war logs' release, saying initially that they could have "potentially dramatic and grievously harmful consequences." But after the rhetoric against me and the leaks reached a fever pitch in the wake of the release of the State Department's cables, he tried to tamp it down in a press conference. Gates pointed out that the U.S. government has always been full of leakers—even citing John Adams complaining about how all his negotiations with foreign nations had been published—and said that the last time the diplomatic community had raised the alarm that foreign governments might not want to share information with the United States (when Congress began having true oversight over the CIA, in the 1970s), nothing had actually changed.

"Governments deal with the United States because it is in their interest, not because they like us or trust us or because of our ability to keep secrets," he said. "So, other countries will continue to deal with us. Is this embarrassing? Yes. Awkward? Somewhat. But the longer-term impact? Very modest." His statement was admitted at my court-martial, although he declined to testify on my behalf. The fact that he was a public figure, speaking for the U.S. government, gave that statement special weight, and I was glad of it, for all the good it did.

Soon after I was returned to the United States, my aunt came to visit, and I told her that I intended to hire a civilian lawyer, David Coombs, rather than depend solely on military attorneys. (This is common in high-profile trials.) Coombs, then in his early forties, wasn't strictly a military lawyer, but had served as a lieutenant colonel in the reserves. I knew he would understand what it meant to be a military person, and how to speak to the military people who'd be deciding my fate. He wore his dark hair close-buzzed, and kept his suits and ties traditional, but he truly understood and was politically sympathetic to my point of view.

I was consumed with building our case. Not just out of hope for my own freedom, but out of a desire to get the facts straight. I cared about the way history would portray my actions, and I was terrified that the real truth of what had happened would be steamrolled by the government's muscular public relations narrative. After all, while I was being kept in a cage in one-hundred-degree heat, they had already been seeding the media with stories that painted me as a traitor not just to other soldiers, but to every single American.

In our earliest conversations, I asked Coombs what my sentence might be. He told me the only way to project a sentence was to compare a case to similar cases, but there were no cases like mine. His hope was that I'd get a sentence I could serve and get out and live some of my life. I thought that was wildly optimistic. Here I was, jailed like a terrorist, denounced as a traitor. The deck was thoroughly stacked against me. I never felt like I could speak freely in front of my lawyer; I still wouldn't be remotely surprised to learn the government had obtained a warrant to record all of our conversations.

I had spent very little money while I was in Iraq, so I had savings, which I used to give Coombs a down payment for his services. Courage to Resist (CTR), a nonprofit started by a Marine Corps Desert Storm veteran named Jeff Paterson, also provided financial support. Paterson had abruptly become a pacifist during his service, and one day he'd lain flat down on the tarmac, stopping all planes from flying, until he was arrested and court-martialed. His support was critical.

I never saw myself as a pacifist or a conscientious objector, like Paterson. I worried that CTR might eventually find my beliefs at odds with theirs. But Coombs helped convince me that what we eventually started calling "the campaign" was about more than just my own court case. It was a larger political effort. Although at the time I had only a limited sense of the impact I'd had, my arrest—and the information that had come out through my disclosures—had helped rejuvenate an antiwar movement. Things got complicated fast: all the groups expressing support for me clearly had their own agendas and views. My ability to tell my story had always been constrained by the limits of social convention; now it was not just limited but co-opted.

Despite the insulation of solitary confinement, I began to understand that to some people, I'd become a cause, one that was more important to them than my fate as a flesh-and-blood person. There was the me who I was and wished to be—and there was the Private Manning that the world was imagining and reading about: a figurehead, a placeholder, a symbol. I feared that I'd be associated with views I didn't actually have.

In 2013, the International Peace Bureau gave me an award for my "outstanding work for peace." Colonel Ann Wright accepted on my behalf. She was an antiwar activist who'd been a senior officer in the military and resigned from the State Department over her objections to the 2003 invasion of Iraq. I was flattered to get the award, to get *any* award, but what she said stood in contrast to my actual beliefs.

When I saw a transcript of her speech, I decided to write a statement, which I released to *The Guardian*, explaining my point of view: "It's not terribly clear to me that my actions were explicitly done for 'peace' . . . I feel that the public cannot decide what actions and policies are or are not justified if they don't even know the most rudimentary details about them and their effects." At that time, I thought of myself as a transparency advocate above all.

I burned a lot of bridges with that statement, especially with the older antiwar community. But I thought what I had done was better understood as a direct action in the service of transparency than as a symbolic action intended to secure peace. I knew some activists would not be happy with my statement or my approach, but dogmatism and purity don't convince anyone who's not already a true believer. If I was going to be imprisoned for the rest of my life, it was important that people understand the nuance of why I did what I did, and the long tradition of direct action that I believed my actions were part of.

And to be clear, my assumption was that I would get life without parole. After what I had already gone through in Kuwait and Quantico, as far as I was concerned, I was already dead. I hadn't felt alive since I'd been taken into custody. Still, I fought and I fight still for the right to tell my own story and to be heard.

I turned twenty-three in December 2010, in administrative segregation at Quantico. I was allowed to write a wish list of books and publications for my birthday and Christmas. I asked for the nerdiest publications they allowed. *Science*, *Nature*, and *Scientific American* kept me occupied. I was, and remain, a voracious reader, of all kinds of books, on all subjects, written from disparate, sometimes even abhorrent, perspectives. At that time, I was preoccupied with processing what I had seen in Iraq. I read Sun Tzu's *The Art of War* and Carl von

Clausewitz's *On War*. I loved YA novels, and was especially taken with a series of epistolary novels told through the text messages of teenaged detectives. I must have read 150 books in my time at Quantico.

Coombs's first priority was to get me out of solitary. We argued that this was cruel and unusual punishment, and filed under the military rules and regulations for identifying problematic pretrial conditions. The brig's own mental health experts had recommended that I be removed from injury-prevention watch. My records showed that my behavior was "excellent," to the point that the mental health staff correctly intuited that I had fully internalized an awareness that I was being meticulously monitored. But the military wouldn't budge.

Quiet, behind-the-scenes petitioning for my release from isolation didn't help. In mid-December, the journalist and lawyer Glenn Greenwald wrote about my conditions for *Salon*. In January, David Coombs spoke to a reporter at *The Washington Post*. My confinement in solitary became a cause: a support network that had sprung up to help me after my arrest organized a protest outside Quantico. They carried blankets, meant, symbolically, for me. This brought some pressure to bear on my situation, but rather than improving my conditions, it drew retaliation. The next day, four guards, rather than the usual two, came to take me out of my cell for recreation time. They were confrontational and aggressive. One told me to turn left; when I complied, another one screamed, "Don't turn left!" I stopped, and the first marine berated me for not following his orders. Another yelled at me to say "Aye, Sergeant," instead of "Yes." At the recreation room, this Kafkaesque hell continued while they removed my leg restraints. I took a step back as soon as the shackles were off. I felt dizzy, panicked. My heart pounded, and I was afraid I'd fall, so I sat down. The guards started to walk toward me. I backed off and put my hands up. "I am not doing anything. I am just trying to follow your orders," I shouted.

They let me walk for an hour, but back in my cell afterward, the brig commander, Chief Warrant Officer James Averhart, came by to chastise me. "I'm the commander," he said. "You still have to follow brig procedures," I answered, without thinking.

Averhart left—and immediately ordered me back on suicide watch. This, in itself, threw me into near-suicidal crisis. "Why are you doing this to me?" I cried. I grabbed my head, pulled my hair. "Why am I being punished? I have done nothing wrong." I felt like I was losing my mind.

What little I had left was now taken away from me. My hour outside the cell each day for exercise: gone. I was trapped in a cage, again. I asked an official if there was anything I could do to get off suicide watch. He said no.

In January 2011, Coombs ramped up his advocacy. We filed a complaint that specifically targeted a couple of the officers who were responsible for deciding how I was treated. This process requires the commanding officer to explain and justify their treatment of a soldier. Each side is allowed to mount a case before a judge.

The paperwork, and the emails that the military had to disclose, revealed a contradiction in the government's case. While the official story remained that my solitary confinement was for my own mental health (an assessment that was made without the weigh-in of actual mental health officials, which military rules didn't require), internal emails revealed that the government justified my confinement as a matter of national security—not in order to protect me.

This was useful for our next legal move, an Article 13 motion. This military code statute holds that the "arrest or confinement imposed . . . [shall not] be any more rigorous than the circumstances required to insure . . . presence" at trial. This was months and months after my first, failed, halfhearted suicide attempt in Kuwait. At this point, I had no inclination to self-harm. The government claimed, in effect, that my efforts to get out of solitary had nothing to do with wanting to feel human again, but rather that I only wanted the freedom to kill myself. I already felt dead, though. Killing myself wouldn't have changed anything. Being around other people would have. Alone, I moved deeper inside my own head. I worked through complex math problems. I read. I waited.

Nine months after I'd entered solitary confinement on American soil, the master sergeant came by my cell and told me to pack up my things. "I don't have any things," I reminded him. But the Pentagon had decided to make a change. The marines opened the door and allowed me to be unrestrained, a feeling I hadn't had in almost a year. For just a moment, I remembered what it was like to walk around unencumbered, remembered myself as a person, not a prisoner. I held on to that memory long after my restraints were reimposed, during the comically short drive to the airfield in yet another armored black SUV.

14.

We drove about five hundred meters to a big hangar at the Quantico airfield. Old guys in suits were milling about clutching important-looking papers, their thin comb-overs whipping in the wind. They led me to a small plane, kitted out for ten or so people. The plane was a wood-laminated wonder of outdated cutting-edge military tech, the most futuristic flying command center the 1990s had had to offer. This time, I was told where we were headed: Fort Leavenworth, Kansas. The deputy director of operations for the military corrections system met me on the plane and took personal custody of me.

My restraints were removed for the plane ride, but I was surrounded by U.S. Army Criminal Investigation Division (CID) agents. They brought MREs—"meals ready to eat"—and the head of security chatted with me. He told me he had been given orders to move me only that morning, and that they hadn't even had time to properly fuel the plane. We touched down for a short refueling stop in Ohio, then landed at the Fort Leavenworth airfield, where sergeants met us in an armored police van. For reasons I still cannot comprehend, they ordered me to keep my head down, and drove the vehicle right up to the door of the Joint Regional Correction Facility (JRCF), where I would spend the next six years.

The transport had been urgent and strange, but at least I had been carried there without chains, in the company of other people. Grief settled in: I was certain I was headed back to solitary confinement. But inside the prison, the JRCF guards removed my restraints, instructed me to shower, handed me a uniform, and escorted me to a regular cell, where I was issued all the things I'd been forbidden in Quantico: toothpaste, shower shoes, towels.

After a meal, I went to see Dr. Galloway, a kind woman who would become my psychologist until my release. She assessed me and determined I was no longer suicidal. Solitary confinement, she said, would be incredibly harmful to me. After more than eleven months of solitary, it was cold comfort, an ironic validation that my placement had been intentionally punitive and not, as publicly claimed, medically necessary.

I learned later that the military had made a big press show around this consultation: the undersecretary of the army released an official statement concerning the change in my status, answered questions about how much better my conditions would be in Fort Leavenworth, and offered words of concern for my care and well-being, promising that my pretrial confinement would be "the best we can provide."

Several days after I arrived at the JRCF, the government's dog-and-pony show began to make sense. In fact-checking ahead of the next round of publications, reporters had been asking government officials questions that tipped them off that more disclosures were imminent and revealed the subject of those documents: Guantánamo.

Seven hundred files on the Guantánamo military prison were about to be published. The world would learn, from the files of specific detainees, more details about the interrogations they'd faced. The public would learn more details about how many of the detainees were low-level foot soldiers, or didn't have any useful intelligence. They would see the inhumanity of conditions at Guantánamo, and the flimsiness of the military's intelligence rationale for maintaining such a useless gulag.

In other words, although I can't say for certain they were related, the U.S. government got the heads-up that this information might hit the press while I was in the same kind of extended solitary confinement used at Guantánamo, and they rushed me somewhere nicer.

At the JRCF, I discovered just how much I had been altered by the previous year. Moving around without restraint left me in shock: I was physically and psychologically so unused to freedom that it unsettled me. I waited for the shackles to come out at every moment, repeatedly asking the guards, "Am I supposed to be unrestrained? Is this allowed?"

"Of course," came the answer. But I worried that the soldiers who failed to restrain me were going to get in trouble. I feared that this was a test, or a trick: someone wanted to argue that I'd manipulated my escorts into letting me slip the cuffs, so they could punish me even more. I was terrified to be outside of my cell. Even this small measure of liberty made me deeply nervous. Would it be ripped away again the minute I got used to it? I was hyperaware that any perceived mistake, any allegation of defiance, could create an excuse for the government to throw me back into solitary confinement, to punish me by any means necessary.

After so long in solitary confinement, I struggled with the most fundamental things. Regaining normal speech was challenging. I couldn't remember how to talk without shouting and sandwiching my responses around the rank of my interlocutor: *Yes-Sergeant-yes*, as the Marine Corps guards had demanded. It drove everyone at the JRCF nuts, but I was too well trained. Little by little, I regained my balance. I willed my own self into existence again, and not for the last time.

———

At first, none of my fellow prisoners knew who I was. I was just the new person, and other prisoners tried to make friends. But any kind of social contact felt impossibly uncomfortable. "I'm sorry," I would tell them, "but I don't know if I can talk to you." And I would return to my silence. I'd sit in the back while they watched TV. Or I'd return to the self-soothing habits I had formed in solitary, pacing in my cell, back and forth, back and forth. Finally, after about a week of self-imposed isolation, a guard at the prison told me I was allowed to socialize, that I probably *should*. It took three more months for me to actually relax a little bit around other people, to stop feeling so skittish.

The sheer deluge of mail I received marked me as different from other prisoners. The flow of cards and letters was overwhelming. I read them all. Most were kind, the writer expressing why my actions had affected them in a particular way. People sent me their life stories, in detail.

I could never reply. My lawyer had made it very clear that anything I put in writing could be used as a statement in my court-martial, and the prison staff had been instructed by one or another government factotum that all my interactions and conversations—which included my correspondence—had to be recorded. To that end, every day one of the soldiers was assigned to act in the role I called the Clipboard Cop. This person followed me around everywhere and wrote down every-thing I said. If I tried to see what had just been recorded, the soldier would snap the clipboard protectively up.

Fort Leavenworth became my universe; my family and friends and anyone else from the outside world, except my lawyer, faded into a background of distant memory. I was concerned that any conversation I had, no matter how intimate or how trivial, could be used against me in my trial.

The prison guards were children. They were soldiers, eighteen or nineteen years old, never having so much as sniffed a deployment but given a badge of authority. They were the post–Abu Ghraib generation, and they received specialized training in detention operations. They loved nothing quite so much as enforcement, flexing their authority. The doors closed every night at 10:05 on the dot, lights out.

By the time I reached the JRCF, I was long past depression; I was just passing time. Breakfast was at 5:10 a.m., and if you weren't in line promptly, you didn't eat. I would crash back to sleep every morning after chow until 9:00 or 10:00. To fill the long hours, we'd watch a lot of TV, mostly sports.

Exercise—now that I was allowed it—became a release, a way of getting high. I ran sometimes; it took me about six miles before I hit euphoria. But my true addiction was to a HIIT cardio program that we could play on the DVD player. At first, a whole group of us did the workout together, but after a while, I was the only one doing it. I'd do it every day, jumping and sweating alone, forgetting for precious minutes myself, my surroundings, the terrifying future. I got into even better shape than I'd been in in Iraq. I liked feeling strong and alert again. I tried to ignore the way my body grew ever more masculine.

In Quantico, I couldn't focus on anything long enough for a thought to take emotional hold. But once I settled into a routine at Fort Leavenworth, everything I'd pushed out of my mind came flooding back. I thought about gender constantly. About appearance and affect. About what, essentially, gender was or could be for me. I considered my own conceptual lexicon around gender and identity with care.

I couldn't keep a journal to work out my feelings or keep track of my thoughts, though; my cell was searched, and anything I wrote down was photocopied as legal evidence. I couldn't use the internet. My surroundings limited and frustrated me. My lost hope for transition was a constant burden. I had fewer opportunities than ever before to assert my own gender, but no amount of external restriction could constrain my thinking—which got sharper and more clear—or the comfort I found in my own imagination.

My case proceeded slowly. The government delayed my court-martial over and over because, despite charging me with twenty-two counts, of varying severity, it hadn't yet built its case. The investigation, still underway, involved complex coordination between the military and civilian agencies. Most of the charges were about the actual act of disclosure—which I admitted I'd done. But the most controversial charge was "aiding the enemy." It was an unprecedented application of law, basically accusing me of what amounted to treason for being a source.

I followed it all as closely as my lawyer did: the minutiae of military rules of evidence, how the court-martial was to be set up, our planned strategies and approaches, the motions we intended to file, and the order of operations for filing them. This was something I had control over, unlike the narrative about me in the press. I became, functionally, the paralegal on my case. David Coombs was the only person working on the case full-time, against the huge prosecution team. I worked for hours in the prison's law library, researching and drafting portions of the motions. David printed out every single page of the discovery and brought them to me in file boxes. I was authorized to have two at a time, and I savored them the way some prisoners reveled in the arrival of a package from home.

The government's strategy was to inundate us with too much information, to bury the gems of solid evidence that we needed under mountains of irrelevant bureaucratic paperwork. But I had nothing but time on my hands, and I wasn't billing for it. Preparing for the court-martial became my life. It was a logic puzzle, not an existential morass. A tactical battle, with rules to be followed and leveraged. I didn't want to deal with my emotions, but this was something I could focus on.

At the time, my case had the dubious distinction of generating more paperwork, by volume, than any other military criminal case under the U.S. court-martial system. There were eleven thousand pages of investigative reports from all the interviews the government had conducted with four hundred potential witnesses. On the law library computer, I typed out a running file of summaries for David, so he'd know who the government was likely to call, and what they'd say, before the prosecution presented us with its witness list.

Even when I watched TV to relax, I'd have file folders with me. At first, I was focused on the factual details of my own case, but over time, I started to develop a broader sense of the federal, state, and military legal systems. It was no real surprise to learn that the law is often unrelated to and often quite at odds with—commonly held notions of justice. But the logistics and bureaucratic machinery of the system fascinated me. The admissibility or inadmissibility of important evidence in court, for one thing, floored me. I came to understand that the question of guilt mattered less than the ability of one party to *prove* something with some inspired procedural maneuver.

And in my case, the government was using every procedural tool at its disposal to gain ground. I'd embarrassed it, disclosed unflattering truths, made officials' lives more complicated, and revealed just how poor the army's security procedures were. The government clearly felt the need to throw the book at me with all possible force, and it threatened to charge me with offenses that could carry a life sentence.

I had begun to see myself discussed on TV news soon after my arrival at Quantico, and once I was at the JRCF, the many implications of being a public figure became clear to me. I told David we needed to hire a public relations firm. This wasn't going to be just a court-martial. I felt that this was a war over the meaning of America, both here and abroad. David's role was to fight in the courtroom, but he did publish our defense motions on his personal blog, which was a way of ensuring relative transparency around how the case was proceeding—or, rather, not proceeding.

Whether it was due to inertia, the complications of coordinating multiple agencies, or because it suited the government's purposes, discovery took forever. The government's key evidence was kept out of our hands until the last possible minute. My team wasn't even invited to participate until 2012, nearly two years into my time in jail. Once discovery began, the government tried to pressure me to plead guilty, and to take responsibility not only for my own disclosures, but for things I had not done.

One afternoon, I was pulled out of the prison and taken to a separate secure location for what amounted to a high-pressure sales pitch for life without parole: David was waiting there, along with the government's legal team. The prosecution lawyers queued up a very fancy PowerPoint and began to take us through their arguments, with all the evidence that had been assembled against me, along with their theory of the case. They were clearly having trouble finding evidence to prove that my actions had caused measurable harm. They cherry-picked what they did have to try to convince me I could never win and that it was in my interest to plead guilty to all the charges the government brought, rather than to exercise my right to a trial. Major Ashden Fein was the lead prosecutor for the government. His efforts to convince me did not work.

Besides, taking their deal would have meant setting a precedent, one that would have allowed the government to use the same tools and weapons it was using against me against everyone—for instance, to go after someone who was just acting as a source to a journalist. This weighed on me, but so did the dull terror of imagining a life sentence in prison. Or worse: a conviction for "aiding the enemy" could mean life without parole—LWOP. These were high stakes, and I could not, with the rest of my life on the table, decide how to proceed. For more than a year, my team and the prosecution went back and forth over terms, and Coombs and I went back and forth over whether to take a plea.

The government wouldn't budge on two things that I couldn't imagine agreeing to: They wanted a minimum sentence of forty years and a conviction for "aiding the enemy." And they wanted my full, complete, and absolute cooperation. I wasn't comfortable with any number above a twenty-year sentence. And while I was willing to plead guilty to some of the charges, I refused to plead guilty to something I had not done. I had acted as I had because I wanted the American people to know what was being done in their name. The truth was not negotiable.

The government's case was built around computer forensics from one of the largest and most complex investigations ever conducted. But it was also flawed, incorrect in places, and in order to agree to its terms, I would have had to perjure myself.

The prosecution's timeline was based on what its investigators had found on my MacBook. Some of their circumstantial theories were correct about when I'd leaked and what I'd sent, although they had zero physical evidence to back it up. But in one crucial instance, the government had gotten something big wrong. They alleged, incorrectly, that I had uploaded the video of an air strike in Garani, Afghanistan, in November 2009. In fact, the government now alleges that a systems administrator at the Department of Energy's Brookhaven National Laboratory had, that December, attempted to crack a file containing the video and was terminated for "inappropriate computer activity."

I understood why the government tried to pin it on me. It didn't suit its case, much less the narrative of me as the biggest national security threat in the history of the American military, to consider that an entirely *different* person with classified access might have leaked months earlier, without being noticed, the same information that I had found in the JAG folder. Our forensics team, which I assisted, was able to show when I had uploaded the Garani video: 2010, not back in 2009, as the government was alleging. They rushed forward with the charge anyway.

We went in fighting, even from the pretrial hearing, to determine whether I needed to undergo a full court-martial. Coombs argued that the investigating officer, Lieutenant Colonel Paul Almanza, needed to recuse himself because he worked as a prosecutor for the Department of Justice, which worked to build a case against WikiLeaks (and Julian Assange) after my disclosures. The request was denied—the investigator argued that he wasn't involved with that prosecution—which sent a message that the deck was stacked against us in an unfair and possibly illegal way.

There was also the fact that of the forty-eight witnesses—digital security experts, military officers, psychologists, even the secretary of state—Coombs wanted to call for the pretrial, only twelve were allowed, ten of whom were also prosecution witnesses. Coombs also publicly suggested that part of the reason the government was so keen for me to plead was that they wanted me to become a witness in a larger conspiracy case.

The public had not heard me speak since I'd been jailed. I was simply a symbol, a silent-film actor onto whom people projected their love and their hate, their politics and their fear. In November 2012 I gave testimony in a pretrial hearing at Fort Meade, in Maryland. The press seemed to be surprised by the reality of me: I was outgoing, careful, and articulate on the stand. I don't think it was what anyone had expected. The news was filled with images of me in military fatigues, wearing glasses and smiling a little. Someone snuck a recorder into the courtroom and uploaded my testimony, and the internet roared back.

The government was surprised, too, that I'd decided to get on the stand. Most lawyers would prefer that their client not do so, because they can make a poor impression, commit an unforced error, or otherwise open themselves up to attack.

The military judge, Colonel Denise Lind, asked me to explain why I intended to plead guilty (to some of the charges) if I believed my actions had been motivated by the greater good. It *was* complicated: I needed to plead to the specific offenses that described what I'd actually done without admitting a broader wrongdoing that I had not committed. "Your Honor," I replied, "regardless of my opinion or my assessment of documents such as these, it's beyond my pay grade—it's not my authority to make these decisions."

Part of the pretrial proceeding concerned whether the government had treated me unlawfully during my confinement, particularly during the nine months at Quantico; we argued that because I'd been punished so harshly without a conviction, my case should be dismissed. The prosecution downplayed, and even lied about, my conditions, claiming, for instance, that I'd been allowed to make telephone calls when I hadn't. The government also revealed that my gender and sexual identity had made my punishment worse. I signed some of the letters from jail as Breanna Manning, and Marine Corps Master Sergeant Craig Blenis testified that this, along with my admission to Sergeant Adkins that I suffered from gender dysphoria, had created a "red flag" for potential self-harm. This, he said, justified their "protection" of me via isolation. When Coombs asked Blenis why my gender issues might make them think I'd hurt myself, he replied, "That's not normal, sir."

Other people, especially when they first got to Fort Leavenworth, liked to ask me about what I'd done. I'd shrug off questions with my stock line: *I don't talk about my case. It's big and complex.* Some people liked me just because of what I'd done. They'd been locked in prison by the military, after all. *You put the biggest black eye into the fucking military that we've ever seen and that is fucking cool*, went that line of thought. Many people hated me for the same reason.

I developed friendships, including a brief connection so intense that I wept when my friend was convicted and transferred out. I also developed enemies, like a charming and amoral man who'd spent a bunch of time in prison before his wrongful conviction was over-turned. The government had decided to re-court-martial him, and he was back in pretrial detention, as a seasoned inmate. The experience had left him arrogant: he tested the limits of the rules all the time, got in a lot of fights, and deliberately baited the guards. One of his special-ties was yelling as loud as he could to get them mad. It worked on me, if not them: I'd shout back at him to shut up. "I just want some fucking peace and quiet!" We'd go back and forth in front of the guards, which he loved—it gave him a feeling of power over both them and me—and I hated. I didn't want any more black marks on my record, especially not while I was still waiting for trial. One day, as he needled me for the umpteenth time, I couldn't take it anymore. If I let him push me around, that would mean I was someone people could take advantage of. I grabbed him by the shirt and punched him four times in a row, as fast and as hard as I could. I didn't do it out of anger. I punched him to make sure that everybody knew that I couldn't be fucked with. The guards saw it. I was back in solitary.

By then, I knew exactly how long it would take me to go loopy in solitary: nine days. After nine days, I would get so bored that any sound would be instant, overwhelming stimulation. Before then, I could entertain myself, hollering, monologuing nonsense soliloquies at the guards, walking, dancing to the music in my mind.

This time, I was there for only three days. I paced back and forth and did the side straddle hop that we'd learned in basic training. I did push-ups and crunches when the guards weren't looking. This time, I could read books, and the writing I read in solitary confinement imprinted itself on my brain like nothing else. I ruminated on articles I had liked in *The New Yorker* and *The Atlantic*, publications I was able to receive at Fort Leavenworth, and this kept me more or less content.

But it wasn't the last time I would be alone. In the beginning of 2013, the government pulled me out of the general population and placed me in an observation cell. I hadn't done anything wrong; I wondered what the hell was going on. It turned out that Aaron Swartz, the open-source activist, had taken his own life. I believe the government knew that he and I had mutual friends and worried that I'd hurt myself as a copycat. It is also possible that they imagined some legally significant connection between us—they were reaching out to a lot of my acquaintances from my Boston days, asking questions about me.

I hadn't known Aaron, really, IRL, but we had many people and ideas—and chat rooms—in common. Like me, he'd been a target of the U.S. government, prosecuted for his work in trying to make closed information—the kind kept in expensive academic databases like JSTOR—free and available to everyone, in violation of copyright law. Aaron had cared deeply about my case. In fact, when the news began to surface of how poorly I'd been treated at Quantico, he'd filed FOIA requests for more information about my conditions. Just a few days after he'd filed a request about me, the federal government arrested him for the first time, for guerrilla file sharing.

During the long pretrial period, as we negotiated, the government asked us to stipulate that certain pieces of evidence were true, to speed up what would certainly be a slow, fact-heavy trial. I wanted us to agree only to stipulation of expected testimony; in other words, what we agreed witnesses would be likely to say on the record about relatively procedural things, like whether the chain of custody had been correct, or when a particular document was filed. The government wanted us to stipulate when I'd uploaded certain things, for instance. But they had gotten many of the facts wrong, drawing conclusions based on conjecture rather than forensics, and I wanted that on the record. I wanted the public to hear the parade of witnesses who'd challenge the official narrative, contradict those supposed facts.

The bargaining was complex. I thought we reached an agreement—but not an official plea—with the prosecution: it was pleading guilt "by exceptions and substitutions." In other words, a mixed plea—guilty to some charges, but not to others.

In order for my sentence to be reduced, I would have to plead guilty to the "aiding the enemy" violation. They would drop some of the charges that I refused to budge on. I would face trial on failure to obey a lawful order, transmitting classified information, and stealing government property. This would allow the court case to focus on the consequences of my action, rather than the factual back-and-forth about what had happened. We also asked that the court-martial be decided by a military judge, rather than a military panel; getting one person to see the case our way seemed more achievable.

But after all that negotiation, there was no deal. The military wanted to make an example of me and put me in prison for the rest of my life. There would be no version of a deal for me unless I agreed to the one they'd laid out, one that involved copping to things that just hadn't happened. The moral compromise and the precedent a plea would set just weren't worth the years they would shave off a sentence.

15.

They boxed me in. By choosing to prosecute me with unauthorized disclosures under an obscure and vague federal law, the government had prevented Coombs and the team of lawyers that the military assigned me from presenting a real defense. I couldn't argue that what I'd done was morally right.

The Obama administration's crackdown on media sources was more extreme than that of any previous administration. Because of the way the federal statute is written, we had only three choices from that point forward: argue that I was mentally incapacitated when I made the decision; argue that I didn't make the decision at all; or present evidence of mitigation. We were barred from arguing that no damage to the United States occurred.

The only legal strategy that made sense to us was mitigation. This meant showing that I was a good person put into unusual circumstances, and that the government had repeatedly ignored signs that I was being pushed to the limit, sweeping all my difficulties under the rug because they desperately needed my skill set. And we could argue that the results of the leak hadn't been nearly as severe as the government claimed and none caused any provable damage or injury to any person.

I *hated* mitigation. It felt like conceding, like admitting that I had done something traitorous, when I thought of what I had done as my democratic and ethical obligation. I wanted to fight fire with fire, and show how much propaganda about me was circulating. Coombs urged caution, and reminded me over and over again that the burden of proof was on the government to show that my actions had caused any harm.

My legal team used everything it could, including arguing that gender identity had pushed me to a breaking point. This strategy continues to weigh on me. The legal system forced me to effectively denounce who I was. I hate that my gender had to be brought up in court. While it's true that I felt overwhelmed by keeping my gender secret, there simply was not a causal relationship between that issue and my decision, and I worried that the argument we were forced to make gave ammunition to those who want to pathologize trans people, to suggest that being trans is itself a sickness or derangement. The truth of the matter was that, despite all the stresses that probably contributed in certain ways, I acted as I did because of what I saw, because of the values I hold.

The lawyers insisted I didn't have any other choice. I couldn't plead not guilty to everything, because I had in fact disclosed information marked, however arbitrarily, "classified." I couldn't plead incapacitation, the military version of the insanity plea, which is even more stringent than the already rigorous civilian version. Depression, stress, and anxiety wouldn't cut it, either: just about everyone in the military wrestles with them. You're *expected* to be able to function that way. I had been diagnosed, in my post-arrest psych evaluation, with mild Asperger's syndrome, as well as the possibility of fetal alcohol syndrome. We discussed both as possibilities for incapacitation, but felt that each was a stretch. Bringing up the stress over my gender identity would help some on this front, but wouldn't get us all the way there; it didn't feel like enough to comprise a defense by itself. Besides, we worried that pervasive transphobia would mean that disclosing my gender would actually work against us.

I also was just not ready to talk about my gender in the press, or even to most of the people in my life; mostly, I had talked about it only online, in chat rooms or instant messages. I wanted so desperately to transition, but had never imagined doing it in front of the whole world. Before my arrest, I had been considering trying a stealth-mode transition after I left the army. Not a big-deal coming out, just quietly doing it, and then going about my life as a woman. That option was taken from me. Before I could even tell my *family* about my gender issues, a writer named Steve Fishman published a much-quoted exposé on my life in *New York* magazine. My gender was made public. (Fishman might have contacted my representatives, but I can't remember, and I certainly do not remember having a chance to respond about the specific question of my trans identity.) This is how my family learned that I was trans. There had been speculation online, but nothing so visible. I was outed; it was devastating. For people who were already inclined to view me as crazy, this was one more piece of evidence.

I hit one of my lowest lows when that news broke. My family and friends had already dealt with losing me to prison. Now at least a few of them were grieving the person they had imagined me to be. More than that, I'd had my agency taken from me. I had lost forever the opportunity to identify myself to the world on my own terms.

———

By the time we finally went to trial, I had been detained for more than three years. I saw dozens upon dozens of detainees come and go from Fort Leavenworth during that time. The right to a speedy trial is . . . complicated. We'd had several false warnings, trial dates for which we prepared, only to have them postponed over and over again. In each instance, the government said it needed more time, and Colonel Denise Lind, the presiding judge, acceded to their requests. In June, however, she put her foot down.

The Howard County jail, a low-slung cement block of a detention center in Maryland, was near Fort Meade, where all the hearings and meetings for my court-martial took place; I lived there during the trial. I wasn't officially in solitary confinement at Howard County, but it felt that way: I was alone, separated from any other prisoners, a spectacle on display. Whenever I had to see a lawyer outside my prison, it involved a heavily armed SWAT team in a three-SUV convoy.

As the trial began, the courtroom was filled with press; older activists with shaggy beards and tie-dyed shirts; groups like Veterans for Peace, Iraq Veterans Against the War, and Occupy Wall Street; and the Chelsea Manning Support Network, a nonprofit organization that helped raise funds for my legal defense and subsequent appeals. Many of the activists in attendance were older—boomers with a lifelong, Vietnam-related commitment to pacifism. They gathered outside Fort Meade, in groups of fifteen or twenty, holding up signs with messages such as I SUPPORT MANNING, and cars going by would occasionally honk at them in support. I appreciated the sentiment, but inside the courtroom, they were loud in their civil disobedience, sometimes interrupting and slowing down the proceedings. I watched Judge Lind get more and more irritated, and worried it would turn her against me. At that moment, I was laser-focused on trying to win the court-martial: for me, this wasn't a great symbolic action, it was my life.

I told my father to stay away. He would just cause trouble, get me upset. My sister, my aunt, my cousins, and my mother all came to the trial. A forensics-based case isn't exactly thrilling to sit through, and I didn't feel that I needed emotional support in the courtroom; I needed to be able to focus. Besides, I knew that the press would hound them.

Colonel Lind was a tiny woman in her fifties who drank Diet Coke all day long and peered over a pair of bifocals at the papers on her desk. Lind was a centrist by nature, and her sympathy was with the government's case. She made this clear from the very beginning of the process, when she denied our motion to dismiss the charge of aiding the enemy. And she made it even more clear at the outset of the court-martial, when she granted a reduction of just 112 days from my future sentence, to make up for my cruel pretrial treatment—far less time than the nine months I'd served in solitary at Quantico and the fifty-nine days in Kuwait. I got the sense, from the questions she asked from the bench and the way she directed the proceedings, that Lind had come into it with her mind already made up.

After all the pretrial negotiation, I was facing twenty-two charges, mostly for circumventing security measures and improperly storing classified material, as well as theft and unauthorized disclosure under the Espionage Act. In February, I had entered guilty pleas for ten of those charges. These were the smaller charges related to the technical substance of my actions. I was willing to admit that I'd broken the law when I leaked the documents: we agreed with the government in substance on what happened. But that wasn't enough for the prosecution. They wanted to say that I'd acted with a malicious intent. That kind of intent would make the charges, and the consequences, far more serious.

I wasn't willing to say that I'd done something—treason—that I just hadn't. And so we were to fight for the outcome of the remaining twelve charges, which included the accusation that I'd deliberately aided an enemy (like al-Qaeda) by releasing what I had. If I was convicted of that, it carried a potential penalty of life in prison. It would also set a dangerous precedent, that anyone who gave national security information to be published online for the public to read was committing treason.

The lead prosecutor for the government, Major Ashden Fein, was, to put it bluntly, an enforcer. He was a Texan, thirty-four years old, just six years out of law school and twelve out of West Point, with a graying blond crew cut and broad shoulders. As the decorations on his uniform showed, he had more deployment experience than the average military lawyer: he'd served in Iraq himself. Fein was exceptionally aggressive in the pretrial negotiations. He'd studied under my lawyer David Coombs at the Judge Advocate General's Legal Center and School and was a theatrical litigator, with bombastic speech patterns. He would summon the full weight of his big stage presence at every opportunity.

One night, one or more people from the government's team entered the courthouse and accessed the court reporters' transcript machine. I found it deeply ironic that anyone on a team prosecuting me would improperly access a government employee's computer. After we alerted the court, the judge admonished the government.

Fein used the classification system as a weapon against me. He requested that the most limited amount of information possible be released publicly—with huge redactions in even that. My right to a fair public trial was annihilated, because of the very structure of my court-martial. Actually, it was effectively *two* courts-martial: there were the hearings that the world saw, and then there were the classified hearings, which were completely sealed. Not only did they present a fuller picture of what had led up to my decision, but just about everything that seemed broadly favorable to me appeared only in the classified evidence. Twenty-four of the witnesses the prosecution called gave their testimony, at least in part, under those conditions of secrecy. Judge Lind declared, "The overriding interest of protecting national security information from disclosure outweighs any danger of miscarriage of justice." In other words, the very thing that had helped me decide that leaking was worth it—the arbitrary, self-dealing, and occasionally manipulative use of the classification system—would be weaponized against me.

The control this gave the government verged on Kafkaesque. For example, the cables that I had leaked, which anyone in the world could call up via a simple Google search, remained classified. And each time a subject the government had deemed classified came up, the courtroom would be cleared and the whole building would be swept for bugs. Everyone had to turn off and hand in their phones. Then we could go back in. The reporters, already frustrated at being shut out of the classified portions, began to get nearly as exasperated as I was with the theater of the prosecution. Most of the evidence in the early stages was less about the content of my work as an analyst—much of which *is* classified, and justly so—than it was about the claims of damage that I supposedly did to American interests abroad, which was not classified. But the court was emptied for discussion of that, too.

The only people who ever heard, and probably the only people who ever will hear, the full version of my time and my work in Iraq are my lawyers and the government psychologists and psychiatrists who interviewed me in the wake of my arrest. In the press, the government downplayed my level of access, probably because it would have looked worse for the army; most people without deep knowledge of the military or clandestine services seemed to assume that a private could only know *so* much, when in fact lower-level analysts—whose job it is to filter, to prepare advisory reports—have in some ways broader, deeper, more specialized knowledge than people farther up the chain, who need to operate in the realm of headlines and takeaways and big-picture thinking. The government argued that what I did was dump information, but in fact it was a selective disclosure. There was a lot that I saw and had access to that I didn't reveal, and will never reveal. A true accounting of what kinds of classified information I handled—one I still can't give because I would go back to prison yet again if I did—would add crucial context. What I saw helped me make the decision to disclose.

On June 5, 2013, day three of my trial, one of the biggest news stories of this century hit. Edward Snowden, a government contractor for Booz Allen Hamilton, had sent classified NSA documents to reporters at *The Guardian* and *The Washington Post*. The Snowden leak showed that the United States was running a global surveillance operation in partnership with governments around the world. Most alarming to readers of the news in the United States was the revelation that, via a top-secret program called PRISM, the government was spying on American citizens, and tech and telecommunications companies were allowing them virtually free rein. In internal slides, the NSA set out the goals of being able to "Collect It All," "Know It All," and "Exploit It All."

My reaction to this news was complicated. I support Ed generally, but on a personal level, the timing was difficult for me. It sucked all the air out of my defense. Virtually all of the press packed up and left, and I couldn't blame them. This was a huge, important story on their beat. And while public opinion had been shifting toward our side since my arrest, all of a sudden, they could claim me as the *bad* leaker, the one in jail, the one who couldn't give an interview, the one with the supposed personal issues. Ed was the hero. I had been arrested before I could get my narrative, my side of the story, out there, and now my second chance at doing that had been bumped off the front page.

The judge addressed the Snowden leaks on the record. She announced that coverage of his leaks would in no way affect her ability to adjudicate the case. I believe that to be untrue: the government was unable to go after him, since he'd fled to Russia. And so I became a captive scapegoat. My court-martial offered the government a chance to send leakers a message at a crucial time.

The government made its case first, and chose an interesting method of going after me. They highlighted my strong record as an analyst and the specialization of my training, and then flipped around and wondered how I could have betrayed all of the trust that was placed in me. Their case downplayed my sexuality and gender dysphoria, I suspect in part because talking about sexuality and gender would have highlighted just how the constraints of Don't Ask, Don't Tell—which had been repealed in late 2010, just months after my arrest—could have huge, negative ramifications.

There was nothing I wanted more than to testify, to explain what I had done and why. I wanted the platform. But doing so would have meant going outside the rules: the prosecution had filed a motion that barred me from explaining my intent, on the grounds that intent wasn't relevant to the court-martial, and thus should be kept out of evidence.

I wanted to defy this, to try to speak my piece. I needed people to hear my voice. And if the judge shut me down, the world would watch it happen. David strongly recommended against it. If I insisted on testifying, I would be subject to brutal cross-examination. Besides, he said, there was nothing I could say that wasn't already in the evidence we were planning to bring, and most of what I wanted to say would be expressed by other witnesses. The testimony of a corroborating witness will always carry more strength than that of the defendant, who has skin in the game. I acquiesced.

During the trial, my only emotional releases were exercise and food. David would bring in burgers and pizza for me. It was the good stuff, which I hadn't tasted in years at this point. It tasted like freedom. I read all the papers, even though we got them a day late in prison. I was also interested in finding out how Early Bird—a now-defunct DOD aggregation service that rounded up the most relevant news for the military and national security communities—was portraying the proceedings.

The government did its best to keep a tight lid on the trial: transcripts weren't released, and recordings of any kind weren't allowed. *The Guardian* had a thorough live blog, by Ed Pilkington and Alexa O'Brien. David had successfully prevailed upon the court to allow him to publish redacted defense motions on his personal blog, which also served as a source for reporters.

But what I was most concerned about was how the bigger outlets, the ones that actually shaped how the public responded to me—cable news, *The New York Times*, *The Washington Post*—were presenting the case. Would they just take the military's line and assume that there had been meaningful damages as a result of the leak? Would they cover the trial—witness after witness, expert after expert—by presenting as hard facts hypotheticals about what the government feared *might* happen, rather than reporting what had actually happened?

My legal team worked hard to build relationships with the press. I cared about the *Times* most of all. Its coverage was, I thought, mostly evenhanded. Charlie Savage, a national security reporter assigned to the trial, was someone whose work I particularly admired. He had won a Pulitzer Prize for his coverage of the Bush administration's use of executive power, and had aggressively covered the ways in which the Obama administration calcified into permanence so many post-9/11 methods of surveillance and detention. (He later wrote the book *Power Wars* about that subject.) Charlie didn't just take what the government said at face value, but pushed beyond what he was being told in order to describe the truth.

The case proceeded at a snail's pace, in part because Major Fein needed to consult with a retinue of lawyers representing various agencies before giving his reply to any of the judge's questions. The prosecution's large team of consultants took up approximately half of the courtroom. After each question, they'd all huddle in the corner, discussing their response for two or three minutes. The pace was excruciating.

Many of my former colleagues testified. Seeing the people I'd served with made it feel as if no time had passed since I'd been in Iraq. Other colleagues refused to cooperate with the investigation. They lawyered up and declined to speak. The ones who did go on the record were honest and defended me, a testament to the loyalty and professionalism of our field. Some of those witnesses came to visit me once they finished their testimony. We couldn't talk about the case itself, but they'd ask me how I was doing, and we'd just shoot the shit.

The Admin was the major exception. On the stand, time and time again, she would start with the facts, and then things would get weird. Her stories contradicted both themselves and what other witnesses had said. Coombs was able to destroy her in cross-examination, tangling her in the details.

One incident she described happened in a room where, conveniently, just the two of us were talking, so there was no one to contradict her version of the story except me. She'd asked me what the flag meant to me, and I had replied with a constitutionally based skeptic's argument: *I have no loyalty to a flag, that's just a symbol. It's not why I signed up. What matters to me is protecting my comrades.* I was loyal to people, not to propaganda.

That part of her story was true. But she then claimed this was just the beginning of an anti-American, disloyal rant. That I had gone on to say that I hated the flag, and that I began talking about my hatred of the flag all the time. She claimed that she suspected me of being a spy, and had reported that suspicion multiple times.

That was not just outlandish, it was easy to disprove. Over and over,

Coombs asked witnesses upon cross-examination if they had heard me make anti-American statements, or if anyone had raised concerns about that to them, and each time the answer was a clear and simple *no*.

What made it most embarrassing for her, and the prosecution, was that the Admin's initial pretrial statement had been factual. She didn't bring up the allegations of disloyalty until the full extent of the investigation (with the charge of "aiding the enemy") had hit the news. The government latched on to her story, which suited their case. In what turned out to be a tactical error, they made her into the star witness of my alleged traitorousness.

Yochai Benkler, a lawyer and digital-network theorist at Harvard, took the stand and explained that in an era of decentralized media, online activist groups were filling the new role of getting information to the public. This development wasn't in the government's interest, of course; while the government could lean on newspapers and trade favors, "it's very hard to suppress information once it's on [the web] . . . So in order to prevent this distributed leaking, it's necessary to increase the fear, as it were, or the constraint on potential leakers." He also pointed out that until my leaks were published, the Pentagon effectively considered WikiLeaks a journalistic outlet, and that the most respected newspapers and magazines around the world—*The New York Times, The Guardian, Der Spiegel*—had coordinated directly to publish the war logs.

Fein tried to make it seem like I'd started hunting around explicitly on behalf of WikiLeaks as soon as I got to Iraq. He pointed to a list they'd posted of their "Most Wanted Leaks" for 2009, and tried to claim that I'd been looking for the Garani video in November, just two weeks after I'd gotten to Iraq. But this backfired on him, too—first of all, we had evidence that I hadn't uploaded the Garani video until the spring of 2010. Second, the video wasn't even on the most-wanted list. Third, the vast majority of things I'd posted weren't on it, either. (Coombs said that this was as if I'd showed up at a wedding with a gift that neither the bride nor groom wanted.)

We were surprised, in fact, at how well the court-martial went. Other than the Admin, the government didn't manage to get any witnesses to disparage me. The forensic evidence lined up with my story as I'd told it, of course, and could not be made to mesh with the prosecution's conspiratorial narrative. But even things that were factually in our favor sometimes went against us. The prosecution was particularly focused on the disclosures related to Guantánamo, trying mightily to argue that suspected terrorists might look at the detainee assessment briefs and learn something important about our strategy. Not so, said Colonel Morris Davis, who'd been a prosecutor at the U.S. detention facility from 2005 to 2007. In his opinion, the information contained in those briefs was not specific enough to be of use to terrorists. It was like reading "baseball cards," he said. "Other than causing embarrassment to the country that it was released, I don't see the enemy could gain anything of value from reading the detainee assessment," he said. "If you are trying to gain some kind of strategic tactical advantage, the detainee assessment brief is not the place to get it." Cassius Hall, who worked for the U.S. Army Intelligence and Security Command, said that more than 60 percent of what was contained in the SIGACTs was already in the public domain. The prosecution simply could not prove that my disclosures had risked anything but the exposure of America's own inflated self-image. Still, the prosecution's narrative seemed to be holding sway.

After a month and eighty witnesses, the prosecution rested its case. Next, Coombs led my defense. We agreed with the government's own investigators on the facts of the case and what the computer forensic evidence meant. They'd conducted a massive investigation, and we weren't disputing the findings. That agreement became the strongest aspect of our defense. We could then focus on disproving the malicious intent that the government was accusing me of, which—unlike the rest of the case—had no concrete evidence backing it up. They had a conclusion, but nothing to prove it. The whole thing was insinuation, and as a result, the government's own investigators became our strongest witnesses. We used them to show that the prosecution was extrapolating way beyond what the forensics actually showed. During closing statements, at the end of July, Major Fein spoke for most of the day. He characterized me as a "traitor," which I continue to reject. "These are not the words of a humanist," he said, referring to my description of the SIGACTs as "beautiful and horrifying." (In Iraq, I wore a dog tag that described my religion as "humanist.") "These are the words of an anarchist." (An innocuous characterization, even a downright badge of honor.) He accused me of seeking "notoriety." Coombs, in his closing, demonstrated how arbitrarily the government classified and declassified information, and how cavalier it was with the classified information in its care. He set forth how frequently the network crashed, forcing us all to burn backup CDs, how it was common practice for us to watch movies and TV or download our own software onto official computers. He outlined all the ways in which the army had created the conditions for me to grow alarmed about what the military and State Department were doing, as well as just how absurdly insecure the network was.

In his closing arguments, Coombs showed the now infamous video of the 2007 helicopter attack that killed the two Reuters reporters. He called me "a young, naïve, but good-intentioned soldier who had human life and . . . humanist beliefs central to [her] decisions, whose sole focus was, 'Maybe I just can make a difference, maybe make a change.'"

"Guilty," read Judge Lind. "Guilty, guilty." She went down the sheet of charges, repeating the word for seventeen of those twenty-two charges, six of which fell under the Espionage Act. The severity of my sentence and the fact that I had spent years in prison before being convicted for unauthorized disclosure under the Espionage Act were unprecedented. After all, I'd disclosed information to the public rather than spying. A precedent now existed; a chill had been created.

I avoided life in prison only because the judge rejected the government's most extreme, ridiculous—and, for me, dangerous—gambit: the charge of giving information to an enemy. I was not guilty of treason, in other words. Lind also declared me not guilty of having leaked the Garani video, siding with my timeline over the government's on the disclosures.

Then there was the sentencing portion of the trial. This was the most tense, fraught phase yet. Rather than reconstructing the actions I'd taken, it focused on the mindset that had brought me to the point of acting. Judge Lind had limited discussion of my motivations during the main portion of the court-martial; now, they were the heart of the matter. Sentencing, in military court, is almost its own mini-trial; the military code doesn't have strict sentencing guidelines, so each side must again make a case about degree of wrongdoing and severity of punishment.

The witnesses my team called were meant to show my state of mind in the lead-up to my action. In particular, they wanted to show that I had been pro-military—that I was a disillusioned person, not someone who had never believed in the aims of the organization I was joining. One witness was Lauren McNamara, previously known to me online as Zinnia Jones. She read from those instant messages we had sent each other in 2009, while I was at Fort Drum. She testified that I "was concerned with saving the lives of families in foreign countries . . . and [the] soldiers themselves and making sure they got home safe." She affirmed that I "considered human life to be valuable above all." The prosecution, upon cross-examination, tried to cast my involvement in activism as a bad thing. They had her read something I'd IM'd before even going to Iraq, trying to show that my belief in direct action meant I'd been determined to do something dangerous. "Activism is fun," I'd typed late one night. "It doesn't do much good unless you get hurt, however."

Coombs explained that I was an idealist, that I'd done what I had because I believed it to be in the public interest. He reminded Lind that I had been just twenty-two, and that I had believed no one in the American public could support the kind of war that I myself had been shocked to see. An army therapist who had treated me was brought to the stand, explaining that I couldn't have sought meaningful therapeutic help for any of my problems, given Don't Ask, Don't Tell. He explained, carefully, how this supposed policy of quiet tolerance had ended up leaving me isolated, abandoned, without a network of confidants, how a "hypermasculine" environment had made affirming my gender impossible, giving rise to all kinds of ancillary stresses. My sister, who had visited me in jail several times before my trial, took the stand and spoke about the difficulty of my childhood, my mother's alcoholism, and the way it had shaped the contours of my universe.

Coombs also sought to show that my unit had been improperly run. Several witnesses criticized Master Sergeant Adkins as careless toward information security. That, the defense implied, had made it easy for me to burn a disc containing thousands of restricted documents.

Adkins was later demoted, as a consequence of his role in this saga—a role that was in fact principled and just, and more or less unrelated to my disclosures. He had declined to follow Don't Ask, Don't Tell and report to his superior the picture I had sent to him in which I was presenting as a woman. He had believed my work in the already understaffed department was too vital. Maybe he also recognized the army's obsolete, homophobic, transphobic policies for the damaging baggage they were.

During sentencing, the prosecution attempted to show that I was a narcissist with a superiority complex. This backfired at least once, when a witness (an army psychologist who'd treated me in Iraq) was asked about the time I had described other soldiers as "ignorant rednecks." The witness replied that he, too, had called his fellow marines rednecks. The courtroom cracked up. The prosecution also lasered in on proving that I had caused harm to the United States' standing and diplomatic interests abroad. Most of the prosecution's argument about measurable damages, however, happened when the courtroom was cleared. Four witnesses testified exclusively there, two about what the disclosures had meant for our relationship with Pakistan. In the public part of the court-martial, Patrick Kennedy, a State Department official, said that the leaks had a "chilling effect" on "frank discussions." Robert Carr, who had chaired a Defense Intelligence Agency task force meant to assess potential damage from the leaks, testified for Fein that "folks might choose not to talk to us anymore because the information that came out could be detrimental to their livelihood." But on cross-examination, he couldn't name a single specific instance in which this had happened. He tried to connect my disclosures to the death of an Afghani at the hands of the Taliban, but the man who died hadn't appeared at all in the diplomatic cables, and Lind ordered this part of the statement removed from the testimony.

Another witness, Commander Youssef Aboul-Enein, part of the Pentagon's Joint Intelligence Task Force for Combating Terrorism and a military advisor to the George W. Bush administration during the initial invasions of Iraq and Afghanistan, argued that the SIGACTs' evidence that the United States had killed civilians would help America's enemies with fundraising and recruitment. He could point to just two instances in which the terrorist organization had used anything obtained from the SIGACTs, though: once in 2010, in its English-language recruitment magazine *Inspire*, and in a video the following year by Adam Gadahn, an American who'd joined al-Qaeda and become a spokesperson. On cross-examination, Aboul-Enein said that while the SIGACTs might reveal a pattern of U.S. military activity, al-Qaeda hadn't had any tactical victories as a result of my disclosures. Once again, the narrative was set forth: nothing bad has actually happened—but it might have. I wanted to scream. People on the ground in Iraq and Afghanistan could see the locations of U.S. military bases and convoy routes. They didn't need to look at documents online. Yet the government was so afraid of these disclosures—afraid of the global public learning true information about how our conduct abroad stood in stark contrast to our own stated principles.

My lawyers wanted me to make a statement apologizing to the government for the damage that I'd done. They thought this would help me get less jail time. It got heated, and they said it was in my own best interest. But I saw it as admitting to damages I hadn't caused.

We went back and forth over what I would say, arguing for hours. I drafted my own statement that I wanted to read, in which I explained why I'd done what I did, and accepted responsibility for my actions and whatever consequences might result from those actions—but didn't admit to having caused damage. In the end, though, I listened to the lawyers. Here is what I read: "I'm sorry that my actions hurt people. I'm sorry that I hurt the United States. I look back at my decisions," I said, facing Colonel Lind, "and wonder how on earth could I, a junior analyst, possibly believe I could change the world for the better over the decisions of those with the proper authority."

I still believe that this statement hurt me. The prevailing news story became that I had acknowledged damage was caused. The organizations and protesters that had done so much to support me wanted me to be a prisoner of conscience, and if you admit to having caused damages, you're not a prisoner of conscience.

By the conclusion of sentencing, I felt devoid of emotions. I had ceased to allow myself to feel hope. When the judge read the thirty-five-year sentence she was meting out, along with dishonorable discharge and forfeiture of all my pay, I wasn't upset so much as numb. I didn't cry. It had been more than three years, and this court-martial had become my life. I couldn't imagine anything other than prison, and that's what my life would be for the foreseeable future. A life without freedom until I was in my fifties, a life doubly restricted, an outcome impossibly cruel and unusual, because I would be forced to live as a man.

The protesters sitting behind me began to yell and jeer. The government was prepared; security escorts instantly whisked me and David out of the courtroom and into a side vestibule and kept us there until they could clear the courtroom.

"Look, it's over," I said. David began to cry. He had urged me to trust the system, he said, and it had failed me. "It's all right," I told him. "It's all right." I felt a strange sense of relief. At least now I had numbers. A finite number of years to count down, to turn over in my head when I couldn't sleep. If you get LWOP—life without parole—you don't have that rosary bead to count. With numbers, you'll get parole eventually. Thirty-five years was a long time, but it wasn't life.

16.

If I was going to be confined for years, I needed to liberate myself from some self-imposed constraints. There was no reason anymore to play along with masculinity, and every reason to finally take the opportunity to be me. At the Leavenworth County Courthouse, immediately after the trial, I legally changed my name to Chelsea Elizabeth Manning.

I had decided to come out as trans a couple of weeks before the end of the court-martial. My gender identity had become a very public issue, and I was determined to take back control of it. My lawyers felt that coming out during the trial would compromise the case itself, undermining our argument and distracting the press from the narrative we were trying to tell. (Both the world and the court system were transphobic.) But we were past that worry. So I made a statement: *Here's who I really am. I want the law to recognize it.* Breanna, a name I'd tried out before, felt wrong. I'd played under the name Chelsea in video games a decade before, and it was a neighborhood in Manhattan full of dance clubs where queer people could feel totally at home and normal and welcome. (Now, of course, the neighborhood is completely unrecognizable.)

I gave a statement to David, who sent it to the *Today* show for the anchors to read on the air. "I am Chelsea Manning. I am female. Given the way that I feel, and have felt since childhood, I want to begin hormone therapy as soon as possible. I hope that you will support me in this transition." (The statement read on air was a little different from the one I'd written; David had accidentally subbed in "female" for "a woman.") It wasn't until several days later that I understood just what a big story this became. I thought David was exaggerating when he told me that—and then the mail started arriving. A deluge of it, full of lovely supportive messages, many from people in the trans community, who poured out their own life stories to me.

I went from the clerk's office to intake at the prison. I was taking my first steps into the confinement where I assumed I would spend the next three and a half decades, but I was doing it as myself.

Prison was like a small town, four hundred people with nothing to do but hang around one another all the time. The first day back at Fort Leavenworth, in the new, long-term section where I'd be housed, I introduced myself as Chelsea. I said I was trans, and that I'd just come out recently. But many people already knew about it. They'd seen the news. Not everybody respected it at first. Some guards and inmates were truly assholes, but then again, we had all been raised in the same casually transphobic culture. And I hadn't earned their trust yet.

This part of Fort Leavenworth housed permanent residents who were figuring out how to live together; it was not a temporary jail where everyone was still swaggering and posturing and uncertain. Soon after I arrived, an inmate grabbed me and pulled me aside. The guard shrugged and told me to go talk to him. This was the beginning of the indoctrination process. The inmate told me that everyone knew who I was, but they didn't care. It wouldn't be a subject of discussion. He gave me a rundown of the housing unit and the rules for prison: *This is who gets what gym equipment and when. Here's the right table for you to sit at, here's the right hallway. No snitching, of course, but also no dry snitching—asking a question that draws attention to something against the rules, or mentioning something within earshot of a cop. Oh, and guards get called cops, because that's what they are. The real policing is self-policing by inmates.* He assigned someone to be my escort for the next day, to make sure the rules had sunk in.

Somehow, supposedly just by accident, nearly all the white prisoners end up in one section of a housing unit, all the black guys in another, the Latinx in a third. The shared electric kettle, which we used to make coffee and warm Kool-Aid, was where most of the interactions among the groups took place. There were elaborate rules around who got to use the kettle and when, so it became a hub for the exchange of information and gossip. It was our church, school, office, and bar.

Life settled into a routine. Often, I skipped breakfast in favor of sleep; this wasn't like pretrial confinement, where they dragged you out for chow. I did manage to get up on Sundays, when there were omelets made with real eggs, not the fake stuff or stale muffins. Food and sleep were among our only pleasures, and they were allowed in prison. The menu comforted me.

I became addicted to cardio—my HIIT workouts on the indoor rec days, and running on the outdoor days. There were other runners, but they cycled in and out, and ran in groups arranged by pace. I mostly ran alone. I didn't like to talk; I didn't want to think. I wanted the euphoria, the runner's high. If I wasn't sprinting, I'd put on headphones and listen to pop with as much thrumming beat as I could get on the Kansas City FM stations. I'd circle the track faster and faster until my mind went blank. I'd count in a rhythm: 1, 2, 3, 4, 1, 2, 3, 4. Notice my breathing, in and out. I'd look at the cloud formations over the flat horizon, measure the time by the sinking sun. When it was finally dark, it was time to go back in, to remember everything I'd been trying to numb away. I'd finish with one last sprint as hard as I could, a finale that got me as tired as possible. I'd sink into the freedom of sleep the minute I hit my pillow.

Compelling the prison, and the military, to actually treat me as a woman was difficult. I filed the first necessary administrative request the moment I was processed into Fort Leavenworth after my court-martial, which meant entering into another protracted legal battle. Before my court-martial had even begun, I'd decided to research how inmates in the federal prison system had managed to get appropriate treatment while incarcerated, so I could then develop a similar case for the military's parallel system. The argument, which had been upheld under the Eighth Amendment's ban on cruel and unusual punishment, was that getting hormone treatment was, for a trans person, a medical necessity. I told David Coombs about my plan; he didn't think it would be possible, since it had never been done in the military. And so I presented him with a memorandum of law that I'd written up, with my theory of how we could actually make it happen.

The first thing that I had to do was show that I had a diagnosis of gender dysphoria. The government had already done some of that work: the psychologist who had evaluated me for the trial had confirmed my dysphoria. What we needed was for the government to acknowledge that, so I had deliberately asked David to bring it up in the court-martial, which would make it re-admissible in another court as fact, without us having to line up a whole set of witnesses and prove it all over again.

After I came out publicly as trans in 2013, David referred me to the ACLU. Chase Strangio, my next lawyer, joined the team. Chase is also trans, and quickly became not just my lawyer but a role model. (He has since successfully argued in front of the Supreme Court for a landmark ruling that enshrined workplace protections for the queer community.) Over the years of my sentence, we became true friends. He'd call every couple of weeks and of course we'd talk about my case, but also about politics, his life. I'd tell him what was happening to me in prison, how I was feeling, and who was messing with me. He listened. He cared.

My legal team had sent a letter to the Pentagon and the army asking that I get treatment for gender dysphoria, which would include hormone therapy and the freedom to follow female grooming standards. But the Pentagon did not allow me those things, and formally replied that the military did not "provide hormone therapy or sex re-assignment surgery for gender identity disorder."

Chase made a few adjustments to the argument I'd laid out, most importantly changing the jurisdiction: he felt that pursuing our case in the federal courts first, before the military courts, would help us. Federal judges tend to feel more pressure from the public, and trans rights were by then becoming more visible. That wasn't something I could ever have predicted. Some trans-rights advocates saw my public statement that I was trans as a turning point, one that helped push the issue even further into the public consciousness. Whether that's true or not, I now have a lot of friends who came out directly in the wake of my own public affirmation.

The federal case law was solid. This was clearly an Eighth Amendment violation—a blanket denial of medically necessary care, in direct contravention of the medical advice of multiple doctors. The government's purported rationale—that providing me with hormone replacement therapy (HRT) would in some manner compromise the "safety and security" of the prison—was nonsense. The facts were undisputed, and the law was clear, but bringing the case itself hinged on the long and tedious "exhaustion of administrative remedies." I would have to go on the fool's errand of asking the military correctional system for medically necessary clinical care that I already had a right to, and then go through the entire process, all the way from grievance (a complaint) to multiple appeals, before I was even allowed to plead my case to a court.

The government and judicial system had generally never ruled in my favor. I had little confidence the courts would come through, even if the moral imperative seemed clear.

And the stakes felt even higher than my court-martial. It wasn't just about preserving my own life, but about establishing a precedent that would actually help other people make it through theirs. I wanted the government to know I was uncontrollable, uncowed, capable of direct action.

The law library quickly became my favorite place in the prison. I think I spent more time there than the people who actually worked in it. I filed FOIA requests, not just related to my own case, but also to things in the news that I wanted to know more about, like the Insider Threat Program, a wide-ranging surveillance program through which the government targeted its own employees. (I passed information from the training materials I obtained via FOIA to Ed Pilkington of *The Guardian*, who used it in a story.) I filed for information about other inmates' cases, and about the way the military used quotas to shape the parole process unfairly. I discovered, via FOIA, that Fort Leavenworth, violating its own code, wasn't issuing people verbal warnings before they went to formal punishments, such as solitary confinement (known as the special housing unit, or SHU), and I passed the intelligence on to the writers of the internal prison newsletter. Suddenly, the policy of verbal warnings was actually followed. My belief was reaffirmed: information is power, and it is power that should be held by everyone.

I became a jailhouse lawyer, giving advice to other prisoners who were scheduled to go before the administrative board for appeals. I'd type them scripts for cross-examination, or help them write a declaration that they could submit in lieu of an improvised verbal statement. Sometimes they'd pay me with prison currency: goods from the dining hall, contraband they'd somehow acquired. I'd become an expert in the ways the law could be used against prisoners; I wanted to use that knowledge. Keeping people out of the SHU was my top priority. I wanted that thing to be burned.

For the first year I was in prison, my official job was working in the dining facility, handling the 3:00 a.m. breakfast shifts. The hours were more difficult than Iraq, and almost as bad as the ones at Starbucks, which had changed daily. I started out scrubbing pots and pans—the most miserable, sweaty job in the whole prison, ending every day covered in dirty dishwater and food waste—and worked my way up through the hierarchy to filling food trays to be taken over to the inmates in the SHU, which was much easier and far less grimy.

No one got to leave until everyone's work was done. The sooner we finished, the sooner we got to go back to sleep, after all. I'd yell, almost like a drill sergeant, about how this was a collective effort and we all needed to pull our weight. No one wanted to look bad in front of everyone else for wimping out. I got in my first fight this way. A tall, skinny white guy from my own section just refused to work. He told me I was spending more time organizing people and bossing them around than doing the work myself. Then he added a crude insult. I saw red. "If you have a problem with me, and with anyone else who just wants to go back to their cell," I said, "let's work it out."

I told him to meet me at the freezer, where prisoners "worked it out" hidden from security cameras.

After that, some people started to call me La Jefa—the boss. They started addressing me using feminine pronouns—a sign of real respect. It was not lost on me that I was respected as a woman only after I had engaged in some archetypically masculine bullshit.

I despised visiting the barbershop. We had to go every two weeks to keep that close institutional crop. I hated the sound of the buzzing razor, the sight of those piles of hair. It meant that once more I'd be a boy, literally cut back with every quarter inch of shearing to a version of myself I hated, over and over and over again. I'd try to miss my appointments, but the guards were strict about attendance.

The barbers, on the other hand, were kind. They were prisoners, too, though they'd been trained as cosmetologists for their prison work. They could see my pain. They could feel my body tense, sense how anxious the whole thing made me. I'd freak out every time and start telling the barber that I didn't want to do this, I couldn't bear it again. They went slow, talking me through it very carefully. "I know," they'd say gently. There was no judgment. They'd get me talking about something else, anything else.

Sometimes, they'd wash my hair, to make it feel more like a beauty appointment than a ritual shearing. And each of the barbers made sure, very carefully, that he left my hair at two inches every time—the longest length allowed. One barber asked if he could shape my eyebrows; he said he wanted the practice. And so from then on, he'd thread my brows into a feminine shape, a small thing that made me feel more like the person I knew I was. It touched me deeply.

I wasn't the only trans person in our housing unit. In late 2013, the dining facility was closed for renovation, and we ate in the gym. Everything was temporarily socially scrambled, our usual table arrangements thrown into chaos. There was a break from territoriality, the usual de facto segregation. A person from the Latinx group sat down next to me and began to talk quietly about my transness. "I feel the same way," they said. "I have these feelings, and I never got a chance to deal with them." Not long after, they were transferred to a medium-security facility in Texas. (Texas was a jurisdiction where prisoners couldn't legally change their names, which meant that a trans person couldn't do what I'd done in Kansas.)

Most of the prisoners now called me by feminine pronouns and used my last name or called me Chelsea. Even the transphobes at least largely respected me. But there was one guy—white, blond hair, glasses, lanky—who'd been convicted for murdering civilians. He came into the dining facility one day not long after he'd arrived and began needling me about my gender. If this guy thought he was doing something original that was going to cause some kind of fresh pain, he was extremely incorrect. Being an out trans person had quickly thickened my skin. I was surrounded by people who say the meanest possible things to you, so you learn to be twice as hard, and twice as ready to rip someone apart. I went straight back at him. *Look at you, you skinny-ass glasses-wearing little general. I wonder how many pencils you've broken today.* He was momentarily stunned. Everyone else reacted. *Oh, I hope you got a sterile dressing for that burn.* He was mortified. He had been taken down by a trans girl, and nobody let him forget it.

The other inmates were supportive of my pursuit of gender reassignment, not necessarily because they believed deeply in trans rights, but because compelling the government to allow me to take hormones was fighting back against the prison. A victory for me would be a victory for prisoners. Eventually, the prison allowed me to wear female underwear, but it was a concession so small it felt insulting. I wanted hormones—a fundamental change to my body and my biological workings—and they gave me a slightly different cut to a piece of cotton. It was as if they were making a mockery of my requests, of my pain. *Change your underwear, but don't change anything else, Manning.*

I jokingly called the prison hierarchy the Sacred Order of the Blue Plastic Chairs: there were four rows in the dining facility, and you could tell just how much power each person had by which row they sat in. I suppose the military mentality dies hard. Eventually, I moved up to the third row, where I had a role as a kind of enforcer. I worked to make sure people pulled their weight and generally stayed in line. When two people were having an issue—stealing, harassment, whatever—I'd conduct the informal investigation. I'd ask the who, what, where, when. I didn't care too much about why. I just needed to assess who was causing the problem, and quietly confront them.

The difficulty, though, is that we were living in a racially segregated totalitarian surveillance state, one designed to pit us against each other. The cops wanted nothing more than the high they got from throwing people in the SHU, and the promotions that came along with cracking down on inmates.

Chow was the activity around which the whole prison revolved. The sections took turns going first, with twenty minutes for each one to make it all the way through the line. The guards controlled the speed with which the units were called, and one day at lunch, shortly before a big inspection was set to take place, one of the guards decided to assert his power by slowing down the food line so that section three didn't get fed. Everyone flipped out, holding their empty trays, yelling bloody murder. This guard did the same thing at dinner, and the next day, again, at both lunch and dinner, until it became crystal clear that this was deliberate, someone acting on orders.

Meals were the only good thing we got every day, and the prison was fucking with them. It messed with our heads, created hostility between the sections, and generally tempted us to engage in behavior that would land us in the SHU. Prison is about control and dominance. On the second day of the crisis, the military police investigative unit (MPI) arrived. They're the guards who cultivate confidential informants. They sat back and watched the panic, waiting for someone to misbehave in an actionable way.

Fort Leavenworth had a prison inmate council, something like a student council for prisoners. After three days of this deliberate baiting, I went to the council with a plan. Following chow time, prisoners had the option of either going directly to their own housing unit or heading to the medical window to pick up medications. There was a rule that prisoners could always get Tylenol, no questions asked. I suggested that every single prisoner go to the window and ask for a dose, which would overload the line dramatically and slow down the whole cycle of the day. We would be fighting back, while still following the letter of the law. It would only work, though, if all eighteen housing units got on board.

By lunch the next day, everyone was in. Every twenty minutes, more people stood up and moved from the dining hall to the pill line, in unison. The line wrapped all the way around the prison. My unit was the last one, so I got to see the reaction in the dining hall. The guards were panicked. They called for reinforcements. Riot cops came in with their kneepads and shields, arrayed like storm troopers all around the line.

As the investigators walked toward me, I grabbed my forehead. "I have the worst headache of my life!" I said.

I was shocked. Both that it had worked and at the extremity of the response. The commander of the prison was there, as were what looked like civilian cops from the outside. I started to worry they'd crack down on me. I worried they had seen me organizing. I was sweating. I actually *did* then get the worst headache of my life. Finally, at 4:00 p.m., the last people in the line, including me, took their Tylenol.

That night, the prison called a lockdown. For dinner, we were served sack lunches in our cells. Some people were thrilled at the success of what we'd done, how we'd stood up to our captors, but a lot of other people were pissed. Yes, we'd avoided the SHU, but instead of solitary confinement, we'd gotten stuck with group confinement, which could be its own version of hell, too.

The next morning, they released the lockdown. At chow, the commandant of the facility stood watching us, flanked by his deputy and a large group of investigators. I was ready for the deliberate baiting of inmates to begin again, but instead, something wondrous happened. Chow proceeded exactly as it was supposed to.

17.

In prison, the house always wins. A week after the protest, just as things started to seem settled, a guard came up to me as I was walking out of chow and asked if I'd thrown a ketchup packet at him. I asked if he was accusing me of something; he said yes, that I had just assaulted him.

I put my hands up and told him I was asking for a lawyer. "Article Thirty-One, UCMJ." I recited the military version of the Fifth Amendment. I needed a lawyer if I was going to be accused of assault. I was now surrounded by a crowd of guards. I repeated my request for a lawyer.

Eventually, they dismissed me. I walked away, toward the medication window to get my Tylenol, feeling their eyes on my back. I thought it was over.

A few days later, I had forgotten about the whole thing. And then, without warning, as I walked back to my cell from lunch, they came for me. Two guards pulled me out of the housing unit and escorted me down the long hallways to the special housing unit, where I would stay pending investigation. Prison investigators searched my cell for hours, hunting for violations. They took pictures, went through all my personal items. They found a tube of toothpaste past the expiration date, which of course had been issued to me by the prison, and charged me, absurdly, with "medicine misuse."

I had the Caitlyn Jenner copy of *Vanity Fair*, acquired subject to the prison's own rules, which they tagged as contraband. They grabbed and removed my books, which included political theory, histories of political organizing, works on and by queer and trans people. They labeled those contraband, too. To all those charges, they added disorderly conduct, a charge they supported on the basis of my having asked for a lawyer. Putting my hands up was characterized as "flailing."

I was only in the SHU for one day, thanks to a disciplinary hearing before a board that could not help but recognize that these charges would have made Josef K.'s interrogators blush. But I got fifteen days of recreation time restriction. It was the first time I'd been in solitary since arriving in the long-term prison, though, and I sort of couldn't believe that, after all that I had suffered and avoided, a manufactured incident with a ketchup packet had landed me there.

But that one day in solitary was when I realized the prison administration didn't mind us fighting. They worked to entrench hostility and segregation, and didn't want us to recognize ourselves as a class with common interests. The scariest thing, to the prison administrators, was when we all worked together. It meant they were losing control.

In September 2014, Chase and the ACLU had filed a lawsuit on my behalf against the secretary of defense, Chuck Hagel, as well as other army officials, for failing to provide me with the medically necessary treatment. The Pentagon was, after all, the ultimate authority over how I, as a military person, was treated; also, Washington, D.C., where we filed, was a more favorable jurisdiction for a trans-rights battle than the district in Kansas where I was physically located. And the army's own doctors had diagnosed me with gender dysphoria four years earlier. I desperately needed hormones. We also filed a motion for a preliminary injunction; we wanted a temporary restraining order against the government. Rather than deal with another round of back-and-forth court motions and arguments, the government began to relent. In December 2014, I successfully demanded access to cosmetics. The Pentagon ultimately made the decision about whether I'd be allowed to use lipstick, a surreal moment. And yet it still felt like a humiliating compromise, a stopgap measure that didn't address the fundamental, underlying issue.

Finally, I was granted access to hormones. On February 16, 2015, after a few weeks of medical appointments, I walked up to the medication window and took my first doses of hormone treatment. I became the first person in the military prison system granted access to hormones, and among the first handful in the military at large: they had, a few months before, begun relaxing the official policy. Chuck Hagel had announced in November 2014 that he was stepping down from his post as secretary of defense. He had been openly hostile to me: After I'd come out, Hagel continued to use my deadname. He consistently used masculine pronouns to refer to me. I don't think it's an accident that military trans rights didn't move forward until he was on his way out from that job. Maybe the Pentagon relented in large part because public opinion was beginning to shift toward demanding trans rights, and it would have been a public affairs nightmare if the story got out that the government was compelling me to live as a man against its own doctors' recommendations.

It also wasn't the end of my legal battle over my gender identity. The military wouldn't let me grow my hair; we repeatedly and formally requested that I be allowed this important aspect of female grooming, and were repeatedly denied.

Hormone therapy, as exciting as it was, weakened years of carefully constructed emotional defenses. The first month is simply a reduction of testosterone. Your sex drive decreases, your muscle mass shrinks. As the weeks go by, slowly estrogen is added. The rush of new chemicals in my body unlocked more feelings, and I slipped into despair. I had never been depressed without also having testosterone to act as a chemical defense mechanism. It was wearying. And then, about three months in, the balance of hormones switched. It was worse than wearying. The familiar endocrine system that for my entire life had regulated my emotions had been dismantled, and it had not yet been replaced by anything coherent.

Everything intensified. Friendships brought joy more vivid and deep—but equally, every pain cut through me. I'd cry for days and days, for the first time in my life. I still got angry, too: I'd go to the woodshop, take a mallet, and just beat the shit out of chunks of wood for an hour at a time.

Connections with people were more intense, as was their absence. Vulnerability lived on my skin. This is widely said to be the hardest phase of transitioning, and certainly it was for me. I had a hard time talking to people honestly about it. I did not feel close enough to anyone to unfold this sorrow before them.

Certainly not to a therapist, who would just report anything I said under the guise of "safety and security," which in a prison can easily function as an excuse to betray patient confidentiality. I hated weekly group therapy: rather than address real problems in our lives, we were given workbooks meant to refashion us into smart, law-abiding members of society. We had to sit and discuss how people had made incorrect decisions, without any acknowledgment of how the system was stacked against certain people.

But I did have support outside the prison walls. That spring, just as I was at my most desperate for someone to talk to, someone put me in touch with Annie Danger, a trans woman and tattoo artist in San Francisco. Annie was a lifeline. We'd talk about the politics of transitioning, how the language used by and about trans people kept changing, and why. We talked about the way trans people are treated. She was there for emotional support, too. I was in the middle of a wild depression: crying a lot, tired, wondering if the flood of emotions would ever end, ruminating on my untenable situation. It was hard to even get up in the morning. This is the part no one ever tells you about, Annie reassured me. *Everyone* hits the wall at three months. Six more weeks, and I'd feel fine again, she promised.

There was, perhaps surprisingly, a queer culture inside the disciplinary barracks, and it was more robust than I might have imagined. The mere act of seeking one another out helped break down the boundaries of the prison's racialized grouping. We intuitively understood the possibility of a different, more inclusive set of organizing principles. On the other hand, many of the relationships we formed on the basis of that shared queer identity were superficial.

But before I started hormones, I could hardly stand to have someone look at me, let alone try to form meaningful connections; interactions that lightly skimmed the surface of social politeness were all I could handle.

With hormones, my ability to tolerate—and even desire—closer connection began to change right along with my body and my sense of it. My skin got softer. Freckles dappled my skin. The angles of my face softened. I began to speculate about intimacy. A few months later, with no change in my diet or my workout, my muscles softened to curves. I was experiencing what medical literature calls "redistribution of body fat." Eight months after I'd begun hormone therapy, people started to notice my shape, even through the baggy prison uniform. As I took shape physically, my mind and heart cleared. I formed closer connections with people, built friendships.

I was careful about my appearance. I wanted it to be immaculate. My uniform was always pressed, and I always had a fresh pair of Chucks from my aunt, who remembered my signature look. Fashion is a vital form of expression that broadcasts identity and puts power on display. I spent hours at the prison library studying fashion history, learning as much as I could about Alexander McQueen and Vivienne Westwood and punk high fashion, about the way Queen Elizabeth I used her ruff and solid colors and heavy jewelry to telegraph strength. I liked these visions of womanhood—tough, self-possessed, self-determining. I began to think about how I would dress when I got out: utility belts and dresses, combat boots, so I could signal that I would fight my own battles.

In some ways, military prison was the only place I ever fit in. This was a group of people who understood the institutions that had both shaped and ruined me. It was a system I was good at. I found solidarity there. Most of my friends preferred reading to watching television. We started discussion groups: history, politics, science.

I read many books in Fort Leavenworth (all told, during my years in jail and prison, I read more than one thousand) and subscribed to more than forty-five publications: *The New York Times*, *The Washington Post*, *The Economist*, *Scientific American*, *Skeptic* magazine. A sports magazine. Every single fashion magazine possible. I read adventure books by the boatload. I read Neal Stephenson and Haruki Murakami. I read tons of trans history—*Captive Genders: Trans Embodiment and the Prison Industrial Complex*, *Some Assembly Required: The Not-So-Secret Life of a Transgender Teen*, as many issues as I could find of *Transgender Studies Quarterly*.

Like many other prisoners, I read *The 48 Laws of Power*, by Robert Greene—but I rejected its worldview, its promotion of winner-take-all manipulation of the systems that try to manipulate us. Instead, the theories I found in Michelle Alexander's book *The New Jim Crow*, about the carceral system, resonated with me. That book was relatively difficult to get my hands on: the title was considered inflammatory, a threat to the discipline and order of prisons. I shared that book with as many people as I could. Same thing with the Ta-Nehisi Coates *Atlantic* cover story "The Case for Reparations," which was also frowned on by the mail room.

My dear friend Lisa Rein—who had worked on Creative Commons with Aaron Swartz and had originally contacted me in prison, out of the blue, to write a remembrance of him to be read at Aaron Swartz Day—began to catalog all the books I'd read, as an ongoing archive. It was sweet, and also in a funny way made me feel like some kind of bygone historical figure. That was difficult for me in prison: I had a sense that people were talking about me as if I were already dead. More often than not, people—my friends, the press—spoke about me in the past tense. I wasn't with the living anymore. My life was over; I was wiped out, written off, forgotten.

And so I began, often with Lisa's help, the deliberate process of figuring out how to still be a person in the wider world. More and more trans teenagers were writing me letters, and their support and clarity about their own identities overwhelmed me. I was used to getting letters from people who were older than me, pacifists in their fifties or sixties. It was harder for me to feel an immediate connection with them. But I recognized these kids. When I was growing up, there wasn't anyone I could see myself in, or connect with, or look up to. I had been like them, and I had ended up having a rough, fast life. It is hard to think about where I was when I was their age: totally alone. I wrote back to as many of them as possible. I wanted to be the person that I'd needed back then.

But I couldn't write as much as I wanted. It took me at least twenty minutes to write each letter. Paper was limited—one hundred sheets at a time—and I needed it for legal research, too. The internet, even accessed secondhand, seemed like a better way to be in touch with more of my supporters. At the conclusion of my court-martial, David Coombs's wife had created a Twitter account for me. I saw it as a way to respond to all the people writing to me, one that would get around the prison's restrictions on the amount of time I was allowed to write letters. For a long time, though, I couldn't get anyone to run the Twitter account for me. Even Courage to Resist didn't want to get involved. Then a public relations firm that did a lot of work for left-leaning causes reached out to me. They wanted to run my Twitter feed pro bono.

Christina DiPasquale, the employee assigned to my account, was incredible. The owner of the firm was less incredible, particularly with respect to his treatment of women, and Christina started a new firm in the wake of his sexual assault scandal. She took me along as a pro bono client. Lisa helped, too. She'd call me over the monitored phone line and read me highlights from that day's Twitter, catch me up on the memes and trending hashtags.

I got a lot of my ideas for how to run my Twitter account from case studies in the *Harvard Business Review*, which I subscribed to, and which had given me so much insight into how the world really works. Everything was hidden in plain sight in the pages of this magazine that many people would assume was dull. Despite my distaste for corporate capitalism, I understood the utility of certain concepts, and imagined myself building not just my own identity but a brand. It would be a radical brand, to be sure, that stood for transparency and against prejudice and government cover-ups. I wanted my mission and message to be clear, reliable, and consistent. The *HBR*'s case studies on social media strategies turned out to be an unparalleled resource. I learned that Denny's had managed, by getting weird on Twitter, to refashion itself from a blah breakfast chain into some kind of online millennial juggernaut. I realized the polished advertising strategies of the past one hundred years were no longer effective. What people actually paid attention to online was connection or emotion.

Emotion wasn't something I was lacking. I had *lots* I wanted to share. In fact, the difficulty was that Christina wasn't always available when I wanted to tweet something—whether it was my reactions to current events or feelings about letters that I'd received.

I also started writing for *The Guardian*, which contacted me after I started tweeting. I initially hesitated, however. *The New York Times* had also asked me to write an op-ed—a piece critical of Iraq war coverage—and the editors had diluted it until it didn't sound like me, and it didn't convey what I had to say. I worried that the same thing would happen at *The Guardian*—but it didn't. The first article was a successful experiment in how they would treat my tone and content. I wrote a piece that was aggressively critical of the government's way-too-statist strategy in the war against ISIS. I had watched ISIS start from its earliest seeds and knew about the important players.

The article did well, so when *The Guardian* asked me to do a monthly column, I took the opportunity. They were the opposite of the *Times*: my editor there pushed me to be more passionate, more direct with my emotions, to explain not just what I thought about an issue, but why I cared about it and what I knew about it from my personal experience. *More fire* was the note I got most often.

The logistics of getting my writing published were painful, and it put limits on how responsive I could be to current events. I'd have to physically mail it out, per the official rules of the prison, along with the proper paperwork. But the minute the letter was in the mailbox, I could call up Lisa or Christina and dictate it. They'd record, transcribe, and send it to my editor, who would send the edits back to Lisa: it was illegal for me to interact directly over the phone, without clearance, with a member of the media. So, as a workaround, Lisa would call me up and talk through edits as I wrote notes on the margins of my printed-out column, and then go back to the editor with my changes.

I got more involved with politics. I wrote a "Bill to Re-Establish the National Integrity and to Protect Freedom of Speech, and the Freedom of the Press," which I proposed on Twitter (via Lisa) and sent to members of Congress. It was meant to outlaw some of the most egregious ways that the Espionage Act and Computer Fraud and Abuse Act had been used against me, so that others wouldn't be put in such a bind for wanting to do the right thing. It also included fixes to the Freedom of Information Act, and would give stronger federal protections to journalists. It was a pipe dream and was treated as such.

Some of the people who wrote me letters in prison became the most important people in my life. Like Janus Rose, a tech and information security journalist just beginning to grapple with her trans identity, who sent me letters and cards from HOPE, the Hackers on Planet Earth conference, a biannual event where, each year after my incarceration, they had a booth for people to write to me. Those letters always meant a lot—it was my community, the hacker world, and so many of the friends whom I'd spent hours talking to online went to HOPE each year—but Janus's letters stood out because she felt a connection she couldn't explain. It's something a lot of trans people feel in the early days, before they even recognize their transness. When I'd felt it, I didn't have anyone to write to.

I also corresponded with Isis Agora Lovecruft, a nonbinary hacker and cryptographer who also happened to be an unabashed anarchist. Isis had admired and befriended Jacob Appelbaum, a WikiLeaks-affiliated programmer who was a towering figure in the Tor developer community. Isis came forward to say that Jake had betrayed that admiration and sexually assaulted them. The allegation became a giant controversy in the crypto and hacker community. Many people sided with Jake. I wrote to Isis, whom I'd never met, as soon as I heard the news. *I believe you*, I told them. *I've had very similar things happen to me. And I had the fear that nobody would believe me or nobody would listen to me.*

They wrote back, and we became such intimates that I think of them as family. Isis kept me up to speed with what was happening in the world of cryptography and cybersecurity; they sent me math books and cryptography papers. I loved the feeling of being part of the hacker community, even from prison.

18.

Sometimes I believed that I had everything I needed in prison. Books. Running. Access to hormones. Enough food to sustain me. Solidarity and fellowship. But I didn't, of course: I didn't have control over my life, didn't have freedom, and was treated by the prison guards as less than dirt. In order to survive, I tried to avoid dwelling on any of that, but by 2016, six years since I'd first been locked up, it had become increasingly clear that prison was corroding my sense of possibility and connection with the future. I began to sink into despair. Anger bubbled up more often.

On the Fourth of July weekend in 2016, I tried to kill myself. The Obama administration had just announced it was overturning the ban on trans soldiers in the military. The secret that had made life so difficult for me in the service wouldn't have needed to be a secret if this had been the law before; what would my life have been like? Would I have had an official support system? Would I have felt so much pain about who I was? I did not want anyone to have to endure what I had—the policy change was a net gain. But I couldn't help but be furious at the official confirmation of what I had long known: my suffering, and that of all trans soldiers before, was unnecessary and unjustifiable.

I'd already spent June in a blind, horrified, hurt rage over the shooting at the Pulse nightclub in Orlando. The only safe space I had left in my memory was the gay clubs, and someone had violently trespassed into my last remaining sanctuary. I couldn't even begin to imagine the anguish of the families and friends of the victims. That July weekend, I called everyone I knew, looking for someone to tell about my sadness, my desperation. No one picked up the phone. I felt more alone and hopeless than I had in that steel cage in Kuwait. It felt like I'd lost everyone I trusted or cared about.

When you're in that kind of mindset, you don't think, I'm suicidal. It's more like, I just want the pain to stop. The attempt was a serious one. I engineered a sophisticated device that I was certain would work. I woke up in the ambulance on the way to the hospital, mostly shocked, and deeply angry, that I had failed to end the pain.

When that summer ended, I was in a dark place. After the first week post-attempt, I was no longer imagining dying, but the world remained bleak. I stopped reading the news: both Donald Trump's steady march and the failures of the Clinton campaign depressed me. In April, my psychologist had given an official recommendation that as part of the medical treatment for my gender dysphoria, I needed access to bottom surgery. As the months went by, and no news came on the medical front, I became hyper-focused on completing my transition with gender-affirming surgery.

Time and time again, though, the DOD gave me the runaround. To drag out the process this long felt like another form of deliberate torture, another way of pushing me over the edge. The denial of gender-affirming care posed an existential threat to me, and they didn't care. The government might have been legally compelled to help me, but knowing how badly I wanted this, *needed* this, gave them the opportunity to punish me one more time.

In order to get the government to do what I needed, I carefully crafted a plan to box in the prison administration with a hunger strike. First, I read as much as I could about the history: Bobby Sands of the IRA. The Guantánamo detainees. And most important, there was Pelican Bay, the maximum-security California state prison where, in 2013, four inmates—alleged members of rival gangs—had launched a hunger strike from solitary confinement to protest the long-term use of the practice. On the first day of the strike, thirty thousand prisoners across the California state penal system refused food. On day three, eleven thousand were still going.

I got in touch, via friends, with some of the radical organizers who'd worked with the Pelican Bay inmates from the outside. They sent me explicit, detailed instructions on how to prepare for and execute a prison hunger strike. I decided I would time it to coincide with the national prison strike, which began on September 9, 2016, the forty-fifth anniversary of the Attica uprising.

I read every bit of case law I could about hunger strikes, particularly in military prisons. Ever since the Guantánamo detainees tried it, the government has claimed that force-feeding hunger strikers is a medical necessity, that keeping someone alive is the main priority, for (as always) "safety and security." That procedure calls for inserting a nasogastric tube into the prisoner's nose and down the throat, and pouring liquid food in. It's bloody and painful, and to get hunger strikers to stop, to break them—and maybe as extra punishment— sometimes the prison will insert the tube without lubricating it. I needed to take away the government's legal justification for doing this.

And so, as a final step, I smuggled in a notarized Do Not Resuscitate order. I didn't consult my lawyers. This wasn't exactly the course they'd have recommended, as supportive as the ACLU was of my larger battle. Everyone in my life would have tried to talk me out of what I wanted to do, and so I talked to almost no one about it.

I delivered the DNR along with a statement. I released it to the press at the same time I started the hunger strike, so there was no way the DOD could try to suppress it. "I need help," I wrote.

> I am not getting any. I have asked for help time and time again for six years and through five separate confinement locations. My request has only been ignored, delayed, mocked, given trinkets and lip service by the prison, the military, and this administration. I need help. I needed help earlier this year. I was driven to suicide by the lack of care for my gender dysphoria that I have been desperate for. I didn't get any. I still haven't gotten any. I needed help. Yet, instead I am now being punished for surviving my attempt. When I was a child, my father would beat me repeatedly for simply not being masculine enough. I was told to stop crying—to "suck it up." But, I couldn't stop crying. The pain just got worse and worse. Until finally, I just couldn't take the pain anymore. I needed help, but no one came then. No one is coming now. Today, I have decided that I am no longer going to be bullied by this prison—or by anyone within the U.S. government. I have asked for nothing but the dignity and respect—that I once actually believed would be provided for—afforded to any living human being. I do not believe that this should be dependent on any arbitrary factors—whether you are cisgender or transgender; service member or civilian; citizen or non-citizen. In response to virtually every request, I have been granted limited, if any, dignity and respect—just

more pain and anguish. I am no longer asking. Now, I am demanding. As of 12:01 am Central Daylight Time on September 9, 2016, and until I am given minimum standards of dignity, respect, and humanity, I shall—refuse to voluntarily cut or shorten my hair in any way; [refuse to] consume any food or drink voluntarily, except for water and currently prescribed medications; and [agree to] comply with all rules, regulations, laws, and orders that are not related to the two things I have mentioned. This is a peaceful act. I intend to keep it as peaceful and non-violent, on my end, as possible. Any physical harm that should come to me at the hands of military or civilian staff will be unnecessary and vindictive. I will not physically resist or in any way harm another person. I have also submitted a "do not resuscitate" letter that is effective immediately. This shall include any attempts to forcibly cut or shorten my hair or to forcibly feed me by any medical or pseudo-medical means. Until I am shown dignity and respect as a human again, I shall endure this pain before me. I am prepared for this mentally and emotionally. I expect that this ordeal will last for a long time. Quite possibly until my permanent incapacitation or death. I am ready for this. I need help. Please, give me help.

Day one was bad. I stayed in my cell, trying to be smart about when and how I sipped water. (Too much water, and you start to cramp.) Food was a close, visceral memory, one I couldn't shake. I just stayed in my cell, trying to preserve energy. The guards monitored me closely, watching and writing down everything I did. I think they hoped it was just a game I was playing for attention, but I had never been more resolute about anything in my life.

Day two was even worse. This was the low point. Every last bit of stored food energy had been used. I barely moved. But I knew to expect this. From my reading, I was sure that if I could make it to day three, I could get to the end.

On the third day, the prison administration took me out of the general population and put me under observation. They began to document me more carefully, photographing me and the changes in my body. They issued me multivitamins, too, which I took. I expected this. It was the official government hunger strike procedure, which is meant to break you, to isolate you, and to get inside your head. I was prepared. I let my mind go blank, and remained resolute.

After five days of not eating, I'd made my point. The government sent two civilians in suits from the Pentagon to Kansas to assure me, in person, that I was going to be getting surgery. There was even a date, they promised, but I wasn't allowed to know it, in case I cooked up an elaborate plot to escape while out of prison for surgery. Once again, they told me they were withholding the information for my own "safety and security," and that of the country.

Still, it was a promise, in writing. As soon as I got the news, I ate again. They served me chicken, rubbery and dry—but I couldn't eat it fast enough. Almost immediately, I was nauseous, bowled over and sick. My body didn't know what to do with the nutrition. It took two days to feel normal and to eat regularly again. I'd won, but was perpetually reminded that once again, the cost had been both steep and unnecessary. I released a statement to the press via the ACLU.

I am unendingly relieved that the military is finally doing the right thing. I applaud them for that. This is all that I wanted— for them to let me be me. But it is hard not to wonder why it has taken so long. Also, why were such drastic measures needed?

I didn't feel a sense of victory for long. It began to gnaw at me: When would it actually happen? *Would* it actually happen? That same week, I found out that I had lost a long series of appeals before the disciplinary board, which had occupied much of my energy before the hunger strike. I was once again going to solitary confinement, this time for two weeks. They claimed my attempt to kill myself in July had disrupted the safety and security of the prison. I had also supposedly resisted the guards who had come to my cell, although I'd been unresponsive when they'd found me. My charges were also multiplied by small infractions: I'd been caught with a contraband book, about the Anonymous collective, in my cell.

Whether in Kansas or Kuwait, solitary confinement is more or less the same. By then, I thought I knew how it would feel. I knew the cycle of detox from human contact, I knew how and when my brain would warp. But this time, as with the first time I'd found myself in solitary confinement, I couldn't take it. I couldn't imagine the next decades of my life in jail. It was just about as long as I'd even been alive. How many more times would I be sent to solitary? How well would I get to know these tiny rooms? How many times would bullshit charges be used to punish me? How soon would I forget why I even wanted freedom? When would I get my surgery? Or was that another lie, another psychological manipulation to get me to behave?

I tried to kill myself again in solitary. I'm ashamed of it, and at the time I was embarrassed almost immediately afterward by my attempt. I was hurt and deeply lonely. This time, it was more a gesture of anger than anything else. I was taken, while semiconscious, not out of solitary but to a different, more restricted area called Alpha Tier. There, I had even less human contact and was under even stricter surveillance by the prison.

I sank further into the valley of solitary—I felt alienated from my humanity. I was vividly self-aware, but equally dissociated. One night, nearly a week into my time on Alpha Tier, I heard a sudden noise. I could never have been prepared for what came next. I heard two corrections officers I didn't recognize, one of them a woman, begin to talk about a cyberattack on the East Coast and a tweet from a corrections officer that had mentioned me as a target, about new and draconian antiterrorist legislation that would prevent felons from running for office. They didn't sound like corrections officers, though. They talked like people from video games or movies, like bad actors reading a hackneyed script. I heard a pistol firing, and a fight. The woman offered to open the cell door, yelled at me to run, described a bag that contained a passport and firearms, clothing and wigs, told me about escape routes. She said I needed to shave, which I hadn't been able to do in solitary. I stayed put, ignoring her. Finally, the woman said, "I don't think she's going to cooperate."

The U.S. government has a long record of psychological torture. In the prison at Guantánamo Bay, they staged elaborate mock executions. I believe that this was a complicated way to screw with my head, to punish me, to get me to attempt to break out, to get my hopes up, and to utterly confuse me. But I was days into solitary confinement, yet another form of psychological torture. I know what I heard, and what happened to me, but my state of mind no longer belonged to me. It was a terrorism of its own.

By the time I got out of solitary confinement, my supporters and legal team had rallied around me. Nancy Hollander, a prominent criminal defense lawyer, had reached out years before with a gentle, thoughtful letter offering to represent me during the lead-up to my court-martial when I was in solitary confinement. Nancy had not only argued before the Supreme Court but had a background as an activist, one that I admired. Still, she was a civilian lawyer who didn't know as much about the military code as other lawyers I was considering, so I had passed on her offer.

But by February 2014, I wanted to seek clemency. David Coombs had helped me with an initial ask—more or less pro forma, in the direct wake of my conviction, ten days or so after I'd been sentenced, the soonest that it's allowed—but I wanted to try in earnest. I reached out to Nancy with a letter of my own and asked her to take on my case, for the appellate level, and beyond if necessary. She agreed.

Nancy is now in her late seventies. She's tiny but fiery, a true advocate with an obsessive dedication to her life's work. Our strategy was to go at a couple of bylaws that we felt had been used unfairly against us. The government had argued, using the Computer Fraud and Abuse Act, that I'd exceeded "authorized access"—a term just vague enough to capture almost anything to which the military objects, lawful or not.

We decided on a sweeping strategy: to challenge not just my own unauthorized access in this particular case, but also the whole concept. Then there was the government's interpretation of a section of the Espionage Act, which is more or less a misnomer: what I had done wasn't an act of spying, but an unlawful disclosure. The way they'd deployed the Espionage Act in my case set a dangerous precedent. If any disclosure of government information—regardless of the level of classification of the information—to an "unauthorized" person can be prosecuted, that means journalists' sources (and journalists themselves) could be arrested under a law that had been written to discourage people from spying for foreign powers.

The ACLU wrote an amicus brief arguing that this application was overly broad, vague, and a First Amendment violation. We relied heavily on their argument that it restricts speech preemptively, in an unconstitutional move called "prior restraint." This was the same issue involved in the prosecution of the Pentagon Papers' release; we actually based our argument on a *Columbia Law Review* article from 1972 discussing the way the government had gone after those disclosures. This precedent had worried me in the court-martial, but I'd been fighting a more urgent set of battles then. The appeal was a chance to rectify that, but it would be an uphill battle.

When President Trump was elected, in November 2016, I wasn't as surprised as everyone else seemed to be. After living in prison in Kansas with a bunch of conservative-leaning white folks, I knew something sinister was happening. Some people were unwilling to say it in public, but in private, this was the man they had been waiting for. By this time, I believed in worst-case scenarios; my life had been nothing but. I could see the world trending toward nationalism and fascism, fueled by spreading fears of immigrants, Muslims, people of color, queer and trans people. The rule of law had been perverted to override the rule of the people—and soon, the rule of law would be almost meaningless. The country was going in a bad direction, and I just couldn't take it.

In part, that's because I knew the new president might directly affect my life. Trump and the people supporting him saw me as an active enemy of America who deserved to be punished even more than I already was. During the campaign, when President Obama had made a point of talking about closing Guantánamo before the end of his term, President Trump responded on the stump by saying that not only did he want to keep the prison open, he wanted to fill it with "bad people." Who did he mean, exactly? Trump clearly needed villains, effigies to stoke his base, and a trans woman who had (at least in the Fox News narrative) betrayed the military could be the perfect target for him. Besides, Fort Leavenworth was overflowing, while Guantánamo was, by that point, more than half empty. I could imagine the Department of Defense transferring American-born national security prisoners there, to justify the expense of keeping Guantánamo running.

And so, I felt that I just couldn't wait any longer for our appeal to make it through the legal system. Shortly after my suicide attempt, still feeling abandoned and on the edge, I sat down to write a letter.

I addressed it to President Obama, because of course he was the person who had the power to get me out of prison with a stroke of his pen. But I viewed it, while writing, not as an appeal to a president, to the office. I saw it as just a letter to *him*, to another human being. I was used to writing legal memoranda about my situation, couching everything in the armor of the parts of the Constitution and the U.S and military codes that had been violated in order to punish me. I wasn't as used to just explaining, in plain and close-to-my-heart words, what this had all done to me, what I feared it would do to me, why I hoped that I had been punished enough.

Someone had given me a form for a clemency petition to go along with it, but I had little hope of its actually being effective. After all, this was the administration that had thrown me into jail in the first place, and had been tough on journalists and their sources. Writing the appeal felt more like a therapeutic act, a catharsis.

One of our contacts in the White House had told us that, as his final term wore down, Obama was thinking hard about his legacy and was concerned he'd become known as the leak-crackdown president, someone who had been unkind to transparency and to truthful journalistic sources. The White House contact also suggested that Obama would never pardon me, but might consider a commutation. (In other words, they wouldn't erase my conviction, but might redress an overpunishment for the crimes.)

Edward Snowden, still in Russia, was pushing for a pardon; his supporters had taken out an ad in *The New York Times*. But I was sure there was no way Obama was going to do that. He was a lawyer at heart. He wouldn't even consider that kind of thing, especially for someone on the lam. No soon-to-be-former president wants to actively tarnish their legacy with a pardon that turns into a scandal.

I, however, was okay with a commutation, and I thought that was a better shot, given what we'd heard and what I knew of the president's temperament and view of my actions. Obama was a man of compromise; he'd always tried to solve everything by meeting at the midpoint, not by listening to idealists or activists. I tended to think of this as a flaw in him, but it was a flaw we could use to our strategic advantage. We waited until November, once the election was done, to make my push, and started with a proposed compromise. We discussed asking for a commutation to a ten-year sentence, which would have gotten me out of prison in 2020. We would publicly talk about asking for time served—something we could turn into a flashy slogan, a hashtag, #TimeServed. But the official petition request would be for a decade of jail time, which had been David Coombs's original request in the court-martial.

The lawyers read my letter carefully. They made a few small tweaks, and we tried to send it off. The army, however, initially refused to forward my commutation request to the appropriate party at the Department of Justice, claiming that the army clemency and parole board was the only correct clemency review process—even though the presidential power to pardon exists in the Constitution itself. The legal team submitted an attached memorandum of law arguing for the superseding power of the Constitution, and still they refused. Secretary of Defense Ash Carter said explicitly that the Department of Defense would never consider commuting my sentence. However, we sent a separate copy of the commutation request to the pardons office at the Department of Justice for review by the White House counsel and, we hoped, eventually the president.

We also needed to help make clemency seem politically viable. Lisa Rein and Evan Greer of Fight for the Future created a White House petition, using the official government website to do so. They also pushed my lawyers, who, I sensed, viewed the petition as a shot in the dark, to take it seriously. I will never understand how much time, energy, and intensity my friends put into the effort to get me free; no major, large organization would support the effort in the beginning.

The second approach we took was a back channel, attempting to get people in Obama's inner circle who might be sympathetic to my case to raise it directly with him or his staff. Lawrence Lessig, the Harvard law professor who knew Lisa Rein from their shared interest in digital freedom, was among those most crucial to that outreach. And via those back channels, we also made sure to get a physical copy of the petition, and my letter, into the hands of the White House's general counsel, circumventing the Defense and Justice Departments, which both refused to engage. All we wanted was to make sure that the administration would actually give the petition a fair shot.

Initially, our petition generated a lot of buzz. The numbers looked good. (The rules stated that you needed to get at least one hundred thousand signatures within thirty days to get an official response.) Three thousand signatures turned to eleven thousand turned to thirty-five thousand. But that's where we hit a brick wall, until organizational help came through. The ACLU put out a statement saying it supported the petition, getting us another twenty-five thousand signatories. Fight for the Future put its name more formally behind it. And then, just as we were butting up against the thirty-day deadline since the petition's creation and still short more than thirty thousand signatures, Amnesty International—among the biggest NGOs in the world—got on board. Amnesty's public support got us over the one-hundred-thousand line.

I felt a tremendous sense of relief at not having failed all the people who'd worked so hard on my behalf. I had been afraid that the campaign's failure would sap any momentum around my fate as a cause that people cared about. But instead, we'd succeeded. Obama would be forced to at least reckon with how many people wanted me out of jail.

In January 2017, I was working in the woodshop, covered in dust, cutting flag cases made out of beech. As we finished up for the day, waiting to be escorted back to our housing units, several civilian and military security officials walked toward me. The other prisoners quickly assumed I was in trouble again. I was nervous, worried I was headed for solitary confinement or worse. The staff refused to tell me what was going on, and escorted me away. It was like my transfers to Quantico and Fort Leavenworth all over again.

I asked again and again what was happening. They refused to tell me anything, and didn't seem to know what to do with me, either. We moved to the special housing unit, to a cell for a minute, then to an office. Finally, the guards brought me to the protective custody wing. The psychologist who had treated me for six years sat across a table from me. She wore a curious expression on her face. As I greeted her, I glanced at a television behind her. I was shocked to see my own face with a blond wig framing it, the photograph I'd snapped during my day at Tysons Corner, when I was back in Virginia on leave from Iraq. The CNN chyron beamed, BREAKING: OBAMA COMMUTES CHELSEA MANNING'S SENTENCE. I was going to be free.

My first reaction to the news that I'd get out was, in retrospect, muted. I didn't believe that the government would really follow through. I imagined that maybe this was one more bait and switch. I got the news on January 17, but my release wasn't scheduled until mid-May. Until two days before I was scheduled to be released—in other words, the absolute last minute at which the prison could begin working on the release forms and procedures—no one treated me any differently. Life in prison droned on.

We'll never know exactly why Obama decided to commute my sentence. But when a reporter asked him about the decision, he acknowledged that I'd taken responsibility for what I'd done and served a tough prison sentence. Maybe his views shifted over the time he was in office. I haven't asked, and I won't seek an answer; I am grateful that he chose to act as he did.

Up until the night before my release, I still doubted that freedom would actually be granted. The military prison refused to give me a set time to expect dismissal, telling me only that it could happen anytime between midnight and midnight. I needed to be ready to go when they said the word. The day before, I took a shower and put on the prison uniform. Late in the afternoon, I went to sleep in my empty room, on a mattress without sheets or a pillow. Staff woke me up a few minutes before midnight—the first moment of the release date, May 17, 2017—and walked me out for a medical checkup, then through the back gate of the facility. Officials handed me a shirt and slacks. A dress wasn't an option: we had spent weeks negotiating, only to get something that felt gender-neutral. It might not have seemed important, but in my first moments of freedom, I wanted to feel really free, to wear something that showed who I *actually* was. From a tiny airfield outside Fort Leavenworth, I flew on a small plane to New York, with Nancy, Chase, and a security team my lawyers had hired. While I was aboard, I put on women's clothes for the first time—leggings, a tank top, a red hoodie. I finally felt like me.

When we landed, the driver took us to a safe house. The security company we'd hired provided us with a quiet refuge—I still don't know where exactly we were, just that it was somewhere on the East Coast. We spent a few days there decompressing, going back to normal. I ate greasy pizza: normal and boring, but great. I sat in lawn chairs looking at the mountains, talking to Chase about everything that I wanted to do and to be.

Everyone expected me to be in shock at being out, to kiss the ground or something. It did feel surreal to be free—but it also felt like what I'd been dealing with for the previous seven years would never be over. It certainly isn't over now. I can never leave it behind.

This was my first time as a free woman, quite literally. I had spent several years transitioning, so I felt comfortable in my body, in the way it moved and the way I felt. Even in prison, with restrictions on hair length and clothing, people had begun to accept me as a woman. They treated me as a human being. But now I needed to navigate a larger world with this new identity. This meant much more than being a woman; I was a celebrity, and had been made, without consultation, a symbol of all sorts of things, a figurehead for all kinds of ideas. Some of that was fun—when I needed to figure out how to dress, a *Vogue* editor helped me. Annie Leibovitz photographed me for *Vogue*'s September issue, in my own swimsuit. Some of it—the director of the CIA pressuring Harvard University to uninvite me from a visiting fellowship, Fox News seizing upon my very existence as a cheap way to rile up its viewers—was much less so.

But the main upside to my new notoriety was that I could do important work. Activism quickly became almost a full-time job. I went to the Pride parade in New York City; I ran for Senate in Maryland; I protested the Trump administration's policies on immigration and refugees, and the president's reinstatement of the ban on transgender personnel in the military. The political moment into which I emerged is one in which we are figuring out what got us here as a country. What I did during my enlistment was an act of rebellion, of resistance, and of civil disobedience. These form a deep and important tradition in our history, of forcing progress—a tradition we drew on to oppose an increasingly sinister Trump administration. The documents I made public expose how little we knew about what was being done in our name for so many years.

Now we are all left grappling with our past.

Acknowledgments

Thank you to everyone who helped transform this book from an idea into reality: Noreen Malone, Colin Dickerman, Sean McDonald, Nicole Pasulka, Greg Villepique, P. J. Mark, Luke Janklow, Melissa Flashman, Jackson Howard, Ian Van Wye, Ben Brooks, Devon Mazzone, Eric Chinski, Jonathan Galassi, Mitzi Angel, Debra Helfand, Nancy Elgin, Rodrigo Corral, Cecilia Zhang, Gretchen Achilles, Diana Frost, Mark Zaid, Eric Rayman, Sheila O'Shea, Sarita Varma, Lottchen Shivers, Daniel del Valle, Spenser Lee, Avi Zenilman, and Jesse London.

Thank you to the lawyers who have fought for me: Nancy Hollander, Vincent Ward, and David Coombs, with special thanks to Ben Wizner for the assistance and advice. And to the lawyers who are also life-saving friends: Moira Meltzer-Cohen and Chase Strangio.

Thank you to my loving family, especially Casey Manning and Debra Van Alstyne for their contributions to writing this book.

And very special thanks to Janus Rose, Ashna Ali, Lisa Rein, Christina DiPasquale, and Andy Stepanian.

A NOTE ABOUT THE AUTHOR

Chelsea Manning is an American transparency activist, politician, and former U.S. Army intelligence analyst. She lives in Brooklyn and works as a security consultant and expert in data science and machine learning.